Digging Deep

Digging Deep

A Writer Uncovers His Marriages

Boyd Lemon

Outskirts Press, Inc.
Denver, Colorado

Digging Deep
A Writer Uncovers His Marriages
All Rights Reserved.
Copyright © 2011 Boyd Lemon
v3.0

Outskirts Press, Inc.
http://www.outskirtspress.com

ISBN: 978-1-4327-6846-1

PRINTED IN THE UNITED STATES OF AMERICA

For my children, the innocents who suffered.*

*I have changed the names of my children, my former wives and most of the people who are named, but the places are real, and everything else is as true as I can make it.

Table of Contents

PART THREE: Susan: "For Better or For Worse"

PART ONE
Christie:
"'Til Death Do Us Part"

Chapter One

In March 2007, after a lifetime in southern California, I move to Boston to live with Kate, a twenty-four-year-old singer–songwriter and college student. I step out of the taxi onto the icy street and fall on my ass. Welcome to Boston. Only my dignity is injured.

I'm not in a mid-life crisis. I'm too old—sixty-six. Anyway, it doesn't feel like a crisis. Something strong pulls me to Boston, and for the first time in my life I pay attention to such things. I need to get away from the life I have lived. I want to be alone, but I need the comfort of a friend nearby, like a cat I once had, who wanted my presence, but not too close.

Kate fits my needs almost perfectly. She ignores me most of the time. Occasionally, that hurts my feelings, but usually I'm grateful. I feel her comforting presence, even when we're apart. Her dirty laundry on the bathroom floor and unwashed dishes in the sink—I would have bitched at my wives—strangely add to my comfort.

Since, among other things, Kate is so much younger than I, there is no complicating romance.

I'm writing short fiction, and Kate becomes my writing teacher. She recommends books written by Natalie Goldberg, a well-known writing teacher. I read them and more than a dozen others on writing, and attend two of Natalie Goldberg's workshops in late 2007.

Writing becomes the focus of my new life. I decide to write about my three marriages. The need roars inside me, though I don't yet know why. Kate and I discuss potential structures of a memoir, and I write an outline of incidents. I start the first draft.

In April 2008 I visit my daughter, Lisa, in Ventura, California. I sit at her kitchen counter and down the last of a Hendricks Gin martini. On the opposite beige granite counter, Lisa arranges fish sticks in pale blue plastic bowls for her children's dinner. The shrimp for the adults' dinner thaws in a colander in the sink next to her. Emily, four, draws at her table in the family room to my right—"Pooh Bear," she says. Ryan, eighteen months, looking like a baby from a magazine ad, hair the color of straw, sits in his high chair behind me demanding his dinner. I want another martini, but I should be ready to lend a hand with my grandkids if Lisa needs me, and I'm sure she will.

Lisa brings their dinners to the table, tells Emily that hers is ready, then goes back to the sink to check the shrimp. I get up and sit at the table. I shovel strained peas into Ryan's mouth. He still likes the mushy stuff. I try to keep it off his face, but as I scrape it off his chin, he lets more dribble down and smiles.

"Thanks for feeding Ryan, Dad," Lisa says. "As the family's Director of Domestic Operations, I still can only do one thing at a time."

"Glad to help," I say.

A half hour later the children's dinners rest in their bellies. Lisa quietly calms a screaming Emily, who objects to her brother playing with one of the cars to her train. I grab a *Thomas* book from the floor, pick up Ryan and take him to the couch. He sits quietly while I read to him.

The hum of the garage door opening announces the arrival of Lisa's husband, David. Lisa leaves Emily tranquil and grabs wipes to clean Ryan's high chair. David comes through the door. He hugs and kisses Lisa, the messy wipes clutched in her right hand.

I make another martini, while Lisa turns to the adults' dinner, tearing Romaine lettuce leaves.

"We're having shrimp with linguini and green salad," she says.

"Sounds great," says David. I nod in agreement.

David plays train on the floor with Emily and Ryan. With Dad in charge, their anger toward each other of moments ago disappears. Emily pulls her fingers down through her blond bangs to straighten them, as I've seen her mom do to her bangs all her life. Ryan crashes his train into the couch and laughs as the cars topple over.

"Ryan," says David, "it's almost your bedtime—three minutes. Lisa would you set the timer, please?"

"Okay," says Lisa.

David turns to Emily. "When Ryan goes to bed, would you like me to tell you a story about a bride?"

"Yes," shouts Emily, bounding up and, like a referee signaling a touchdown, throws both arms in the air.

David smiles and looks up at Lisa. "How can I help?"

"You can put Ryan to bed," she says.

"Okay, glad to."

When the timer dings, David picks up Ryan, who waves 'bye, his entire face grinning.

After dinner David and I clear the table, and he begins washing dishes. "Thanks, David," says Lisa, giving him a pat on the shoulder.

"You're very welcome," he says, smiling.

"I'll bathe Emily," says Lisa.

When David finishes the dishes, he says to me, "After I tell

Emily a story I have to do some work up in the office, so I'll see you in the morning."

"Okay," I say.

These moments are precious, but bittersweet, I think. When I had a chance to be a father and husband, to be in a family, I didn't have it in me. Three tries, all ending in turmoil, resentment and divorce—a three-time loser.

Lisa's lucky to have a home and family like this. I didn't get to raise any of my children to adulthood. Lisa has a beautiful home, two great kids and, luckily, a wonderful husband who adores her.

It isn't luck though, is it? Through martini haze and dinner wine, remembrances rock me like a California earthquake. I worked long hours too, but I stayed at the office. When I came home, I poured a drink and sat in my recliner. I didn't play with the kids or put them to bed. I didn't help with the meals or wash the dishes. I usually had another drink. The most I did was read a bedtime story, if I was home in time. Often I went drinking with co-workers. Maybe if I'd put as much into my family as David does, I could have had the family I wanted. I could have helped raise my kids and grown old with a loving partner. My chest freezes. My eyes tear. I lose awareness of where I am.

"Are you all right, Dad?" Lisa had come back in. I'd been staring through her. "Yeah. I'm okay."

"Emily's ready for *Goodnight Moon*."

I struggle upstairs and read to her. When I kiss her good night, she looks up at me. God, she looks just like Lisa at that age.

"Thanks, Pa B. I love you," she says.

"I love you too," I say, and turn my head so she doesn't see my tears. When Lisa was her age, I saw her only every other weekend. But what could I do? Her mother left me. Christie was crazy.

Back downstairs, I have another glass of wine and stop thinking about my marriages.

A week later I fly home to Boston. Not long after, on the first spring like day, I lounge on a bench, gazing at the cold blue of the Charles River. Hulls glide silently through the water, bodies perched inside rowing in perfect sync, like graceful robots. The M.I.T. buildings across the way reflect the pale yellow sun, as if it is trying to penetrate my mind

My cell phone rings. It's my third wife, Susan. After we catch up, she tells me she's disappointed that I moved to Boston. She thinks we should have gotten back together—given it another try. Why, after twelve years apart? I think, but don't say.

We've both changed since our divorce, she says. I don't say no. I mumble something about enjoying life in Boston and change the subject. After we hang up, as I'm sitting on the bench by the bucolic Charles River, I feel a knot in my belly. Would living with Susan be any better now? Whose fault was our divorce? Both of us, I suppose. I have never tried to understand how I participated in the destruction of our thirteen-year marriage. When we separated she said that I had withheld my affection for years, that I had emotionally withdrawn from her. What did she mean? Those thoughts enter my mind but float out into the ether without any deeper thought.

Questions of why all three marriages failed the "'til death do us part" test have lingered under the pillow of my mind for years, sneaking out every now and then, but I always shoved them back. I never let them out long enough to gain much insight, just a passing acknowledgement that I must have contributed.

Could I have done something to prevent my divorce from Stephanie, my second wife? I sat on this same bench more than a year ago pondering that question. I had been talking to

Kate when Stephanie called. Kate left the room. I hadn't heard from Stephanie in a long time, but she got right to the point. "I haven't had a job for three months," she said, "and I can't pay my rent or my car payments. I'll be out on the street. Could you please loan me the money? I'll pay you back when I get a job. Please. You're the only one I can turn to."

I hesitated for a moment, thinking about how she had never paid me back when I loaned her money before. "I'm sorry," I said. "I'm not willing to do that." She said she understood and hung up. My muscles were tense, but I was energized, a little pride resting on the guilt that settled in my belly. I did the right thing, I told myself.

When Kate came back, I told her what I had done. "It was really hard for me to say no," I said, "and I don't understand why. I don't owe her anything."

"Well, Boyd," she said, "I think Stephanie was the love of your life."

"Maybe you're right," I said.

Later, I walked and found the bench.

Was Stephanie really the love of my life? How could that be? She was a hopeless alcoholic and drug addict. There was nothing I could have done.

I can't penetrate. Each time I think about my marriages I scrape a little dirt from the surface where the truth is buried. Instead of continuing to dig, I stash the shovel.

In Spring and Summer 2008 I am consumed with writing the memoir. By the end of August I finish a rough draft, nearly three hundred pages.

On August 31st I move across the river to Cambridge. Kate moves to the Cambridge Zen Center to study meditation. The next morning Kate comes over and reads my rough draft on the computer. I have not yet read it all the way through. I sit on the couch reading a novel. In a few hours Kate turns away from the computer screen toward me.

"It doesn't work," she says, shaking her head. "My advice to you is to throw it out. Don't look at it again and start over.

I'm sorry, but you can do better."

I feel devastated. "Can you be more specific?"

"You tried marriage three times and failed. What insights do you have about your role in the failure of those marriages?" She asks.

I hesitate. "I'm not sure."

She wrinkles her brows and looks straight at me. "Twelve years since your last divorce, and you have no insight into what your role was?"

Humiliation rises up through my throat and heats my face. I don't know what to say. "I guess not," I reply.

"That's astonishing," she says. "I always thought you were courageous when you told me you were willing to marry again. Apparently, you're willing to subject yet another woman—and yourself—to the same old suffering."

I can't speak. My throat and chest tighten. I swallow. Tears flood my eyes, the way men cry, not like women, who sob freely when they're in pain.

"If you're going to write about the destruction of your marriages, you'll have to understand your role," she says. "That has to be in the memoir."

After Kate leaves I go over to the computer and read the draft. She's right. It's terrible. It's not me. It's boring.

I walk toward The Plough and Stars, a bar down the street from my apartment. I have always handled my life's traumas by cloistering myself for a few days, looking at what's ahead and moving on, pushing the trauma down to the bottom of a hole somewhere and burying it, never to be uncovered. Isn't that what self-help gurus tell you to do—move on? The problem is that if all you do is move on, you don't learn anything.

I could just avoid marriage. Then I won't have to go through a painful introspection, I think, as by rote I press the button on the pole to light the walk sign at Mass Ave and Hancock Street. Is there something about the way I related to my wives that could be important? Will I ever find peace if I don't understand how I acted during most of my adult life—twenty-seven years? Kate is right. If I'm writing about my marriages, I have to understand my role in their failure. When I wrote that first draft, I didn't do what I'd learned from Natalie Goldberg. I can hear her now, "Dig deep. Write what scares you, not what monkey mind says you should write." I realize now I didn't dig down to the gold that I know is deep within my mind. I didn't get to the bottom of it, nowhere near.

I decide to start thinking about my first marriage. That will be the easiest. Still, like a child standing on the edge of a high-dive board, shivering, afraid to jump, I am held back by fear. I sip my third martini before I can begin.

My stomach churns as I think, through the alcohol, back to when Christie, my "crazy first wife," was committed to a mental institution. Eventually, she was diagnosed as bipolar and cured with medication. I have always believed that she left me because she was insane, that her hospitalization confirmed that.

I get out my notebook and pen. It occurs to me: she wasn't committed until three years after our divorce. Did she have any bipolar symptoms when we were married? There's an interesting question. I don't remember her ever acting depressed. She worried a lot about her work, but that was normal for somebody who had never had a full-time job before. She was never manic. On the contrary, she seemed calm. I feel dryness in my throat, from the gin, I assume, and ask the bartender for a glass of water. I knew Christie was odd after our first date, but I don't believe she was mentally ill, then or during our marriage. I take a long drink of water. I've been deluding myself all these years. I need to take a closer look. I'll start at the beginning.

She was called Christine when we had our first date. Several years after we married, she told me she wanted to be called Christie, but I kept calling her Christine. I wasn't consciously trying to irritate or demean her, but I didn't call her the name she wanted to be called, a telling lack of consideration for her. Maybe she should have called me "Bud."

Our first date was blind, a sorority party early in October of my senior year at the University of Southern California. I had a full tuition scholarship for debate. My friend on the debate team, Sharon, had arranged the date. I'd never been to a sorority party or had a blind date.

On the afternoon of the party, I had second thoughts. What if she was ugly or obnoxious? What if I wasn't sorority girl dating material? I had always been shy, but since puberty I had been especially shy around girls and felt that I wasn't attractive to them. I never dated much.

I decided to walk the four blocks to the sorority house. It was cool out, but I sweated through my deodorant. As I walked down 28th Street, I breathed deeply, trying to relax, but it didn't help. I was so nervous I didn't notice the row of sorority houses. I had clenched my fists so tight that my wrists hurt. I worried about not having anything in common with a sorority girl. I wasn't ugly—average looking, I guessed—awfully skinny though. As long as I could think of things to say to her, I'd be okay, I thought. I had to date. I was marrying age, and I'd never get married if I didn't date.

Just as I prepared for a debate, I thought it was best to prepare for a date. I had planned topics to break the ice- -what she thought of Redlands, where Sharon said Christie had gone to college the first two years; the national collegiate debate topic; what she thought of President Kennedy; where she grew up; questions about her family, such as whether she had siblings and what her father did. As I walked, I went over these topics in my mind, until I realized I had passed the sorority house. I turned around and walked back. Like many of the others, it was one of those old wooden three-story former mansions displaying the sorority's Greek letters, well kept, with a broad front lawn.

My knees trembled as I stood at the big oak door, hesitated a moment, then knocked. A girl let me in and asked whom I was there to see. "Christine," I said. "I'm Boyd." She told me her name, which I didn't hear, and said she would get Christine, then bounded up the stairs. Sharon and a girl I assumed was Christine emerged on the semicircular stairway. Christie stumbled on the bottom stair, but recovered all except her dignity. Her face was still flushed as Sharon introduced us. Christie's hair was brown, medium short, curled at the ends. It sloped down from the middle of her forehead and covered her ears. She had light olive skin. Her face was oblong. Not bad, I thought, a little skinny, but so was I. Sharon led us to the punch bowl. She chatted a little about plans for future sorority events, while I poured punch for Christie and me. Then, the moment I feared--Sharon left.

In less than a minute, Christie and I exchanged the information college students who just met invariably asked about, alternating questions and answers like a script. What year are you in? She was a junior. I was a senior. Where are you from? La Cañada. Alhambra. What's your major? Dental hygiene. Double major—poli sci and speech.

"What's poli sci?" she asked.

Is she kidding? I wondered. I better assume not. "Political science," I said.

"Oh, yeah. Sorry I'm so dense," she said with a weak smile, her shoulders hunched.

After some awkward conversation about the sorority and the university, Christie chattered on about her family. At least it kept me from having to create conversation, I thought. I relaxed a little. Her father was an architect. She had a ten-year-old sister.

"I've always wanted a little sister," I said, "but I'm an only child."

She said her family lived in La Cañada. I had never been to La Cañada, but I'd heard it was a wealthy community in the foothills of the San Gabriel Mountains. I imagined the mansion they lived in—three stories, a dozen bedrooms and bathrooms.

I didn't tell Christie what my father did. He was a blue-collar worker. He wore a blue shirt with his tie. He even wore a blue shirt and tie at home. He was proud of rising from his parents' poverty to the middle class. One summer when he painted the house, he wore slacks and a blue shirt with his maroon tie neatly tied and tucked into his shirt between buttons to keep it out of the paint.

I told Christie I had been raised in Alhambra. She said she knew where Alhambra was. It was on the wrong side of the tracks for dating an architect's daughter. The houses in my neighborhood were small, with the neat, clean look of middle-class America. I was proud to have a date with a professional's daughter. Beneath the pride I felt inferior, but as Christie's awkwardness and self-consciousness surfaced, I gained confidence.

I'd better say something, I thought. I launched into the topics I had planned. After a while, she stifled a yawn. My shaky confidence fell.

Somebody turned up the stereo. People were dancing. A slow song played and I asked Christie to dance. We shuffled stiffly around one corner of the room, careful not to step on each other. Thank God she didn't dance much better than I did. After a while, relief, even warmth broke through my nervousness. It felt good to hold her. She smelled faintly of hairspray and flowery perfume. I pulled her a little closer, but not so close that our bodies touched. She said she didn't like dancing to fast songs. Neither did I. I felt like a klutz trying to dance fast.

After a few people left, I told her I had to get up early to work on my arguments for the debate team, which was true. I had to do well in debate to keep my scholarship. She walked me to the door. "Thanks for coming," she said, as I opened the door.

"Thanks for inviting me," I said. I thought I'd like to see her again. At least she was a girl, and we were on a date. I'm twenty-one; it's time I had a girlfriend, I thought. I wondered if she would go out with me again. I asked for her phone number, and she gave it to me.

"Okay," I said. "I'll call you." We stood in the doorway staring at each other long enough to make it awkward, until I finally reached for her, said, "Good night," and kissed her, a peck on the lips.

I walked home thinking the evening had gone well. I was actually coming home from a date. I felt loose and a bit smug. I was glad Christie was shy and lacked self-confidence. Outgoing, confident girls scared me.

Chapter Two

I drop my notebook in my backpack, leave The Plough and Stars and walk a little unsteadily back to my Cambridge apartment. I fall into an alcohol-induced sleep and wake up three hours later with a hangover. After a few painkillers and chamomile tea, the thought of Christie comes rushing back into my aching head like a high-speed train. I set the mug of tea on the table in front of the couch and flop down. I can't write, but I think about Christie.

I knew after our first date that I had no passion for Christie. Dating her for a while wouldn't have hurt, but I married her. Sure, I wanted to have sex with her, but that wasn't passion. I was twenty-one. I wanted to have sex with practically anyone with a vagina. I jeopardized Christie's well-being, mine and later that of our child, by this passionless, unthinking pursuit. Why did I even think about marrying her?

I knew what passion felt like. I had been passionate about Mary. We dated a couple of times in the summer after I graduated from high school. I was anxious to please her. I daydreamed of her fresh smell and longed for her wistfully when we were apart. I had a hypnotic obsession, a sure sign of infatuation. Her features were exquisite, I thought, and though she wore glasses, her wide brown eyes beamed. Her left cheek dimpled when she smiled. We only kissed—innocently—a few times, but I swooned over those kisses for days. She was only sixteen, and I saw her as pure, so I didn't allow myself to picture anything sexual other than kissing.

One day she invited me to her house. We sat on the living room couch. She held my hand, turned and looked at me with soulful eyes—I didn't know it then, but it was the way girls look at you when they're going to bring you down gently. Then she looked down at her parents' beige living room carpet and broke the news that she just wanted to be "…like your little sister."

I pined for Mary for the next three years. I couldn't get her out of my head. I fantasized dating her, making out with her. I read and re-read the letters she had written me that summer from her parents' beach house. She was the girl I really wanted to date and marry. I tried to will her to be my girlfriend, but it didn't work.

I think I knew after our second date that I would ask Christie to marry me if she didn't dump me, despite the absence of passion. I was that desperate to get married. It was what we did in our early twenties back then. I was afraid I would be alone, that nobody else would have me. I must have thought I was so undesirable that I was willing to marry almost anybody.

I get up from the couch and grab a bottle of wine from the refrigerator and pour a tumbler full. I take two gulps and hold back tears before I flop back down. I know I am going to cry. Wine sloshes onto the couch. I don't care. I finish the glass. I start to cry, this time in audible sobs, the way girls cry. I hope my neighbors don't hear me. I sob until I'm spent and nauseated.

I remember that after we married, Christie and I used to visit our friends Paula and Steve, at their house in Orange County on weekends. We all drank, but I drank so much I threw up. Once at their house I threw up in bed with Christie. And now, thinking about my failures in marriage, here I am using alcohol to numb my brain, avoiding pain and the chance of insight. It hits me. This is exactly what I did during my marriages. I came home almost every night and had a drink or two--or three--if I hadn't already been drinking with co-workers before I got home. I didn't give attention to my wives. While Christie tried to recuperate from work, and while Stephanie and Susan continued what they had done all day—taking care of the house and children—I drank. If I got home in time, they usually cooked my dinner. I wasn't a falling-in-the-gutter drunk. I didn't pass out. Normally, I had no more than two or three drinks. But I used alcohol to soften life's inherent pain and avoid facing my issues. When I divorced I used alcohol to avoid that pain too. I'm still doing it. I sob some more.

I remember sobbing like this after I spent the afternoon drinking with my friend, Mike, forty years ago. I have been aware of a drinking problem since I was twenty-seven and have done nothing about it. I started drinking to feel more at ease in social situations, but it soon went beyond that. And I considered myself smart. I must be missing part of my brain. I go back to bed realizing I can't continue to numb my pain with alcohol, if I expect to gain insight into my marriages. The next day I write what I can remember about that incident with Mike.

That week I write about my lifelong use of alcohol. Kate comes over. I confess that during my marriages, and ever since, I have been using alcohol to avoid emotional pain. Her voice is kind and supportive, but her words are frank. "Are you an alcoholic?" she asks.

I blurt out, "Yes," tearfully, without thinking, surprising my-self, but realizing it is true.

Kate suggests that there may be degrees of alcoholism, and that I might see if I can control my drinking without giving it up totally. "There are occasions when a glass of wine or a drink enhances the experience," she says. She suggests I try drinking only on occasions when it helps me live more fully and never to drink to avoid living. I agree to try. I don't have a drink that night.

Americans trying to avoid pain swallow pills by the billions. I have used alcohol for that purpose. I'm not alone, but I am determined to stop it and deal with my issues head on.

The next day I sit on my couch thinking about how I can best remember and understand what I was doing and thinking forty years ago and how it affected my marriage to Christie, then write about it. I'm stumped. I go over to my books on writing. I see *Writing Down the Bones* by Natalie Goldberg and another of her books, *Wild Mind*.

Natalie advocates writing practice. I wonder if I could use writing practice to uncover my role in the destruction of my marriages. In writing practice you pick a topic—yours or one suggested by someone else. For a predetermined period of time—at least ten minutes, sometimes twenty or thirty—you write whatever that topic brings to mind. You don't think about what you're writing. You just keep the pen or the fingers on the keyboard moving. You schedule writing practice every day that you can possibly fit it in your schedule. Examples of topics I have used for writing practice include, "I Remember....," "The Road I Didn't Travel," "The Worst Thing I Ever Did," "My First Sexual Experience," and "My Best Kept Secret." I have written on dozens of others. At Natalie's workshops we sit regularly and meditate on our breathing and do slow walking medita-tion to calm the mind. Natalie teaches that the combination of regular writing practice and meditation allows the writer to dig deeper into the mind and write our truth, rather than what we think we should write. She uses pen and notebook, but isn't opposed to people using a computer. I remember Natalie saying in class that she used writing practice to write her books.

I pull *Wild Mind* off the shelf and flip to the Table of Contents. I see a chapter titled "Wild Mind," and turn to it. I had dog-eared one of the pages:

"I think what good psychotherapy does is help to bring you into wild mind. This is what Zen, too, asks you to do....This is all about a loss of control. This is what falling in love is too, a loss of control....Lose control and let wild mind take over. It is the best way to write. To live, too."

Natalie says that writing can get you to the bottom of your mind.

I sit back down on the couch and meditate on my breathing for what feels like a half hour. The clock indicates twenty minutes. Then for ten minutes I slow walk, keeping my mind calm. I sit down at my MAC, move the rough draft of my memoir to the trash and begin again to write about dating Christie.

A few days after our first date, I called Christie. I paced as far as the phone cord would let me. "I called to ask if you'd like to go out to dinner Friday," I said.

"Ah...well, I guess so," she said, her voice trailing off. Her response hit me like a punch to the belly. I expected, maybe, at least, "I'd love to," or something similar. I guess she didn't like me much, I thought. *Maybe I should call her back and say never mind. That would be rude; I can't do that.* I hoped she'd cancel.

She didn't. During the short drive to the restaurant Christie didn't say anything. I felt tense. We went in, followed the hostess, and sat down. I broke the awkward silence by telling her the plot to *West Side Story*, which I had just seen with my aunt Carol and cousin Richard.

The waiter brought the menus. "He's cute," Christie said in a stage whisper I was sure he heard. I felt embarrassed. What an odd thing to do on a second date, I thought.

She sat up straight, her hands in her lap. Then she leaned forward, her brows scrunched toward her eyes. "I have to tell you something," she said, and paused.

"Okay," I said, leaning toward her.

"Usually, I can't eat in restaurants. They make me nervous. My parents always forced me to eat everything on my plate when we went out. 'Waste not. Want not,' they said. Then they reminded me of the starving children in China. They wouldn't let me leave until I finished everything. So I don't know if I can eat. I just wanted you to know that."

"I'm sorry. Well, just order something light, and see. I'm not your parents. I don't care if you eat."

"Thank you," she said.

That's why she acted strangely when I asked her to dinner, I thought. For a moment, I was concerned about her stability, but the concerns soon drifted away.

She ordered a hamburger. She grinned when she took the last bite. Riding back to the sorority house, smiling at the windshield, she said, "I must like you. I had no trouble eating."

"That's good," I said. Wow, she said she liked me, I thought. Maybe I should try a French kiss. But it was only our second date, and I was afraid she would think I was too interested in sex. At the door, I lingered just a bit with my kiss. She put her hand on my shoulder and didn't back off.

As unlikely as it may seem, I had never French kissed. On the drive home I wondered—after you stick your tongue in her mouth, then what? I'll do some research. The day before our next date I went to the main campus library and looked up "French kiss" and "sex" in the card catalogue. There was nothing under "French kiss." I jotted down the section number for sex. I wandered around the library for a few minutes looking for the number and finally found it on cards taped to three large bookcases in a small room off the main shelves.

Under the numbers somebody had scribbled, "Fuck you." The bookcases had glass covers and locks. I tried to lift the cover over the middle shelf of one of them. It was locked. I was too embarrassed to ask the girl at the front desk to unlock it.

I'd never had a real girlfriend. Anything related to sex had been traumatic. As I remember, it started when I was six. Barbara and I were wrestling in her backyard. It was a hot, dry summer day, and we both wore shorts and were shirtless. I felt the urge to see what she looked like down there and thought if I showed her mine, she would show me hers. I scrambled up and pulled my shorts and underwear down. "Yuck," she screamed, and got up and ran in her house.

When my parents learned of my evil deed, my father said, "I'm ashamed of you," and beat me at least six times on the butt with the switch he kept on the windowsill by the back door. It stung and then burned. I felt humiliated and confused.

In fourth grade Cathy and I were playing our version of kickball against a wooden backstop in a far corner of the playground. We both fell down going for the ball. She smiled at me and said, "Wanna see my butt?"

She got up, turned her back to me, bent over, then lifted up her pink dress and pulled down her panties. She turned her head around, smiling at me, as I stared at her baby-smooth, pinkish, round butt. Something below looked like a slit. What was that, I wondered.

"Wanna touch it?" she said.

"Sure!" I stepped up and gingerly petted her soft, warm butt.

"Boyd Lemon!" yelled a voice behind me. I hurled myself around, and there stood Mrs. Axelson, my teacher. My gut sank. My knees wobbled. I held my breath. "Cathy, I'll see you in the classroom in five minutes. Go! Now!" said Mrs. Axelson.

I got a lecture from the school principal. I don't know if he believed that Cathy initiated it. Fortunately, my parents did.

When our neighbor's niece, Judy, and I were about ten, in my backyard she made the proverbial offer, but after I showed her mine, she stared for a moment, then ran away without showing me anything.

In seventh grade I thought of Sheila as my girlfriend. One day after school before her mother got home from work I chased her up the stairs to her bedroom.

She said she was going to change. I turned to leave. "Wanna see my tits?" She asked.

"Yeah," I said.

She took off her shirt and proudly displayed her budding breasts. I stared. They looked like heaven to me. Then she pulled down her panties and started a slow, swaying dance. I thought she looked like a heavenly angel.

I heard the bang of the back screen door, like a shot from a rifle. Sheila squealed in terror, then whispered, "It's Mom! Go!" gesturing frantically toward the door, as she grabbed for her clothes.

I walked down the stairs past her mother. As I left, I heard Sheila crying. She shunned me after that. I hadn't done anything, and I felt sad to lose her.

I had no sexual experiences at all in high school. I never had a real girlfriend. I dated a girl in my senior year, but she was just someone to take to school dances and functions. We kissed a little occasionally, with closed mouths, but I didn't even attempt to feel her up. She must have wondered why I didn't try something, but she never mentioned it. I was afraid to try anything. I dated only a few times in college—two girls a couple of times—a goodnight kiss. That was all.

After a few more dates with Christie, I ignored my fear and screwed up my courage. We had gone to a movie, and I drove her home. She turned around at the sorority house front door. I put one hand on her hip, the other on her shoulder and pressed my lips against hers, a little harder than usual, opened my mouth and stuck my tongue between her lips. She lurched backwards, almost falling. "Oh, sorry," said one of her sorority sisters, who had opened the door from the inside.

"Well," she chuckled, and blushed. "Good night."

"Good night," I said. "See you soon."

On the next date we French kissed in my red 1959 Renault Dauphine. It wasn't all that complicated. Her mouth felt like warm, wet velvet. My erection pushed against my pants—the first one with a girl. After a minute or so, I felt her breast on the outside of her blouse. She gently pushed my hand away.

Christie and I had dated for about five months when she invited me to stay at her parents' Laguna Beach home over spring break. We walked on the beach every day, holding hands. I felt proud to have a girlfriend, like I was a normal guy, not so nerdy. We found a little cave that was somewhat private. Laguna Beach wasn't so crowded then. We made out in the cave. One afternoon, I caressed her breasts under her swimsuit top. I was so turned on I leaked on my trunks and had to run to the water to wash off the evidence.

It's hard for me to believe now, but at twenty-one I didn't even know what coming was. I never masturbated to ejaculation until later that spring. I was alone in my apartment. It was hot, and I was in my underwear reading *Tropic of Cancer* for English class. I had a hard-on. I began fondling myself. It felt good, so I took off my briefs and rubbed my cock on the book. The more I rubbed, the harder I got, the greater the tension, until I exploded all over the book. The exhilaration was sensational. Wow, I thought, so that's what a guy does inside a girl.

But, I worried: where do you put your penis to get inside her? In high school health class I had learned that girls have three holes, one where they poop, one where they pee and one where the baby comes out. You must put it in the hole where the baby comes out, but how do you tell which is which? I think I knew less than most guys my age, but I wasn't alone in my ignorance.

The night I had run out to the ocean to wash away the evidence, Christie and I made out on the living room couch. Her parents had gone to bed. I put my hand down her pajama bottoms and caressed her upper thigh. She grabbed my hand and pulled it away. "I want to be a virgin when I marry," she said. "It's not that I don't want to do it with you. It's just I'm not going to do it until I'm married."

"Okay," I said. "I respect that."

That night, in bed, I wondered if she would ever change her mind. I doubted she would. I would have to marry her.

Chapter Three

It has been two weeks since Kate suggested I drink only to live more fully, and not to avoid living. On alternate nights I have insomnia. I'm so exhausted I sleep the next night. I want a drink, but I am sticking to my vow.

When I can't sleep I meditate. I slow walk. I write. I also take long walks in the cool air of the early fall afternoons to try to make me tired. As I walk down Mass Avenue toward Boston's South End, I'm oblivious to all around me. I think about Christie refusing to have sex until marriage.

My thinking is muddled and my mind drifts. When that happens I sometimes treat myself, a suggestion of Natalie and a writer named Julia Cameron. I notice that I am a few blocks from B & G Oysters. I walk there, sit down at the counter and order the Island Creeks on the half shell and a glass of Chardonnay. The wine clearly enhances the flavor of the oysters, so it's okay, I tell myself. I walk back toward Cambridge. The fingernail-shaped new moon rises between buildings.

Diners enjoy the end of the outdoor season in Boston, propane heaters extending the season. I walk faster to stay warm. At home I write about the sexual revolution that raced through our lives when I was in my late twenties.

Most middle-class women in California in the fifties and early sixties remained virgin until marriage. I, like many middle-class men, probably would not have married a girl who'd had sex with somebody else. I believe many men in my generation got married to have sex. I wonder if the covert reason behind this so-called moral principle of no sex outside of marriage was to induce men to marry. It seems like back then men married for sex, and women married for somebody to support them.

In that era guys liked to say, "Good girls go to a party, go home and go to bed. Nice girls go to a party, go to bed and go home." We wanted to date nice girls and marry good girls.

My generation grew to adulthood in a culture that did not discuss sex, believed it a sin to have sex outside of marriage and clung to so-called Christian values, male dominance over females and light-skinned dominance over dark skin.

Although people think of the sexual revolution happening in the sixties, it wasn't until about 1966, three years after I married Christie, that all hell broke loose. Middle-class couples started openly having premarital sex and living together. The old views crumbled like an imploding Las Vegas Hotel. Only six years after Christie refused to have premarital sex with me, Stephanie and I made love and spent the night together on our second date. A week later we moved in together. Nobody we knew thought it was immoral, except her mother. It was like walking out of Disneyland to the real world.

During the heyday of the sexual revolution and a few years later, when the women's liberation movement gathered strength, I was in my late twenties and early thirties--on the cusp between two generations, trying to belong to the younger one, but dragging some of the older generation's values with me, unable to shed them. I desperately wanted to be part of the new generation's sexual freedom, racial tolerance and more liberal views, and I thought I was. I shed those views of the old generation like a snake sheds its skin, but the flesh of male domination stuck.

When I was about eleven, my mother and I saw a provocatively dressed woman walking down the street. "You know," Mom said, stopping before pulling open the door to the grocery store, "Women don't like sex. Well, a few do, but they're cheap sluts. Good women, anyone you'd want to marry, have sex only to please their husbands and to have children. They don't enjoy it. Good women marry men who will be good providers." She repeated her opinion during my teenage years. I believed her.

The so-called sexual revolution came first and strengthened another drastic change in the male–female relationship that continues to evolve--greater independence and equality for women in society, at home and in the workplace. I embraced the sexual revolution. Embracing equality and independence for the women in my life was more difficult. What a surprise! Unlike women's equality, having sex was always a male goal.

The push toward equality and independence for women radically changed every day life for both genders. For the first time, women who were not prostitutes appeared in bars, went out to dinner without a male companion, traveled by themselves and entered the work force in numbers that today make the stay-at-home mom the exception, rather than the rule.

For us on the cusp, how we related to those who were most important to us—our spouses and our children—was hard to change. I knew at a base level that equality for women was right. Putting it into practice in my own relationship was something else. It was harder to change my conduct than to change my mind. One of my favorite songs, which I sang with great enthusiasm, was Bob Dylan's "The Times They Are A-Changin.'" I couldn't internalize some of the changes.

In 1962 these changes were still to come. I never thought about why I wanted to marry Christie, or whether we would be a compatible married couple. Because I believed I was not attractive to women, I thought she might be my only chance to get married, so I kept up the pursuit. I decided to become a lawyer, in part, because I thought it would enhance my chances of marrying her. It would make me a good provider.

At the end of summer vacation Christie moved back to the sorority house for her senior year, and I lived at home my first year of law school. I was determined to ratchet up our petting—to what, I wasn't sure. Pete, my former roommate, was going to be away the weekend before school started. He handed me a key to his apartment. "Here," he said, "maybe you can pat panties with Christie."

I lured Christie over after lunch that Saturday. We made out on Pete's old off-white couch—more off than white—the same one that was there when I lived with him. We lay down, but I kept slipping until I was falling off the front edge.

"This is the most uncomfortable couch in the world," I said, getting up. "Let's go lie down on Pete's bed." We resumed on the bed. I unbuttoned the top two buttons of her pink cotton dress and unsnapped her bra with greater than expected dexterity. I slipped my hand under her bra and touched her nipple. In a moment it was erect. I unbuttoned the rest of her dress. She didn't stop me. She got up and slipped off her dress, but left on her panties. I took off my clothes, stopping at my underwear. I caressed and kissed her breasts. We pushed our hips against each other, our breathing heavy. I didn't have the nerve to put my hand inside her panties. A final thrust, and I came. Neither of us mentioned it. I didn't know if she realized what happened. This "heavy petting," as we called it then, generated an overwhelming desire to have sex, and I have no doubt it spurred me on to propose to Christie.

A few days later I asked her to marry me. I wish I could say I got down on my knees before Christie in a crowded restaurant and proposed to vigorous applause, or while we held hands, gazing at the streaks of red and orange in the clouds as the sun set on Laguna Beach. Or anything, really. The truth is I don't remember where we were or what I said. I do remember what she said.

"Oh…well, I…I don't know. I'll have to think about it."

Her tone was as casual as if I had asked her to go for a walk. It was two months before she gave me her answer. First I worried that she would say no. Then, worry turned to anger for leaving me hanging. I didn't bring it up. I didn't want her to say no, and I was afraid that she would if I pushed her. Maybe she was carefully considering. I didn't. I still had given no thought to why I should marry her, or anybody, or what married life with her would be like. I had no idea what marriage entailed.

Christie recently reminded me that I told her I had given up the chance to go to Harvard Law School to stay in California and marry her. Now, I remember that—another reminder of how desperate I was.

I had started law school at USC in the fall of 1962, racked with insecurities. I didn't know if Christie would marry me. I was worried about my ability to succeed in law school. When I was an undergraduate a professor told me that I was not "cut out for law school." My classmates' insecurity made mine worse. If that wasn't enough, the government had abolished student draft deferments, and I was petrified that I would be drafted and sent to Viet Nam

My fears were compounded by what was known as the "Cuban Missile Crisis." The Soviet Union had started erecting nuclear missile sites in Cuba, and President Kennedy seemed prepared to confront them by blocking a Soviet ship bound for Cuba. Everyone feared the nuclear apocalypse was at hand. After thirteen days of the only confrontation involving nuclear weapons between the United States and the Soviet Union, the ship turned back. Ultimately, the Soviet Union agreed to dismantle the missiles in Cuba, and the crisis was resolved, but those were insecure times.

I tried to talk to Christie about political issues, but she said she wasn't interested in politics. I mentioned that the military was not drafting married men. She didn't respond.

That fall near the anniversary of our first date, we drove in her silver Porsche roadster (a gift from her father) to San Francisco to see the USC–Cal. football game. She let me drive. Driving a Porsche up to San Francisco to spend the night in a hotel with my girlfriend felt like the ultimate sophisticated adventure.

Staying in a decent hotel with a girl you weren't married to required deception back then. We both had to register. Christie registered as Christie Lemon. Otherwise, the hotel might not have let us stay in the same room. She still hadn't said whether she would marry me, but I didn't want to spoil the weekend by bringing it up. As I unlocked the door to the room and followed her in, I felt wicked to be in a hotel room with a girl.

I had brought a bottle of Champagne. I wanted to open it right away and lie on the bed with Christie, but I didn't want to appear too eager. I sat in the chair while she sat on the bed. We talked—about the football team, her nervousness over her last year of school and mine over my first year of law school. She told me that every summer she went backpacking in the Sierra with her parents. She said she felt in a different world when she slept on the ground in the serene beauty there. They hiked into the wilderness for two weeks, everything they needed on pack mules or horses. I felt envious. I had never been on a vacation, except for a four-day trip to Las Vegas when I was twelve.

I couldn't wait any longer. "Let's open the champagne."

"Good idea," she said. I pushed the cork up. It popped and hit the ceiling, part of the champagne bubbling over onto the carpet. "Yea!" we yelled together. I poured carefully into the hotel glasses, handed Christie hers and sat on the bed with her, our backs on pillows propped against the headboard. We drank the whole bottle in about fifteen minutes.

We made out on the bed. Before long we were down to our underwear. Christie slurred her words and talked louder than usual. Her face was flushed. She got up to pee.

In a few minutes the bathroom door clicked open. I looked up. Christie stood naked, grinning. I stared at her slim, smooth body and firm breasts. I had never seen female pubic hair. I was surprised at how much she had. I pulled off my underwear. She came to the bed, still grinning. We thrashed about the bed, moaning, grunting and breathing hard. I was so hard I ached. The adrenalin or testosterone or whatever it was surged from my groin up and down my body. I felt between her legs and put one, then two fingers inside, moving them back and forth. It was warm and wet and lovely. Now I knew which hole to put it in. She felt my hard cock. I put it between her legs, but not inside. We pushed our bodies together rhythmically, harder and faster. My whole body felt like it would explode. Maybe she likes sex, I thought. I sure do. I could have put it in, but I thought she would be angry when she sobered up and realized she had lost her virginity. I feared then she wouldn't marry me. So, I just rubbed my cock between her legs until I came.

She didn't say anything about it, until she yelled from the bathroom, "It smells like celery."

Two weeks later Christie's parents and sister were away for the weekend. We had another sexual romp in her bed. It felt deliciously evil. Again, I didn't try to put it in. Christie spent most weekends with me that school year. She slept in my mother's other twin bed. My parents slept in separate rooms. When my mother went to sleep, Christie came to my room, took her pajamas off and hopped in. I was always naked. We kissed, and I stroked her whole body. I longed to enter her, but I never tried. It always ended the same way—I came on her thigh; she cleaned up in the bathroom, then went back to my mother's room.

On a weekend in late November Christie came in and

stood over me while I sat in my chair reading a law book. "Can I talk to you?" She asked.

"Yeah, I need a break," I said.

She looked straight at me. "I've decided to marry you," she said.

"Great," I said. I stood up and kissed her. That was all there was to it. She didn't say she loved me. Even her acceptance of my proposal was odd. I was glad, but her two- month silence humiliated me. I felt even more romantically inadequate. I was angry, but I didn't express it and soon forgot it. I was afraid she would change her mind.

Chapter Four

I sit on a bench in front of the Inn at Harvard on a sunny October day when Cambridge wears its finest. The mild breeze brushes my arms, not quite moving the hairs. I'm glad to get out of my apartment, where I've been languishing in self-pity. I want to understand what happened to my first marriage. I figure I probably won't cry this time, so I'm safe in public. I take my notebook and pen out of my backpack and write about why I married Christie.

That I didn't seriously consider whether Christie and I would be compatible wasn't as shocking then as it would be now. Marriage is what everybody did then. Most middle-class Americans in the 1950s and 1960s married in their early twenties. Few men elected to stay single, and it was thought that those who did were either Gay—the term then was "queer" —or in some way undesirable. Once Christie said yes, the matter seemed resolved.

Had I given any thought to whether I should get married at all, it would have been that marriage seemed like an ideal way to live. It still seems that way on the surface. You spend a lot of time with somebody who feeds your ego by loving you, giving you a sense of self-worth. You have a big fan at your disposal most of the time. When you're feeling down or insecure, she is there to support you. Your basic needs are conveniently met: someone to share food, sex, and social interaction. Although Buddhists teach that the nature of human life is impermanence and uncertainty, only enlightened monks seem to accept that. Even though before 1963, marriage didn't provide absolute certainty, or permanence, its vows of support "until death do us part," for better or for worse and in sickness and in health seemed as close as we could get.

I feared two things, loneliness and appearing different. I thought the point of life was to seek happiness and avoid pain, not that I thought much about it at all. So I sought to avoid loneliness—painful to me. As an only child I was alone a lot, and I didn't like it. I thought what I felt was loneliness, but I misinterpreted it. I think it was boredom.

Staying single would make me different. I didn't want to be different from my peers. I wanted to be different from my parents. They seemed boring and ignorant. I longed to avoid a boring, lonely life.

I thought marriage would be a way to avoid both loneliness and appearing different. I was twenty-two. Christie was available. It was time.

I needed to feel superior to any woman I dated or married. Christie served that need. I thought she wasn't as smart as I was, or as articulate, and she seemed less secure. Christie was not stupid, but she was slow to understand things. There is a difference, I think—slow versus never getting it. I remember once explaining to her the system of checks and balances among the United States Congress, the Executive Branch and the Judiciary. She just didn't get it for a while. She was not quick-witted and often misunderstood jokes, especially one-liners. She had a sense of humor, but it was uniquely hers. She did not understand other people's sense of humor, often laughing when they were serious and not getting a joke, or taking seriously a remark meant in jest. This made her appear unintelligent. Yogi Berra, or at least, the way the media portrays him, comes to mind. Sometimes Christie's nonsensical remarks were not funny and offended people.

Looking out at Harvard Square I realize I spend a lot of time alone now, but I'm never bored. Writing has taught me about loneliness. It is a solitary pursuit. Through writing I have found I can feel loneliness without despair. It's just another feeling, and it is the human condition. When I'm lonely I live with it; it passes, drops down to my shoes. I don't fear it anymore. Now I own my loneliness.

I remember the loneliness I felt while sitting at my law office desk preparing answers to interrogatories. That was somebody else's loneliness. As a lawyer, I was living somebody else's life, sold to me by my parents and my society. Maybe that's why now I can live with loneliness. It's mine. And my passion for writing and art overpowers loneliness most of the time. When I feel it, sometimes that is when I can dig down deep and get closest to my true self—when no one is around to distract me.

A young woman wearing black walks by my bench in front of the Inn at Harvard. She smiles. As she walks away, her red thong peeks above the low waist of her jeans. My groin stirs. I look away. I walk back home.

In October 2008, the week of my sixty-eighth birthday, I rent a car and drive to Bethel, Maine to view the fall colors in person and continue considering and writing about my marriage to Christie in this serene, inspiring setting. I sit on a bench in front of the bed and breakfast, notebook and pen in hand, gazing at the foliage of tangerine, goldenrod and canary around me, a little early in the season to have turned darker.

I remember my fear that Christie would call off the wedding. Her parents sent her to Europe for two months as a graduation present. She wrote me a few times, but her letters were not romantic. She wrote in detail about what she was doing and seeing, but never mentioned our wedding. She was there with a group of co-eds. I worried that she had met somebody else on the trip or changed her mind and wouldn't tell me until she returned.

She called me the night she returned, two weeks before our wedding day. She said she couldn't see me until she recovered from jet lag. I still thought she was going to renege. The weekend before our wedding she called and asked me to come over. I was scared. I tried not to think about it during the half-hour drive. She opened the door, her mother standing behind her. We hugged, awkwardly, and I greeted her mother. Christie led me to her room, opened a suitcase, and showed me the things she'd bought in Europe. I paid little attention. I clenched my fists.

"Let's go for a walk down the hill," she said. Her parents owned land beyond their yard that they hadn't landscaped. It was covered with trees and brush. We had made out there, since we couldn't be seen from the house. This is where she tells me the wedding's off, I thought. We walked out through the sliding glass door into the stifling August heat. Sweat beaded on my chest and under my arms. Christie led me by the hand toward the gate. She wore yellow shorts and a halter top. The dry, acrid smell of southern California summer brush filled the air as we stepped through the gate. Christie stopped ahead of me and turned around. I looked in her eyes and felt like crying. She pulled me toward her and kissed me. I touched her breasts. She reached up and undid her halter top and let it slide to the ground. I pulled my shirt over my head, and we pressed our naked chests together. We kissed some more. I pulled down my pants and her shorts. She took me in her hand. I came almost right away.

"I see you missed me," she said.

"I sure did," I said.

"I missed you too. The last week I could hardly wait to get home. But we won't be able to see each other again before the wedding. Mother has me booked up with appointments all next week—doctors, the dentist, hairdresser, makeup. Oh, and shopping too."

"But we haven't seen each other for two months."

"Yeah, but after next week, we'll see plenty of each other," she said.

"Yeah." I sighed and gave her a hug.

Our wedding was unmemorable: twenty or so people in a Presbyterian church in Laguna Beach and lunch at a fancy restaurant afterwards, both selected by Christie's mother. Our only friends there were Howard, my best man, and Rachel, Christie's best friend and maid of honor. I figured Christie's mother didn't want a big wedding where all of her friends would see her daughter marry somebody from the "other side of the tracks." They might find out that Christie was going to support me for the next two years. Her parents were against our getting married until I had a full-time job. They didn't think it was appropriate for a wife to support her husband, even temporarily. Our generation embraced a contrary view, and Christie and I didn't see a problem. But I did feel uneasy about it. After all, I was supposed to be the provider.

I had reserved an oceanfront motel for our week's honeymoon in Laguna Beach. I felt proud, almost like an adult, checking into the hotel as Mr. and Mrs. Lemon. I was nervous about performing my husbandly duties on our wedding night. I thought our room was magnificent; it was right on the beach.

Christie's parents hung around for a while. When they left, we walked out of our room onto the sand and took a long stroll before dinner. I was too nervous to enjoy the restaurant's ocean view. Christie was too nervous to eat. I didn't eat much either. I opened a bottle of champagne back in the room, but this time it didn't relax us. Christie talked nonstop about nothing, which is what she did when she was nervous. I said nothing, which is what I did when I was nervous—still do.

When the champagne was gone, she got up and said, "Well, I guess it's time to go to bed, Boyd." She took a bag out of her suitcase and disappeared into the bathroom. I took off my clothes and got in bed, as nervous as when I had debated for a national championship.

Christie emerged from the bathroom wearing a white negligee and see-through panties. Her breasts showed through. She looked funny to me, not sexy. She got in bed. We turned toward each other. Her expression was like that of somebody about to jump off a fifty-foot tower into a puddle of water. We kissed, our mouths dry. I caressed her breasts for a while. She took off her negligee. We hugged and kissed and caressed some more. I finally got hard. I gently stroked her vagina. She was dry. I touched her shoulder, and she lay flat. I got part way up and tried to get between her legs, but put a knee down on the inside of her thigh.

"Ouch," she screamed.

"Sorry," I said. I pushed my cock into what I thought was the right hole.

"Not there; a little higher," she said. I found the hole and pushed, but it wouldn't go in. I pushed again and again until my erection was gone. We tried once more and then gave up.

"Let's just go to sleep and try again tomorrow. It's not a big deal," she said.

"Okay, sorry," I said. It was a big deal to me. I couldn't consummate my marriage. I lay awake. I felt humiliated and unmanly. I would have cried if it wouldn't have made my humiliation worse. Men weren't supposed to cry.

We avoided any sexual contact the next day. I thought about what we could do to relax. As we walked on the beach, I said, "Christie, tonight, why don't we just do what we always used to do in my room at home, and not plan to make love. If it happens it happens, but let's just do what we're used to doing."

"Okay," she said. "That's a big relief."

"And, do me a favor," I said. "No negligee."

When we went to bed that night with our pajamas on, I kissed and caressed her for a long time before I reached down between her legs. She was wet, and I was hard. I got on top of her, careful not to put my full weight on her. I entered her and moved in and out. She arched her hips to meet me until I came. It lacked passion, but at least finally we'd had sex. I felt male. We had no problems making love after that. Christie was never a passionate lover, but I didn't realize that until I could compare.

That Sunday we moved our stuff into our apartment, the same one I'd lived in with my roommate. It felt great to be a married man. One of my life's goals had been achieved. It never occurred to me that it might not be "'til death do us part."

Chapter Five

I walk through the little downtown of Bethel, Maine, peering in cafes and gift shops, until there are no stores. I turn around and head back, my stomach empty, almost aching with hunger. I stop at a café and stuff myself with lamb chops, sautéed spinach and rice pilaf—quickly because it is so loud with inebriated tourists that I can't think. Surrounded by an artist's palette of colors, my irritation fades to serenity on the short walk back to my bed and breakfast. I fall asleep soon after I get into bed, but I awake around two in the morning. I've dreamt about Christie. She was running away from me down a long, dark alley. I tried to run after her but I couldn't—I could only walk.

Wide awake, I fill a mug with water, grab an herbal tea bag from a dark green plastic tray on the dresser. It floats on top of the water. I put it in the microwave, turn it on and pace until my tea is ready. Standing there holding the mug, I think about the dream. I couldn't run after Christie in the dream.

Perhaps, I couldn't be what a husband to her had to be. I had to let her go. My notebook is already open on the old cherry wood desk in my room. I take the tea over and sit down to write, but nothing comes. I've come to this beautiful setting to write, and I can't.

When I get home, for three days I plan to write, but I don't. I'll write when I first get up. Oh, I can't. I'm too groggy. I'll write after my shower. I can't. I'm too hungry. I'll write after breakfast, but it's too late. I have to go to my Pilates class. In the afternoon I have to go grocery shopping. In the evening I'm too tired. This is ridiculous, Boyd, I think. I've never had writer's block. I pick up one of Natalie's books, *Wild Mind*. I don't find anything helpful. Now, I'm really panicked. Good time to slow walk, I think, and I float around my apartment, trying not to think of anything, and surprisingly, I don't. I end up sitting at my computer. I start to write about not being able to write. When I finish, I think of my mother, who seemed to spend a lifetime doing what she didn't want to do. But how could I know that? Maybe her marriage was exactly what she wanted. Something clicks in, and I write about my parents' marriage.

I went into marriage with my parents' marriage as my only model. I hadn't considered what I expected of Christie as a wife. My mother lived for my father and me. She had fathomless patience. She had no friends, except my father's friends. She had no interests outside the home, except to join in my father's choices, and she went nowhere except with him or in pursuit of her household and motherly duties. She didn't even have a driver's license. She kept a perfect home. To the extent that she engaged in leisure, it was to embroider or crochet, or occasionally read a romantic novel at home or listen to a soap opera on the radio. After we got a TV when I was twelve, she watched two soap operas every day.

She was thirty-two when they married, old for her generation.

"If it hadn't been for your father I would have been an old maid," she once told me. The way she said it, I assumed that that would have been disgraceful. And my dad was a good, steady provider, she said.

My father controlled the family. It was no partnership—he was on top. He usually insisted that my mother accompany him where he wanted to go. She loved the movies. She liked romances, and my father liked adventure movies, so of course they usually went to adventure movies. After my father died she complained about that, but I doubt she complained to him. My father didn't consider my mother's needs or wants, and she didn't ask him to. After all, he was a reliable provider, and he didn't abuse her. That was enough for her, I guess. I'm sure he saw himself, as men did then, as a benevolent dictator.

The message to me was that a wife's needs were unimportant, and that she would stay with her husband no matter what, if he provided for and didn't abuse her. I expected Christie to play that role. I didn't think it unfair.

Late one mid-October night I think about Christie and decide to email her. I tell her I'm writing a memoir about my marriages and ask what she thinks was the cause of our breakup.

A few days later she replies. "We were not compatible. And you were a poor money manager. But the last straw was the Led Zeppelin concert."

Led Zeppelin emerged in 1968, and Christie loved them. They played in concert at the Rose Palace in Pasadena that year, and she bought tickets for us and our friends, Paula and Steve. We parked in a lot near the auditorium. Young people, many of them teenagers, rushed by as we got out of the car and waited to cross the street. Out in front of the auditorium the air buzzed with voices. A girl walked by us in an unbuttoned leather vest, nothing, but her, underneath. Inside, an hour later, the music, as well as the crowd, exuded excitement.

Girls danced topless in the aisles.

It didn't sound like music to me. It wasn't pleasant, and it was so loud my ears rang, and my head buzzed. I don't remember anything they played. After about forty-five minutes, a band member stepped to the mike and announced they were going to take a break and be back for a second set that would be the same songs as the first. Anybody who wanted could stay.

"I wanna stay," said Christie.

"No," I said, "Let's go." I turned toward the aisle. Christie followed me in silence.

I don't think it was the Led Zeppelin concert that mattered to me. I believe it was my need for control and its partner, power. Her recent email suggests the same thing, that it was just the last example of my lack of caring for her needs and wants. She was passionate about Led Zeppelin, and I didn't care. Another forty-five minutes of the concert wouldn't have mattered to me. I didn't even try to think of any alternatives to all of us leaving. I could have hung out at a nearby coffee shop for forty-five minutes. How could I refuse to let her stay for that second set? I would never do such a thing now. Nor would most women today silently submit to my control as Christie did. I wasn't aware that I didn't care what Christie felt or wanted.

Perhaps I could have gotten away with my attitude in the first half of the twentieth century. But I read magazines and newspapers and watched TV during the 1960s. Why couldn't I see that a woman born forty years after my mother would demand more from life, more from me, than my mother did of her husband, especially a woman who could earn her own living? Apparently, it didn't penetrate my great analytical mind that it would make a difference. I didn't understand either before or during our marriage that I couldn't control Christie as my father controlled my mother. I couldn't be the benevolent dictator. How could I have been so stupid?

As an only male child of the 50's, I never did anything around the house. When I went away to college, I could not cook or do laundry. Nor had I ever cleaned anything, except my own body. All my life one of my great joys has been learning to do new things. Apparently, housework and cooking were exceptions.

My father never did anything around the house, except to fix things that broke and take out the trash. Sometimes he dried the dishes. My mother did all the cooking, cleaning, laundry, grocery shopping—all domestic chores. My father could not cook anything and did not know how to operate the washing machine. The male and female roles were sharply delineated in their generation, a simplicity that stabilized marriage but enslaved women and burdened men with taking care of an inferior adult. I couldn't see that.

My mother had emergency surgery to remove a kidney when I was about ten. When my father attempted to cook a meal while she was in the hospital, the hamburger patty he cooked was the color of coal. It was like eating wood. The peas tasted like lawn clippings in warm water. I couldn't cut through the baked potato.

"Sorry," said Dad, looking down at his plate.

I put my leftover ground beef in Blackie the cat's bowl. The next morning it was still there, untouched. Blackie would eat anything, including peanuts, corn and even spinach, but not Dad's ground beef. We ate the rest of our meals out.

When I was in law school and after I started working, I expected Christie to cook and take care of the house as my mother did, though Christie worked outside the home on her feet all day. I thought she should do the cooking, most of the grocery shopping, the laundry and the house cleaning, except that I allowed her to have a cleaning lady come in twice a month. How could I have been unaware of the unfairness of my expectations?

For the first six months of our marriage we lived in the apartment I had lived in with my college roommate. I think

Christie was ashamed of it. We never had friends over. The only people who lived in the neighborhood were USC students and poor African Americans.

After we had been married about six months, we moved to a modern, spacious apartment in the northern Glendale hills. In the mornings the little town of Montrose below reflected the sun. In the afternoon the Verdugo Hills formed a peaceful, rural-like view from our living room and terrace. Looking down from my terrace to the town below gave me a sense of importance that I hadn't felt before. I had already risen above my parents' dull, ordinary life. I'd never lived anywhere with a view. My house in Alhambra had a view of the house across the street. The apartment complex had laundry rooms and a pool. I'd never known such luxury.

Christie wanted to furnish our fancy apartment appropriately. We borrowed the money. My parents, who never went into debt for anything except the mortgage on the house, bought most of their furniture used, and what was new had been purchased in the early '40s. When the couch or my father's easy chair became so worn that it embarrassed my parents, they recovered it, usually in a similar fabric and color. I felt a little uneasy about borrowing to buy furniture, but I didn't say anything.

Influenced by her architect father, Christie had strong opinions about what was appropriate décor—Danish modern. I went with her to pick out the furniture, but she made the decisions. Aesthetic matters are a woman's role, I thought. I know nothing about such things. When all the furniture had arrived, it looked odd to me, so stark. I said nothing. It was modern. It must be chic.

After our move we had our first dinner party. We invited a dental hygienist friend of Christie's and her dentist husband. The dinner featured a standing rib roast. I'd learned a little about cooking during college. I rubbed the roast with seasoning, prepared the salad and mashed the potatoes. Christie supervised. I grew resentful. Christie isn't doing her job, I thought. We chatted with our guests in the kitchen, while I finished preparing dinner. Suddenly Christie screamed, and I heard a kerplop. Something warm and greasy slid onto my bare foot—the roast Christie had dropped on the floor. I grabbed the mitts from the floor, where Christie had dropped them, picked up the roast and washed it off. Our guests seemed understanding. As they left, I promised them next time we would try to keep dinner off the floor. Christie went to bed as soon as they were gone, and I followed. It was an accident—I didn't blame her.

The next day was a workday for both of us. When I arrived home at ten that night, Christie was asleep, and the kitchen was in the same mess as the night before—it stayed that way for two more nights. Blue mold grew in the sink, and the kitchen smelled like a landfill. As Christie undressed in the bedroom, I yelled at her from the hallway to clean up the kitchen. She shouted she was too tired to clean up. My retort echoed through the apartment: "It's your job!" I rushed down the hall to remind her that she rarely cleaned up after meals. She ignored me. A little later, I cleaned the kitchen.

After that night, whenever a mess in the kitchen disgusted me, I cleaned it up, with great resentment, often telling her that I was doing her job. We both worked full time, though I worked longer hours. I never tried to discuss with her how we could resolve this issue or propose a sensible division of household labor. It never occurred to me to try to resolve it, or that there was something to resolve. I simply kept demanding that she clean the kitchen, until, eventually, I gave up. I didn't expect to do any housework when I was married. I stuck to what I had learned from my parents, that housework was a woman's job.

From the beginning, Christie never cooked much. We ate dinner out a lot—an ironic change from her fear of eating in restaurants when we first dated. Since my parents rarely had, it was a new adventure that I loved. Besides, all Christie ever learned to cook was hamburger, pan-fried chicken breasts, steak tartare, and peanut butter sandwiches. She took a peanut butter and jelly sandwich to work for lunch every day. I resented that she made no effort to learn to cook. I usually limited my cooking to scrambled eggs and bacon, or pancakes, and steaks or hamburgers on the barbeque on weekends. Sometimes I added rice or baked potatoes and a vegetable to Christie's hamburger or chicken breasts. Once in a while, usually when Christie went to bed without eating dinner, I made myself spaghetti with canned sauce. I didn't consider increasing my cooking skills so we had a wider variety of food to eat. I chose to remain mired in anger and resentment. I didn't see that marriage was a partnership. I could have proposed a fair division of meal preparation. Didn't it occur to Christie to discuss these domestic issues either, or was she intimidated by my dominance?

Although Christie usually left the kitchen a mess, she was strict when it came to cleanliness and order in everything else. She was impeccable with personal hygiene, showering and applying deodorant every day without fail. Her files were always in order, as was her sock and underwear drawer. She saved everything, put it in its place and knew exactly where it was. Her things were important to her. She expressed anger when somebody inadvertently scratched a table or broke a glass—beyond what was normal, I thought.

She subscribed to *Vogue*, the country's most prestigious women's fashion magazine. She saved every copy and stacked them in chronological order on a shelf in our closet. Every once in a while I used to thumb through an issue. They often had some sexy pictures. One day she told me she didn't want me looking at her *Vogues* anymore, because I dog-eared the pages. I complied with her request. Christie is really strange, I thought.

Chapter Six

As I walk through my Cambridge neighborhood on the way to Whole Foods, magenta and tawny leaves flutter to the ground around me. Larger ones sail like kites on a blustery day. My feet crush others on the ground. I feel the chill of the October morning. I recall another trip to the market when I was about twelve—with my mother. I had written about it before and realized that it and similar incidents had a profound impact on my life. When I return from Whole Foods and slowly put away the groceries, it strikes me that the shopping trip with my mother also influenced the priorities I brought to my marriage and, consequently, my relationship with my wife. I sit down at my computer and write.

As always, the market smelled of greens and disinfectant. Ethel, a checker, smiled at me, turned to my mother and said, "I see you brought along a helper. How are you, Boyd?"

"Fine," I said, looking down at the floor.

Mom said, "See you in a bit," and I followed her toward the canned vegetable section. To get there we had to go through the fresh produce. I stopped at a display of big, shiny tomatoes.

"Can we get tomatoes? Please, Mommy, please?"

She looked back at me. "I'm sorry, Boyd. We can't afford tomatoes. Every year they get more expensive. They're ten cents a pound more than last year and my food budget won't allow it."

"But, Mom, just one. I love tomatoes, and they're good for me."

"You heard me, Boyd. No. We can't."

"When I grow up I'm going to buy all the tomatoes I want," I said.

"I hope you do, son. I hope you do."

On the walk home I listened attentively, as my mother told me that my father regretted having to quit school in fifth grade to help support his mother and two younger brothers. His lack of education kept him from advancing further in the Edison Company, she said. She reminded me more than once. My father never discussed that with me, but it was in the air whenever he impressed upon me the importance of working hard to achieve in school so that I could go to college and get a good job—meaning one that paid more and had greater status than his job as a dispatcher for the Edison Company. When I was in high school, he pounded away at his plans for me—to get an engineering degree and get an electrical engineering job with the Edison Company.

I rejected his plans, but not his ambition for me. When I married Christie in 1963, my universe, my single-minded focus was to work hard to achieve the best grades I could in law school. Finishing in the top ten percent of my class would yield a job with a prestigious law firm and, ultimately, status and money. I had internalized my father's ambition for me.

After my second year I got a summer job with the State

Commissioner of Corporations. On the day when grades and class rankings were posted in the law school lobby, I left the office and drove to campus. Grades would be posted in order of class ranking. How humiliating for those who were near the bottom, I thought. I guess they're preparing us for the jungle out there. I hurried to the lobby, nerves on edge, stomach fluttering. It didn't take me long to see my name. I counted names from the top—ninth in the class of a hundred and fifty, up from fourteenth after my first year. My grades were all A's and two high B's. I was elated.

When I got home, Christie was standing at the sink eating a peanut butter sandwich. I told her about my grades and class ranking. She smiled and hugged me.

"Congratulations," she said. "It looks like I married well. My parents will be happy."

My last year I got a part-time job doing research for a professor. I felt that a husband should do all he could to earn money for the family.

When I told Christie she said, "You don't have to work if it's too much, but I appreciate it."

I finished law school second in my class with most of the honors the University of Southern California School of Law bestowed. Christie told me she was proud of me. Her parents, who mostly ignored us, came to the graduation ceremony. These honors didn't come easy. I worked with the dogged determination of a marathon runner. I spent little time with Christie, but she never complained about my long hours of study and work on the Law Review.

The Monday after graduation, I started work at the prestigious downtown L.A. law firm that had hired me, Nossaman, Waters & Moss. In August, while I studied for the bar exam, a few blocks from the law school outraged young black men and boys burned and ravaged Watts in an uncontrolled protest against poverty, police brutality and racism. For days sirens blared and fires raged. I was horrified by the TV images showing the conflagration a few blocks from my law school, but I focused on my studies.

In December, I was notified that I had passed the bar exam, and on January 6, 1966 I attended the swearing-in ceremonies for new lawyers. I had achieved one goal, but now I fervently wanted to be the perfect new attorney. My new goal was to reach partnership in the law firm. That would bring admiration from Christie and my peers, and the big bucks.

On the 110 freeway that first day as a licensed attorney, I spotted the tall, skinny Los Angeles City Hall. I remembered an earlier time I had seen it. I was with my dad in the blue '47 Chevy coupe, headed for the Los Angeles Angels baseball game at Wrigley Field on Avalon Boulevard in South Central Los Angeles. The Angels were in the Pacific Coast League then. I was about nine. The City Hall tower in downtown L.A. came into view, thirteen stories, at the time the tallest building in L.A. Dad pointed out about a dozen men at the side of the road. They wore jeans covered with dirt, and sweat-stained white t-shirts clung to their bodies. They plunged shovels into the dark chocolate-brown earth, and threw the dirt in a pile—almost in unison, like the rowing crews on the Charles. The strings that outlined the trenches they were digging marked an area over five feet wide and fifty feet long.

"Ditch diggers," Dad said. "That's why you need to get good grades in school and go to college, so you won't end up doing that when you grow up."

"Yeah, I sure don't want to be doin' that, Daddy," I said. I wanted to do what the men on the baseball diamond did—play baseball for a living, but in the major leagues back east, not just the Pacific Coast League. I didn't say that. Dreams were not mentioned in our family. Never did either of my parents suggest that I should work at something I enjoyed or was passionate about. Passion about anything was never mentioned or expressed either. Life was all about working hard and achieving, "getting ahead," the American dream. So I ploughed through most of my life directed by that goal, not knowing what really moved me or who I was deep within.

My father reminded me of the horror of becoming a ditch digger whenever we saw laborers. That was the stick. He also showed me the carrot. He started taking me to the horse races at Santa Anita when I was five. We drove the ten miles east to Arcadia, down Huntington Drive toward the racetrack. One time he turned onto a side street. We drove through a neighborhood in San Marino. The green lawns looked like golf course fairways. Flowers of every color bordered the lawns and framed the houses. Gardeners labored at many of them, their pickup trucks overflowing with mowers, rakes, edgers, clippers, and tools I didn't recognize. The houses were three times as wide as ours, stretching out for half a block. I glimpsed swimming pools shimmering in the backyards.

"This is where the rich people live," said Dad. "Doctors, lawyers, executives, people like that. They all play golf on Wednesdays at the country club. Just try getting a doctor on a Wednesday. Must be nice."

"Really," I said, my mouth wide in amazement.

"Yeah, and most of them were born with a silver spoon in their mouth, too."

"Whatd'ya mean, Daddy? I asked.

"Their parents were rich, so they got into top colleges, and made it the easy way. If you're not born in a rich family, it's hard. But in this great country of ours, son, if you work really hard you can have all that some day, too."

"You mean, I could have my own swimming pool in my backyard?"

"You could, if you work hard."

I took my parents seriously. I had chosen the career that would get me all the tomatoes I wanted, that would bring me status and material success, rather than what stirred passion in my heart. I chose what my parents taught me and my society rewarded with status and money, not what was right for me. When I walked into the office that day, I strode, not into a life that I wanted, not a life I was passionate about, but one that someone else wanted. Deep inside I wanted to be a teacher, but I thought they didn't make enough money. These thoughts were not on the surface of my consciousness then, so I hadn't expressed them to Christie.

Soon after I started working, I told her we should save to buy a house. Rent was just money down a rat hole, I said. She agreed. Maybe the swimming pool was not far away.

Within a few weeks I was working long hours. I arrived at the office at nine-thirty, when lawyers usually came in to avoid the worst of the traffic. Leaving before seven was rare; often it was nine or ten. I usually worked Saturdays and occasionally Sundays. I did whatever was necessary to advance my career, including growing a moustache to look older. Christie didn't complain about the long hours at first. I did the complaining. Her response was that she worked hard too—on her feet eight hours a day. I didn't say what I thought—she only worked four days a week. Typically, I arrived home tired and tense. I fixed myself a Scotch and numbed my brain, the beginning of a lifelong habit—addiction is more accurate.

One day my to-do list had grown to fill most of a page, probably more than eighteen items. I had added new items faster than I crossed off finished ones. I sat in my office trying to prioritize the list. My tie squeezed my neck, and I pulled it down. I need to get shirts with bigger necks, I thought. I would grow to hate wearing ties and suits every day, but at first they were a sign of status and made me feel important. My shirts were white, not blue like my father's.

My intercom buzzed. It was Bill, my supervising partner. "Come over to my office," he said. "I want to go over that brief you drafted in the Grossman appeal." As I hurried down the hall, I felt the adrenaline surge.

After knocking, I plopped down in one of the two chairs in front of his desk. His desk was cluttered with stacks of papers, deposition transcripts, law books, and three cups of coffee, only one of which was still warm, I knew from previous meetings.

Bill was examining the first paragraph of the twenty-eight-page brief as if it were a malignant mole. His tall, thin frame, receding light brown hairline and the sharp features of an Englishman made him appear stern. "You use too many commas," he muttered, as he lined out three from that paragraph. "This sentence is awkward. How about this?" showing me the reconstructed sentence. "No, wait a minute," and he sat there reworking the sentence for the next several minutes. "There," he said. "Whadaya think?"

"Looks good," I said. It was a better sentence.

"You use 'argue' three times in this paragraph. Besides, we don't argue; we explain truths." He removed "argue" from the three sentences and rewrote them.

Three hours later we were on page eight. "Now," he said, handing me the draft he had written on, "I want you to go back and outline in detail what you've written. I think you'll see problems in organization. Reorganize it. Then rewrite it. The language needs tightening up. This brief shouldn't be longer than twenty pages. Bring it back to me tomorrow afternoon, and we'll go over it again. I'll be back from court about four-thirty."

He must have seen my look of disappointment before I turned around to leave. "It's not a bad first effort," he said. "Just needs a little work."

"Okay, I'll give it another shot," I said.

Back in my office, I looked at the to-do list again. How am I ever going to get all this done? A few minutes later, my phone rang. Al said, "Boyd, do you have those Eisenberg interrogatories done?"

"Not yet. When do you need 'em? I asked.

"Tomorrow," he said.

"I can't do that," I said. "Bill wants an appellate brief rewritten by tomorrow. I could have it the day after."

"Well, Christ," Al said. "I gave you that assignment before Bill gave you the appellate brief. He always does that. Pisses me off. Well, it's not your fault. I guess day after tomorrow will have to do."

"Okay," I said and hung up. I wondered if I should just do it. I really wanted to keep these partners happy with my work. He said it wasn't my fault, but he wasn't happy.

My stomach felt queasy. I worked on the appellate brief until ten. It was almost done. When I got home, I undressed in the bathroom. I knew Christie would be asleep. I walked quietly into the bedroom, lay down next to her and tried to sleep. I was thinking about Al's interrogatories. I couldn't sleep. I left in the morning before Christie woke up.

I finished everything by noon and gave it to the secretaries to type. About four-thirty Bill called me in. He read the brief while I waited. "This is better," he said.

"Thank you," I said, holding back a smile. He pulled a pen out of his center drawer and started marking it up. By seven o'clock he was on page eighteen. "That's enough for today," he said. "How about a drink?"

"Sure," I said. I shouldn't, I thought, but I'd better go with him. Besides, I needed a drink.

It was eight-thirty when I excused myself and said I had to go. I'd had three drinks; he had five. I didn't consider the risk of driving after three drinks. On the way home, I realized I had forgotten to call Christie to tell her I would be late. She was asleep again when I got home, and I left before she was up the next morning. I hadn't seen her awake in four days.

When we got up Saturday morning, Christie ignored me for a while. I asked her if she wanted pancakes.

"I guess so," she said. "Are you going to the office today?"

"Yeah, I have to," I said. "When the phones aren't ringing I can get a lot done."

"Please stay home, Boyd," she pleaded. I haven't seen you in four days. It's boring around here on weekends when you're at the office. I wanted to go hiking today in the canyon. You don't really have to go into the office, do you?"

"I'm afraid so," I said. "I have a lot of work to do."

Her face flushed. "Your work is obviously more important

than I am," she implored. "You didn't even call me last night." She stormed out of the kitchen.

My muscles tensed. "It's not like I have a choice," I yelled. "You could give me some support, instead of bitching." She slammed the bedroom door.

I felt abused by both my bosses and my wife. I'm doing this for our future, I thought. I don't like these long hours, working nights and weekends. I'm exhausted, but I have to do this to be a successful lawyer, a partner. My mind raced as my thoughts gathered fury. It's twice as hard when the bitch whines about it instead of sympathizing with me. Either I jeopardize my position with the firm, or I make her mad. There's no solution. I was the rat that had gone for the cheese and was now trapped. I labored under this degree of pressure, or worse, in this imaginary trap, for the rest of my marriage.

Christie was not a workaholic. She only worked four days a week. She didn't have to work more. She made more money than I did for the first three years I was a lawyer. She spoke with pride about how much she made.

When I was home with Christie or in the car going someplace, Christie deluged me with nonstop talk of personal details about her patients. How they were able to tell her so much with her hands in their mouths, I don't know, but she seemed to know a lot about their personal lives. Especially at home after dinner, Christie went on and on about Mr. so-and-so's son, who was a rabbi and somebody else whose teeth developed so much plaque he had to come in every three months and took two visits to get it all off. One woman must drink gallons of coffee every day, because her teeth were stained brown so badly. Mr. Jones' wife died of breast cancer three months after diagnosis—and on and on.

I had no interest in these details of her patient's lives, and I never understood why she thought I did, or if she gave it any thought. Occasionally, I was able to divert her to another subject, but then she sometimes accused me of interrupting. She was right, of course. I should have said something as sensitively as possible, but, instead, I just tuned her out. Sometimes, my attention drifted so far that I didn't realize she had changed the subject, and was actually telling me something I might want to know. Once while my mind was off somewhere, she told me she wouldn't be home the next Tuesday night, because she was taking her sister to a movie. When next Tuesday night arrived, and she wasn't home, fortunately, the first place I called was her parents. After the consequences of not listening to her had occurred several times, she rightly accused me of not listening to her. I denied it.

In contrast, I never talked to her about my clients or my law cases. When I mentioned that once, she said, "Good. I'm glad you don't. It would bore me."

We did have some laughs over the names of some of her patients—back when I was still listening. When she had a patient with a name that she thought was funny, she would pronounce it in an exaggerated manner and laugh. I remember one named "Meepos," a name Christie found hilarious. She would emphasize and draw out the double "e", raise the pitch of her voice and make a popping sound on the "p"— "Meeeeeppos." She said he was a short, stout, bald-headed accountant, a perfect Meepos. She loved unusual names. Why else would she name our cats Mordecai and Hadassah?

When Christie was interested in something, she was fanatic. At first, it was cleaning teeth. Then it was Judaism and finally rock music. Her fanaticism included talking constantly about it.

I realize I'm hungry. It's after three, and I've been writing since seven o'clock without eating. I get up from my computer and fix lunch. Afterwards, I sit back down and gaze out the window at what is left of the colored foliage and picture the trees and bushes covered with snow. I'll write some more, I think. I have become obsessed.

Thinking back to my work situation in the sixties, although I thought I was trapped, the lock was on the inside, and I had the key. There were many alternatives I could have pursued, but I didn't consider any at all. I didn't have to stay in the private practice. I did nothing but complain, harbor anger and resentment of Christie, and withdraw into myself.

I no longer believe that Christie was trying to make it harder on me. I believe she was expressing her needs, trying to enjoy my company and to connect with me, and I ignored her. For starters, I could have had a calm, reasoned discussion with her to seek a resolution of those needs, to show her that I was trying, that I cared about her and her needs. I could have suggested marital counseling. Instead I berated her and made her feel worse. Neither of us was able to address the issues between us without rancor and accusation. It never occurred to me that addressing the issues was necessary.

By drinking after work near the office and at home, when I had the opportunity to relate to Christie, I exacerbated the inattention and blinded myself from awareness of it. I avoided some of the pain of my unfulfilling work. With alcohol as my aid and ambition to succeed as my guide, I forged ahead toward what I feared most—loneliness.

Chapter Seven

Remembrances of my marriages that used to be buried deep in my mind leap to the surface. Now that I have started to write about them, I find that once they penetrate my mind I can't drive them out, and I don't want to. On an Indian summer October evening I feel them there. I decide to fix sardines and crackers for dinner and stay in to write.

I don't often write my remembrances immediately. I give them time to simmer. Many aren't relevant to my memoir or, on further reflection, are not true or real. I have signed up for four of Natalie's workshops in 2009. She calls it an intensive, because everyone who signs up commits to come to all four weeklong workshops during the year, one in each season. So I will be writing and listening to the same people read their writing for four weeks during the year. Most of the week is in silence: no talking to anyone except in class. I know from my previous writing workshops that silence removes distraction and allows you to focus more deeply on writing.

Much of writing practice results in what Natalie calls garbage. Even she admittedly writes garbage. But if you dig deep and keep the pen moving (or fingers on the keys)—don't stop— for the allotted time, not censuring what you write, some gems will come from deep in your mind, she says.

In writing this memoir I often use "I remember...." This time, after I finish my sardines, I sit at my computer and start writing for a half hour on the topic, "When Did My Marriage to Christie Start to Crumble?" I let what I write sit for a few days. I read it. Not too awful, but it needs a lot of work. I spend most of the day revising it. I revise it three more times. Rarely does anything from writing practice end up in a finished piece as originally written. Because of the nature of writing practice— keep the pen moving; don't think, just write—it always needs revisions, sometimes major, sometimes minor. Most of what I write never makes it to the memoir.

Christie didn't complain about my long hours of studying in law school, and she didn't complain about them practicing law at first. But signs of problems occurred early. Less than three months after our wedding my father had his third heart attack. He died the day John Kennedy was buried. Christie didn't go to the funeral. "I hate funerals, and I have a cold," she said. "I feel lousy. The last thing I need to do is go to a funeral."

I answered the query, "Where is your wife?" what seemed like a hundred times.

"Oh, she's not feeling well," I said each time. I was angry. I had a right to be angry. But I couldn't, didn't express my anger. I needed my wife at that funeral, and she didn't come.

One evening when I arrived home from work, Christie stood in the kitchen facing the sink, her shoulders slumped more than usual, head down. She turned and looked up at me. "I was fired today," she said, her voice shaking. "Dr. Teller fired me."

"Why?" I asked.

"He didn't say. He just said it wasn't working out."

"I'm sorry." I reached to hug her, but she turned away.

"I'm going to bed," she said. It was only eight o'clock.

I'm sure you'll have no trouble finding another job, honey," I said. I didn't know what else to say. She didn't talk to me about it anymore.

A few days later she told me she was going to an interview. She said she was very nervous. "You'll do fine," I said. I felt so sorry for her. She got the job.

This was the second time she had been fired. The first time she had said something to a patient that he complained about, and the dentist told her there had been too many patient complaints. I thought I knew what was happening. Christie was socially inept. She often said things that were not appropriate, such as on our second date when she stage whispered about the waiter, "He's cute." She asked people she didn't know well personal questions. More than once I heard her ask casual acquaintances what they paid for their home or car. She even asked people how much money they made, and bragged about how much she made. At inappropriate times, she mentioned vomit or shit or the gore of cleaning someone's gross mouth. She spoke her mind on politics and religion to strangers. She seemed oblivious to what might offend people. I heard her tell an acquaintance that her dress was ugly, and a friend that she didn't like her hairstyle. She once told a friend of mine that his tie was hideous. I lived in fear that when she attended some Nossaman Firm social event—fortunately, there weren't many—she would insult one of my bosses. I don't think she meant to offend or insult, but she often did. She had a blind spot.

It was as if she had been locked in a closet and not allowed to interact with people most of her life. Maybe her parents kept her away from interacting. She told me they made her afraid to talk to people, but she didn't elaborate on what they did.

She said she hated her parents. They always criticized and

never praised her. They made her feel stupid and inadequate, she said. Several times when I was dating her I was with her when one of her parents told her she was stupid and wouldn't let her finish a sentence, scoffing at what she was saying. She told me it was worse when she was a child. This was one explanation for her lack of self-confidence, her shyness and difficulty relating to people, I thought.

I couldn't know, but suspected, she was making inappropriate remarks that offended patients and the dentist. I didn't feel this was anything I could help her change, so I never said anything about it. I guess I could have suggested therapy or a class originated by Andrew Carnegie, "How to Win Friends and Influence People," but I didn't.

Along with her lack of social grace, Christie claimed she was physically uncoordinated and awkward. I know she couldn't catch a ball or throw one accurately. But I think her claims were exaggerated due to her lack of self-confidence. Later in life she became a skilled mountain and rock climber and at the age of sixty-eight still excels as a rock climber.

Christie's social ineptness served me. I was shy and insecure about my social graces. Christie made me feel sophisticated and socially skilled by comparison. That went a long way in making me feel superior to Christie, a need I apparently had.

I believe that for most obnoxious human characteristics, there is a beneficial side, and that was true of Christie's. Whenever she expressed her feelings or opinion about something, I knew she was totally honest. She didn't say things just to be nice. When she told me she liked my tie, I knew she really did. When she told me I was really smart, I knew she honestly thought so. In a way, to me, her social ineptness had its endearing side.

When I first met Christie, I didn't know it, but she had only one friend, a girl that had lived across the street from her all her life, Judy. In two years living in her sorority house, she made no friends. I knew that, but I didn't appreciate what that said about her. She rarely went out of her way to do anyone the smallest favor, even her husband. Once when my car died on the freeway on the way home from work about nine o'clock at night, I walked to the nearest gas station and called a tow truck. Then, I called Christie and asked her to come and pick me up. This was years before our divorce. It would have taken her about twenty minutes to get there. She told me she was too tired and was going to bed. "Take a taxi," she said.

I'd heard her react similarly to requests from co-workers and the few friends she finally made after she started working, giving some unconvincing excuse for why she couldn't help them. My somewhat educated guess is that her parents were her models for that behavior. She had no idea that such selfish behavior angered people.

The summer after Christie and I married she suggested we take a week's vacation to Sequoia National Park—my first real vacation. I have loved traveling ever since. I had never seen such beauty. The huge two-thousand-year-old Sequoia redwoods made me a nature lover for life. One day, we hiked eight miles through woods, on the edges of narrow canyon trails, past cold rushing streams, clear green ponds and foaming waterfalls. I was awed by the clean, clear serenity of the woods. The sweet, green smell has stayed with me. At the end of the hike I collapsed onto our bed with that strange mix of joy and physical exhaustion. I admired Christie's energy in the woods and her knowledge of the flora. I was grateful to her for expanding my life. Her passion was contagious. We took vacations every year—the Oregon Coast, Mexico, a driving trip to Austin, Texas. I admired and respected her then. Maybe I even loved her. But I didn't know how to show it.

Vacations also meant more sex. I had read somewhere that the average married couple had sex twice a week. I didn't consider whether our circumstances were "average," whether average included wives that worked outside the home, whether length of the marriage made any difference in the average or whether average had any significance at all. I took the average as my minimum right as a husband.

After our wedding night failure, our sex life, seemed what I thought, was average for the first couple of years, though there was no passion. Then it got less stimulating for me, and I assume for Christie. Still, I wanted sex twice a week. We rarely tried oral sex, and when we did, it didn't seem satisfying. We experimented with a few different positions, but the missionary position seemed best. I put no more effort into trying to satisfy Christie sexually than I did her other needs. She didn't ask for anything. Nor did I. I thought it was just supposed to come naturally. In a couple of years, we had sex less frequently. I complained to no avail.

After the bar exam in August 1965, we explored the mountains and valleys of Colorado for two weeks. By the second week, Christie complained that she felt tired and nauseated. The whites of her eyes and her skin were yellowish. With four days left of our vacation, she asked if we could go home. I was upset. Studying and taking the bar exam had been exhausting and emotionally draining, and I wanted that vacation. I told her she could just rest as much as she needed to. I wanted to go on. She didn't protest.

Except for her surgery, my mother never got sick, or if she did, she didn't complain. She soldiered on. All Christie did for the last two days of the trip was lie in the back seat of the car and complain. The last night, she went to bed as soon as we checked into the hotel. I drank four Scotch drinks called 'Rusty Nails' in the bar. I staggered back to the room. The next day I had to help Christie walk to the plane at the Denver Airport.

The day after we got home, I went to work. Christie went to the doctor. She called and told me she had Hepatitis B. She had gotten it from a patient, she said. Dental hygienists in those days wore nothing for protection from their patients' blood. There was no treatment for Hepatitis B, except bed rest to allow the body to rid itself of the virus. Without bed rest, or with a weakened immune system, it could be fatal. She could not get out of bed for eight weeks and needed frequent bed rest for another four. Then she could gradually go back to work.

My mother agreed to take care of Christie until she could get out of bed. I continued working late and going out to drink. Nothing changed for me, except I got no sex. Neither my mother nor Christie mentioned my failure to take care of my sick wife. It didn't occur to me that, although my mother could take care of her physically, Christie might need her husband's support and company.

During our courtship and marriage we discussed religion occasionally. Christie was raised Presbyterian and I Baptist, but neither of us had gone to church since high school. We agreed that we couldn't buy into the Christian dogma. But, she said, her love of natural beauty stimulated a feeling that there must be some force beyond what we sensed as reality that created and maintained order in the universe and maybe even some kind of life or consciousness after death.

A class in Philosophy in college had sparked my interest, and during summers I read books by Descartes, Nietzsche, Sartre and Camus. I suggested to Christie that we take a class together in philosophy. She thought that was a good idea, but said she was nervous to take a class with me because I was so smart. "You'll probably get an A, and I won't," she said.

"So what," I said. Who cares about the grade! We can just audit the class if you want."

"No," she said. Then I might not be motivated to study."

We took a Western Philosophy class at Glendale College and enjoyed it. We both got A's.

One of the philosophers we studied was Jewish. I don't recall which one. I think that led Christie to read about Judaism. She went to several services at the Wilshire Boulevard Temple, where they practiced Reform Judaism, the most liberal and least dogmatic. I went to one or two services. I thought it was interesting and not as dogmatic as Christianity, but I didn't care for what dogma there was.

One day she told me that she needed religion and that Judaism was the only religion she knew that she could believe in. She asked me if I minded if she formally converted. I didn't care and said so. I went to the conversion ceremony, and Christie started going to services nearly every Friday evening. I joined her on Friday evenings occasionally and on High Holy Days. I thought I was being a good, supportive husband by not objecting. Maybe the truth was I just didn't care.

By June 1966, we had saved the down payment on a house. Christie wanted to live in the San Fernando Valley. There were more Jews in the Valley than in most other desirable areas of L.A., she said.

We found a house she liked in a new development in Granada Hills, for $36,000. We had it professionally landscaped, including a custom patio and arbor in the backyard. She picked out more furniture at Plummers, a high-end furniture store in Pasadena, while I stood around bored. It was more Danish modern, bright blue chairs and an orange couch in the living room. A teak couch with blue and green plaid fabric adorned the family room; for the bedroom she chose a plain rosewood headboard with rosewood dresser and nightstands.

I felt proud that, at twenty-six, I owned a new three-bedroom home that was fully furnished and landscaped. A few months later I bought a new Porsche on credit. I didn't want to be a lawyer driving my dad's '63 Nash Rambler while my wife drove a Porsche.

Chapter Eight

In a few days I leave for Norfolk, Virginia for my daughter Jennifer's wedding. I have not been sleeping well. I'm exhausted. I sleep only three or four hours a night. I'm tired all the time, but when I go to bed I can't sleep. I take herbal sleeping capsules, but they don't help. I know I'm deeply troubled by what I have unearthed about my treatment of Christie. Two nights before I leave for the wedding I walk the block to the nearest liquor store and buy a small bottle of Scotch. I'll talk to my doctor about non-habit forming sleeping pills when I have my annual physical next month, but I don't want to replace one drug with another. Right now I'm desperate to get some sleep. The hell with Kate and her not using alcohol to avoid living; I'm going to avoid living so I can get some sleep. I drink half the small bottle and go to sleep. Maybe if it helps me sleep it is helping me to live more fully.

I feel okay the next day. As I walk across the Harvard Bridge toward the Back Bay, a chilly wind blows off the Charles River.

I button my winter coat and walk fast. I don't think about my marriages, but when I get home I sit down at my computer and write. Sometimes, mindful walking opens up my mind.

My parents, the media, and popular songs had left me with the conviction that when a couple married, the two were one—with the husband in charge. The Bible and traditional wedding vows to "love, honor and obey" lent support. The wife's influence was confined to homemaking, childcare, minor tasks and home decorating. Along with the husband's power came his duty to take care of his wife—as if she were his puppy. He protected her physically and supported her financially. Women were seen as weak emotionally, and the husband provided emotional strength, not crying or panicking or acting irrationally in the face of crisis, as it was assumed a woman would do. A loving wife sacrificed her needs for her husband. She always acted in his best interests, not her own. I expected that of my wife. I was on the generational cusp, and I didn't notice what was beginning to happen in the male–female relationship. I hadn't considered what happened when the wife worked full time and contributed financially as much as or more than the husband.

I finish thirty minutes of writing practice. I wonder what memoirs on marriage have been published. I log on to Amazon.com. and look at a few. At the bottom of the screen is one of those blurbs, "People who have ordered …have also ordered…." One of those is *The Feminine Mystique* by Betty Friedan. I think that book was out when I was married to Christie. I Google it. It was published in February 1963, six months before Christie and I married. I remember it was on all the best-seller lists.

I didn't read *The Feminine Mystique*, but early in our marriage I read in the media its thesis that women are victims of a false belief system that requires them to find identity and meaning in their lives only through their husbands and children. I agreed with its thesis and other media advocacy of women's rights, intellectually. But I didn't apply it to my own life.

Near the end of my marriage with Christie I read in the media of bra burnings, protest marches for women's rights and other expressions of women's equality. Law schools were sending thousands of women graduates to prestigious law firms. The Nossaman Firm hired Pauline Newman from the University of Texas Law School. She was one of the smartest, most ambitious and competent young lawyers I had known. She was a pretty, independent, emotionally strong woman. She was married and pregnant when she arrived. One partner rolled his eyes when he heard. A co-worker told me she was in a business meeting with a client and a partner of the Firm when she went into labor. That was on a Friday. She had the baby that night. Monday she was back at work until her supervising partner made her go home.

Working with Pauline and other women attorneys made me think of women as equals in the workplace. I saw that a woman could be a peer, a partner, with extraordinary strength and resourcefulness. Yet, though Christie was a professional making more money than I, I didn't look at her that way in the context of our marriage.

Before we married, Christie and I talked about having children. I never considered not having children. I didn't weigh the advantages and disadvantages. I always assumed that some day I would be a father. The overwhelming majority of couples had children back then. People looked at childless couples with pity if they were unable to have children, or as self-centered if they chose not to have them. There was part of me that longed to be different, but not so different that I would be unmarried or childless. I would have felt inferior, a failure in an important aspect of life.

I rebelled against my parents' bigoted views of race and their right-wing political stance. I yelled at my father more than once. I refused to become the electrical engineer he wanted me to be. I refused to allow him to control who my friends were when he told me I couldn't continue seeing Howard because he was white trash. I thought my parents were ignorant and boring, and I didn't want them around my friends. I could rebel that much, enough to confound my father and make him despair. That's as far as I could go. I couldn't be unmarried or childless, if I could help it. I didn't give any more thought to what raising children entailed or whether deep down I wanted to undertake the responsibilities, whatever they were, than I did to the same issues about marriage. I was like a child who demands a pet without considering whether he was willing to care for it.

I told Christie I wanted two children. She agreed. We decided to wait a few years so that we would have some time to do things we couldn't do with a small child. I had no idea what the responsibility for a child involved. I had never been around a baby. I saw them as live dolls. I wasn't concerned about my lack of knowledge because I assumed Christie would take care of the child. I doubt if my father ever changed my diaper or fed me, but since Christie said she wanted to go back to work as soon as practical, I knew I would have to play some secondary role in helping her. And even I believed that the decision to get pregnant should be a joint decision.

After we'd been married nearly four years, I told Christie we should start trying to have a baby. She said, "Well, okay." Her voice lacked enthusiasm, but then it usually did unless she was talking about cleaning somebody's teeth or hiking in the Sierras. She stopped taking the pill and had one period afterwards, but missed the next one.

I went with her to the doctor. After I had read most of the magazines in the waiting room, she came through the door smiling, the doctor following her. "She killed the rabbit," said the doctor. "Congratulations."

"Thank you," I said. Christie and I hugged.

While Christie was pregnant we ate dinner out most of the time. On May 8, 1968 we drove to Encino and had a fancy prime rib dinner, with drinks before and dessert after. The money we spent eating out bothered me. For the first time I was concerned about finances. Without Christie's paychecks it was apparent we would go into debt. We already owed on some of the furniture and had a big car payment for my Porsche. But I didn't say anything.

Early the next morning, she woke me and said she was having what she thought were contractions. She wasn't sure. The doctor told her to meet him at the hospital. My nerves were charged with excitement, but I tried not to show it. I think my hand shook, as if I'd too much coffee, as I picked up Christie's suitcase to take it to the car. Christie was quiet. For a change, she didn't talk when she was nervous. *Maybe there's a point when she's beyond nervous—scared—that she doesn't feel like talking, not even about teeth*, I thought. We drove to Valley Presbyterian Hospital. She winced, hunched over and put both arms around her abdomen. "I had a contraction, but it wasn't too bad," she said afterwards.

She finally said she was scared. I nodded. I didn't know what to say. She had hired a retired nurse, Suzanne, to help her with the baby for two weeks after she got home. She asked me to call Suzanne from the hospital. I didn't think that Suzanne was necessary, but I deferred to Christie. She was adamant that she would need help, and she didn't want her mother.

We arrived at the hospital shortly after nine. After we filled out the paperwork, a woman in pink told me where the fathers' waiting room was, and wheeled Christie to her labor room. Fathers were not allowed in the labor or delivery rooms then. For a few minutes I read the book I had brought, then got up and walked down the hall and back. I sat down and read some more and stood up again. No other fathers-to-be were there until about three. Then a young guy with long blond hair walked in and nodded at me. We didn't talk.

I went to the cafeteria for a snack, but I wasn't hungry. I returned to the waiting room and read some more. I looked at my watch a hundred times. I had no idea what was happening. Was Christie okay? How much longer? Why didn't somebody report something? Maybe I should go ask. At about four o'clock I heard a desperate scream from the inner sanctum. It was Christie. Her screams came frequently and louder and longer. I thought she was a wimp. Other women weren't screaming.

My muscles were clenched. I had made up my mind to ask what was going on when a man in a white gown, surgical cap and green mask dangling below his chin came bounding through the door.

"Mr. Lemon?"

"Yes," I said with a shaky voice.

"I'm Doctor Forbes. You have a daughter. Congratulations. Mom and baby are doing fine." We shook hands.

"Oh, thank you," I said, heaving a huge sigh.

"You can see your daughter in the nursery in about five minutes. Right down that hall over there. Congratulations again." He went back through the door.

I stood there, excited. I kept looking at my watch. Like a sprinter kneeling in the blocks, watching the man with the gun to signal the start, I waited. When the five minutes were up, I walked down the hall. I wanted to run. It was quiet. The room had windows from floor to ceiling. A dozen babies under pink and blue blankets with red, wrinkled heads lay in bins on carts that looked like what produce men in grocery stores use to stock fresh vegetables. A nurse was rewrapping one of the babies as if it was a mummy. Most of them looked to be crying, though I couldn't hear the sound through the glass.

I searched for Lisa. We hadn't been able to agree on a girl's name. I put up with Christie naming our cats Mordecai and Hadassah, but I wasn't as tolerant about names for my daughter. Christie wanted Rachel or Hannah. Those are the only two I remember. I didn't like either. We finally agreed on Lisa.

The nurse looked out at me and then looked around at the babies. She went over to one of the tables and pointed down. The card on the bin said, "Baby Girl Lemon. 19 inches, 5 lbs. 5 oz." It was Lisa.

Oh my God! She's so tiny, I thought. Her face was red. No hair. She lay in the bin, eyes closed, serene. I stood and stared through the window at her. It was hard to fathom that a few minutes before she had been in Christie's body, unable to breathe for herself or see the world. Birth seemed like the only real miracle we humans could perform. Here she was, a combination of Christie and me, yet also her own unique self. It was, like the concept of God, beyond my comprehension. This couldn't be solely the result of a random mixture of chemicals and electric impulses. There had to be divine guidance or intervention. At that moment, at least, I believed in God, a belief that was renewed when I witnessed the births of my other children.

I felt embarrassed when a few tears emerged. Thirty-six years later I wept unabashedly when I saw Lisa's first baby in the hospital nursery.

The doctor walked over, stopped, and looked in at Lisa. "Tiny little girl," he said. "You can see your wife in that room right at the end of the hall on the left."

I walked down the hall to see Christie. "It's a girl—Lisa," I said.

"Yeah, I know," she said. "It was really hard. I don't want another one."

"Well, you don't need to think about that now," I said.

Christie's comments and sullen attitude deflated my elation, but as I drove home, it returned. I felt like my body was lighter than air, like if I got out of the car I would float up to the clouds weightless. At home I called everyone, had a celebratory Scotch and fell asleep on the orange couch.

Christie and Lisa came home on Mother's Day. Christie

handed the baby to Suzanne and went to bed. Lisa, still with a wrinkled, red face and no hair, looked small and fragile. Suzanne handed her to me, helping me adjust her head against my shoulder. I was afraid I would crush her just holding her. I didn't feel like a father yet. Suzanne led me to Lisa's room. With great care and slightly trembling hands, I laid her down on the changing table, and Suzanne showed me how to change a diaper. I followed Suzanne as she carried Lisa to our bedroom. She handed Lisa to Christie and gave her some pointers about nursing. I gazed at the tender sight of my baby on her mother's breast—another dream come true.

Early one morning in my apartment I take out my notebook to do writing practice. I decide on the topic, "What have you tried to do to make a difference?" I'm cheating a little because I know exactly where I'm going. I had often thought about my work on Robert Kennedy's Presidential campaign and had discussed it, but I had never written about it.

One of the activities I pursued to break the tedium and stress of law work, and to feel like I was making a difference, was to work on political campaigns. I also thought that someday I might like to get directly involved in politics in a way not yet defined in my mind. I was a passionate supporter of Robert Kennedy for President. A month before Lisa was born, I signed up to work on his campaign. He was going to appear in Ventura and Oxnard. When Lisa was ten days old, I left to spend four days and nights in Ventura preparing for the events on Kennedy's schedule.

When I got back home, I was heady. Christie greeted me coldly.

"What's the matter?" I asked.

"How could you leave me for four days with a new baby?"

"Suzanne is here," I said.

"That's not the point." She turned around, strode to the bedroom and slammed the door.

At some level I knew when I left for Ventura that I was being insensitive to Christie, but it didn't occur to me that if I explained to her how important it was to me, she might have understood or at least not been as angry. At that time of my life, at the age of twenty-seven, I had unbridled ambition to succeed, but I was not happy as a lawyer in private practice. I saw working on the Kennedy campaign as a potential means to work that would be fulfilling. I was zealously liberal. Robert Kennedy, if he were elected, could provide me an opportunity to do something meaningful for my country, to help the poor and disadvantaged, to end the senseless killing in Viet Nam, to finally treat African Americans as human beings -- equal to whites. I was optimistic that he would be elected, and that my life could be changed in a direction I fervently wanted. I just didn't communicate these feelings to Christie.

At the end of his Ventura appearances Kennedy waited at the Point Mugu Naval Air Station for a plane to take him to his next campaign stop. It had not yet arrived. My campaign staff supervisor pointed at a door and asked me to wait with Kennedy in case he needed something. *Wow, why am I so lucky?* I wondered. I walked over to the door. A Secret Service agent glanced at my lapel pin indicating I was on the campaign staff, and nodded. I knocked. Another agent opened the door. Kennedy, his thick hair hanging every which way, as usual, sat on a folding chair by a metal government-issue table in a Spartan room with smudged, off-white walls. He stood up. I introduced myself, and we shook hands. His toothy grin, which I had seen so often on TV, mesmerized me.

An hour before, he had charged unexpectedly out of an open-air convertible through a crowd of thousands of cheering supporters and entered a modest Catholic church in a poor Oxnard Latino neighborhood. Panicked Secret Service agents fought through the crowd chasing him. I sat two cars back. The Secret Service agent in our car yelled, "Shit, what the fuck is he doing?" I held my breath for what seemed like minutes. I'm sure everyone in the motorcade was thinking the same thing. It had been less than five years since his brother had been assassinated in a similar convertible in Dallas. He strode back to the car, people hanging on him, and jumped in, his coat nearly torn off. Somebody had ripped the cuff links off his shirt.

Nobody else but the Secret Service agent was in the room. I sat down across from Kennedy and asked if there was anything I could do for him. He thanked me and said no. I said I thought the Ventura and Oxnard appearances went well. He said he was very pleased. I didn't know what else to say, so I asked the question I couldn't resist.

"I'm curious. Why did you take such a risk in leaving the car to go in that church?"

He seemed to think for a moment, then spoke quietly (and this is almost verbatim), "I wanted to go where the people here go. I have chosen to be a politician. I have to be involved with the people. I won't be intimidated. If I'm killed, so be it. It's a risk I have to take."

In a moment, his California campaign manager walked in and told me I could leave.

Two weeks later I watched from the ballroom floor of the Ambassador Hotel as he finished his victory speech. I was so high with the thrill of his victory in the important California Primary I could hardly contain my enthusiasm. I had yelled my voice hoarse. My hands stung from clapping. I literally stood on my toes watching him walk off the stage, certain that he would be the next President of the United States.

I stood around talking with fellow campaign workers for a few minutes. The events that followed forever erased from my memory what we talked about. Suddenly, I heard screams coming from somewhere beyond the ballroom. They were not victory screams. Seconds later somebody yelled, "Bobby's been shot." Then more screams filled the huge room. I had no idea where he was. People started running in all directions. I stood frozen for a moment. I didn't see where any of the campaign workers had gone. I ran for my car and turned on the radio just in time to hear the news flash, barely audible through the background noise, that he had been shot. My body deflated. My chest sank into my belly. It was so unbelievable I couldn't cry. I don't remember driving home or telling Christie. I'm sure it was one or two in the morning when I got home.

Two nights later I sat in the bar of a Chinese restaurant in L.A. Chinatown with Christie, Lisa, and our friends, Bob and Pam. Somebody turned up the TV set. "Senator Kennedy died a few minutes ago of massive brain damage caused by the assassin's bullet," said the newscaster.

I stared at the table, not seeing it. Still, I couldn't cry. I didn't know how to mourn, so I didn't, outwardly. Christie said nothing—ever—about Kennedy's death. I watched the funeral on TV by myself. When Andy Williams sang the Battle Hymn of the Republic, I sobbed.

I have lived with a deep sense of loss ever since—for the country and for me. I believe my life would have been profoundly different if he had lived. For years, occasionally in the forefront, usually deep inside, cynicism prevailed in me. I lost my optimism for my future and that of my country. Within five years, our President, a presidential candidate, and our most revered civil rights leader had been murdered. All over the country college students were beaten, and at Kent State killed, for protesting the war and racism. As a child of the serene fifties, I found it hard to face what was happening. The final blow was the election of Richard Nixon.

Having finally written about Kennedy's role in my life, I feel a little lighter. I don't know if the world would be a better place had he lived. Nor do I know I would have led a better or more fulfilled life. That life was not meant to be for him or me. But writing about it brought some closure that was missing before.

You can do writing practice anywhere. All you need is paper and pen or laptop and a reasonably comfortable place to sit. I usually write at home, but sometimes I want to get out. I walk a couple of blocks to my favorite café, sit in a comfortable chair or couch with a cup of apple cinnamon tea, and write. On breaks I people-watch and eavesdrop.

After Suzanne left, Christie said she was panicked at the prospect of taking care of the baby by herself. I just listened to her frequent complaining. Christie didn't change Lisa often enough, and she developed diaper rash. I began changing her when I was home. I didn't say anything, but I resented it. One night Christie said she was too tired to feed Lisa, and asked me to feed her, and went to bed. I muddled through on Christie's instructions. After that I often fed Lisa. My resentment built.

Christie went back to work when Lisa was five months old. Our next-door neighbor took care of her while Christie was at work. When I was home, I usually changed Lisa's diapers and fed her. When she started to crawl, Christie bought a playpen. If she wasn't asleep, Lisa was in the playpen when I got home from work. When Christie picked her up from the neighbor, she put her in the playpen and ignored her. I told Christie I didn't like Lisa being in the playpen so much. I thought it would retard her development.

Christie erupted. "I never wanted this baby in the first place. It was your idea. I shouldn't have gone along with it. You take care of it." She stomped down the hall and into the bedroom. We never talked about having Lisa in the playpen after that. I made no effort to deal with the issue, and neither did Christie.

One Friday night when I came home inebriated after a few drinks with Bill, Christie launched a tirade about my working such long hours. "I work hard, on my feet for eight hours, and I have to come home and take care of a baby myself. I'm exhausted. Obviously, your job means more to you than your family. Why did you want a baby anyway?"

"You agreed to have one, and my job supported her and you for five months," was all I said before I headed for the kitchen to fix myself a Scotch.

For the first five years of our marriage we had rarely argued. To me, arguing meant the relationship was failing, something I couldn't face. I had never seen people who care about each other argue. My parents never argued in front of me. I thought arguing in a personal relationship was an indication of disrespect. And I was imbued with the common human weakness of wanting to avoid confrontation. After Lisa was born, arguments began to erupt. They consisted of a few angry outbursts by both of us—a charge and a defense—with no attempt to resolve the issue. Neither of us knew how to argue productively.

I was unhappy with my job. I felt burned out. There couldn't have been a better law firm to work for, I thought, but working so hard to help rich people get richer for the rest of my life was unappealing. My drinking increased; my time at home shrank further.

After a while Christie stopped complaining about my working long hours. I think she no longer cared. She had given up on me.

All my life I had been deeply conflicted about being different from other people. On the one hand, I feared being different. I wanted to be a respected professional, a person my parents wanted me to be. I wanted the little wife with the house and the white picket fence and the 2.2 children. I didn't want to be considered Gay or odd. I wanted to fit in. My fear of being different drove me to become a lawyer, marry, have a child and do most of what was expected of me.

But I feared being like my parents—ordinary, dull and boring—never doing anything exciting, just living as everyone expected them to live. I was determined not to live their boring life. They rarely did anything outside the house that would be considered entertainment, except going to horse races and baseball games for my father and, infrequently, a movie. They didn't travel. They had no interest in art or music. They read no fiction, except the occasional romance novel my mother read. They didn't have a record player. I asked for and received one for Christmas when I was about ten and then bought a Hi-Fi with my own money when I was a teenager. They rarely dined in restaurants and then only in cheap diners or coffee shops. They were like the Puritans, dedicated to hard work and "getting ahead." Pleasure and entertainment were for people who had already gotten ahead.

My fear of being ordinary and dull drove me to act impulsively at times and take unwise risks—to take drugs, drink excessively, work for a legal aid foundation, volunteer for the ACLU, march against the war in Viet Nam. I dared to be different on occasion. Once, I went to a party wearing Stephanie's (my second wife's) pink, yellow and purple striped pants, so tight on me they looked like the tights male ballet dancers wore. People laughed. I got the attention I wanted. When I was married to Stephanie I took cocaine to Tokyo and Hong Kong. When I was married to Susan, I bought racehorses. I wasn't a dull, conservative nerd.

Once when Christie's fifteen-year-old sister, Jean, visited for the weekend, Christie asked me if Jean could have something alcoholic to drink. "She says our parents let her and she likes the way it feels."

"Well, I guess it can't do any harm as long as she stays in the house," I said. I was thinking of harm to me, not to her.

"What do we have?" asked Christie.

"Well, maybe she'd like a Tequila Sunrise," I said. "It tastes pretty good."

"Okay," said Christie.

I went to the kitchen, took out the orange juice, Galliano, grenadine and tequila and mixed the drink over a large glass of ice.

"Mmm. This tastes good," Jean said, and she swilled it.

Christie drank water. She rarely drank alcohol.

Within a few minutes Jean asked if she could have another.

"I guess so," I said. "But you might want to drink the next one a little slower."

"Okay," she said. "But it tastes so good."

The three of us sat in the family room playing Monopoly for a while. I made Jean a third Tequila Sunrise and myself a third Scotch.

"I'm tired. It's been a hard week," Christie said. "I'm going to bed."

"Okay. Good night," I said.

Jean and I sat in silence for a moment, sipping our drinks. Her face was flushed, and her eyes were wet, pupils dilated. She pulled a joint out of her purse.

"You mind?"

"Not if you'll share," I said.

As we passed the joint back and forth, I tried to think of something to talk to her about. "Do you have a boyfriend?" I asked.

"Yeah," she said. "I'm not allowed to date until next year when I'm sixteen, but next weekend my parents are going away, and Nate's coming over. I'm kinda nervous about it. I really don't know what to do."

"What do you mean?" I asked.

"Well, I've never really even kissed a boy before, you know, French kissed."

"Don't worry. You'll learn," I said.

She looked away. "Maybe you could teach me," she said.

"Well...I suppose I could."

She scooted closer to me. I looked directly at her—a baby, too young. Christie had gone to bed early every night for a week. I was horny. The conservative Boyd, afraid of being different, said don't do it. Another Boyd said go for it. I didn't think about what harm I might cause Jean or Christie or my marriage, or that it was flat out wrong.

I embraced her, and we kissed. Her lips were open. Our tongues met and we kissed for what seemed like forever. My erection felt like it was about to burst from my pants. I pulled her down on the couch and put my hands under her sweater, caressing her breast outside her bra. She sighed. I unsnapped her bra and felt her flesh. I wondered if she knew what my hard-on pushed against her thigh was. I unsnapped her jeans and put my hands down the back of her panties, pulling her against me, kneading her ass. She moaned and pushed her tongue deep into my mouth. I started to move my hand to the front. I could fuck her, I thought. I really want to, but that would be stupid—statutory rape that could land me in prison and cost me my license to practice law, not to mention my marriage. I'm twenty-seven. This is my wife's fifteen- year-old sister. This could profoundly hurt her. Am I crazy? "We'd better stop, Jean," I said.

"Yeah," she said. "We should." I got up and went to bed. I lay awake, sick at what I had done. *I can't do that again. What was I thinking?* It was so wrong.

Two weekends later Jean and her boyfriend came over. In a half hour they disappeared. The sound of their lovemaking came from under the guest room door. I felt relieved, rescued from temptation.

I think it was at this point that Christie exhibited another of her strange characteristics. She talked about strange things that most people wouldn't discuss, and she would bring them up out of nowhere, unrelated to anything else that was being discussed. After telling me she had bought condoms for Jean for this weekend, she said, "You know Lynn."

"Yeah," I said. Lynn was Jean's best girlfriend, and she occasionally came over with Jean.

"She's coming over tomorrow," said Christie.

"That's fine," I said.

In nearly a whisper, Christie said, "You know something funny about Lynn. She has an abnormally large clitoris that hangs down way below her vagina." Christie giggled. "When she walks, if she's wearing panties, she almost has an orgasm. So she usually doesn't wear panties or tight pants. Even the friction from walking stimulates her. Isn't that weird?"

"Yes, it is, Christie," I said.

When I saw this poor girl the next day, I couldn't look at her.

It was 1968. It seemed like everybody under thirty was smoking pot. When Bob, one of my associates at the law firm, asked me if Christie and I would like to come over to his place and smoke pot, I said, "Sure." Christie said she wanted to. We went over to Bob's apartment in Manhattan Beach. His girlfriend, Pam, was there. We sat around and shared a joint. I felt numb, incredibly relaxed, content. This is so cool, I thought. Possession of marijuana was a felony in California then. If caught, Bob and I would have been disbarred. We smoked with Bob and Pam several times, and once or twice more with Jean.

A few months after Lisa was born, Christie told me Jean could get some LSD for us, and she wanted to try it.

"That would be fun," I said. "We just have to be careful."

One Friday after school Jean came over with Nate, and we all swallowed the little pieces of paper that presumably had acid on them. Lisa was asleep, hopefully for the night. We were all scared. We'd heard tales of people on acid having bad trips, and even jumping off cliffs. I was comforted that there were no cliffs around our neighborhood. But it was agreed no one would be left alone.

For a few minutes we all sat staring at each other. "Does anybody feel anything?" I asked. In unison they replied no. I felt a twinge of energy, then a rush. The furniture looked bigger. I walked around the house. The chair I had been sitting in followed me. The orange in the living room couch shimmered with light and overwhelmed the room. I could see the orange on my arm. The room seemed brighter. We all agreed it was too bright, and turned off most of the lights.

I had a hard-on without even thinking about sex. I went up to Christie, kissed her and started feeling her breasts. She pushed me away and went out back, "...to be by myself," she said. Jean and Steve watched her through the sliding glass door. They started fondling each other and kissing. Soon they were on the floor fucking right in front of me. That made me even hornier. This is wild, I thought. I'm not leading any boring life like my parents did. I sat on the glittering orange couch.

As I watched Steve and Jean, I thought I should have fucked Jean when I had the chance, but, even on acid, I knew it was a bad idea.

Christie and I had been married five years. Gradually, she had more and more headaches and less and less energy for sex. I had no interest in her most of the time. We rarely had sex after she got pregnant. I still made no effort to improve it. I never asked her what she liked or told her what I liked. I stopped doing anything romantic—no more flowers or candlelight dinners. Like sunlight at dusk, sex had faded from our marriage. I rarely noticed it. I had no sexual passion for Christie, once the novelty wore off. But my sense of loyalty, shyness or cowardice, I don't know which, kept me from cheating.

It didn't occur to me that our loss of interest in sex might be a symptom of a dying marriage. Marriage was forever.

Jean, Nate, and I smoked some pot that first night we took acid, but when I offered the joint to Christie, she said she didn't want any because she was afraid it would make her paranoid. It made me mellower. Jean said she and Nate were going for a walk. I told them to be careful. I was afraid to go outside the house, except in the backyard. Christie said she was too. I turned the outside light on, and went out the sliding glass door to the backyard. I felt buoyant and mellow at the same time. The grass seemed brighter and undulated in waves up the side of the hill. The oranges on the trees were brighter. Even the light seemed more yellow.

I couldn't sleep until the acid wore off, and I felt exhausted when I went to work on Monday. I took acid one more time a few weeks later. That time I walked around the neighborhood and marveled at the flowers and plants. They were phosphorescent. The sidewalk kept moving—up and down and sideways. That scared me, so I went back to the house.

Inside, Christie was smoking a joint and handed it to me. She stared at me. I heard Jean screaming and Nate moaning in the guest room. "I hope they're using something," I said. Christie continued to stare at me.

"Why are you staring at me?" I asked.

"I wanna fuck," she said. Christie never used that term. She always said, "make love."

"Great!" I said.

She headed for the bedroom taking her clothes off and dropping them on the floor as she walked. She asked me to go down on her, which she rarely wanted. We fucked and licked each other for what seemed like hours. Christie couldn't get enough, and I finally couldn't do it anymore. Afterwards, she didn't remember demanding so much sex. She took acid several times more, but she never again wanted sex like she did that night.

I didn't take acid after the second time. I wasn't comfortable with hallucinations, and I was exhausted for a week after I took it. I also thought it was irresponsible when we had a baby. What would we do if we were both high on acid, and Lisa got sick? When Christie took acid, I took care of Lisa.

Once Christie demanded to breast-feed when she was on acid. I grabbed Lisa away from her. She started screaming at me. "She's my baby! She's my baby!"

I took a bottle out of the refrigerator, went out to the back-yard and fed Lisa. Eventually, Christie calmed down.

Chapter Nine

Except for generalities I can't seem to write anything that rings true about the end of my first marriage. It's not a problem with my writing; it's a problem with my thinking—not thinking deeply. My mind is foggy. I'll meditate, concentrate on my breathing, then try again. Maybe the fog will lift. It doesn't. I don't look at the memoir for several days and then come back to it.

After more than five years of marriage, Christie said, "I would like to have my own checking account to deposit my pay checks in. We can work out what I pay for and what you pay for, but I want control over my own money."

"I can't agree to that, Christie," I said. "You have no experience managing finances. It's the husband's role." She frowned. But she didn't argue or raise the issue again. Years later, she told me she thought I was a poor money manager, and that she resented my controlling the finances. She didn't mention that when we were married. I wondered why she would want her own checking account.

Around the same time, she said she wanted contact lenses, a new and expensive invention at the time. I told her she couldn't; we couldn't afford it. She bought them anyway. I retaliated by not giving her cash I had intended for her birthday—curious that I would give my wife cash for her birthday. Not very romantic.

I felt that, as the husband, I should make the major financial decisions--even when Christie was supporting us. For the first three years that I practiced law, Christie, as a dental hygienist, made more money than I. That didn't affect my view.

It didn't occur to me that she was trying to assert independence, that at twenty-seven she wanted to be a whole person, not just part of me. And at some level I knew I wasn't doing a great job managing our money. We had so much debt that I proposed we sell our Porsches and buy Volkswagen bugs so we could pay it off. Christie didn't object, but at the dealer, as we walked over to drive away our new Volkswagens, she turned around and, with wet eyes, looked longingly at her Porsche.

We were earning today's equivalent of more than $200,000 a year. I had no experience managing that much money. We lived paycheck to paycheck, not saving any. Spurred on by the likelihood of greater future earnings, we spent more than we earned. We had bought a house with two mortgage payments that stretched us to our financial limit, perhaps beyond, and a third mortgage loan of $5,000 for landscaping. We bought my Porsche, expensive furniture, dinners out, vacations, cameras and I don't remember what else. We talked more about money than anything. We both spent, but since I controlled the finances, I must accept responsibility. It definitely put stress on our marriage. I don't recall Christie complaining, but I should have perceived her stress from the amount of time we spent talking about money.

During the last couple of years of our marriage the guitar-playing folk singer, exemplified by Bob Dylan and Joan Baez, was wildly popular. Christie and I both loved Bob Dylan and had all his records. We spent much of our time at home listening to music. Christie was probably the only person in the country who subscribed to *Rolling Stone* and *Vogue*. Christie also liked hard rock, but I didn't. In the last year of our marriage we went to a Judy Collins concert, a love-in in Griffith Park and another at the Orange County Fairgrounds, where I watched a couple make love among the crowd at the concert.

Christie loved to hike and travel. I was so focused on my work that I didn't share her enthusiasm and didn't have time for it. She worked four days a week, eight hours a day. I worked sixty-hour weeks, sometimes more. It faded in and out of my consciousness that Christie and I were growing further apart emotionally, physically and in the time we spent together. Alcohol dimmed it further. But at some level I felt the distance between us.

One evening, after singing along with Bob Dylan, to the extent that's possible, I suggested to Christie that we take guitar lessons together. I had always wanted to learn to play a musical instrument, and the guitar seemed the easiest. I thought it would give us something to do together. Christie said she thought it would be fun. For several months we took lessons once a week from the wife of a friend of mine. We learned to play chords for "Scarborough Fair," "This Land Is Your Land" and several other popular folk songs. I sang while I played. Christie was too self-conscious to sing, claiming she couldn't carry a tune.

I thought I was doing something to reduce the widening gap between us. I didn't realize it, but it was too late. And it was during this time that I refused to let her stay for Led Zeppelin's second set.

I still insisted on control. Because her father was a successful architect, Christie was used to having the best of everything—a Porsche, expensive clothes, expensive vacations, a lavish home professionally decorated with the finest of furnishings. After we took guitar lessons for a few weeks she wanted a Fender guitar. I told her, no. At our level of skill, an inexpensive guitar was good enough. She looked sad, but as usual when I denied her something she wanted or told her what to do, she didn't argue or protest. She just hung her head—probably what she did when her parents denied her something. She was afraid to argue. She once told me she was afraid to argue with me, because she could never win, since I was a champion debater.

One day Christie said that one of her patients taught guitar, and she wanted to take lessons from him. He played rock. I went with her for the first lesson. Dan had long hair, old jeans, a dirty brown shirt, hippy sandals and several days' worth of beard. I didn't care for him, so I went back to my friend's wife. I didn't try to connect. Christie continued with Dan. She started going several times a week. I noticed that although she claimed she was too tired to do anything with me after work, she wasn't too tired to take guitar lessons with Dan. I was sad and jealous that my wife didn't want to be with me. It didn't occur to me that she might feel that way when I went drinking with my co-workers.

A few weeks before Lisa's first birthday, we left Lisa with our next-door neighbor and drove out to the Mojave Desert. Christie told me she loved it there. I had never been. I was entranced by the wildflowers and the huge, quiet expanse of the landscape. We found a secluded spot on a little rise with a fifty-mile view, and spread out a blanket on the sand. We shared a joint. In a few minutes we took off our clothes and made love beneath the big, lustrous sky, the sweat from our efforts drying quickly. We fell asleep in each other's arms.

On Lisa's first birthday Christie baked a chocolate cake, unusually domestic for her. We slathered it with chocolate frosting and put it on the tray of the high chair. Lisa smeared it all over her face and pink dress, as Christie and I laughed. We gave Lisa her presents—toys, books and clothes. I helped her rip off the wrapping paper, while Christie snapped a whole roll of pictures. Then we went out for pizza and beers. Lisa, with few teeth, licked the tomato sauce off the slice we gave her. I fed her strained peas and beef. We went home and put Lisa to bed and practiced guitar. I got through all the chords without a mistake.

After putting the guitar back in its case, I set it down in the bedroom closet. I walked up to Christie as she was getting ready for bed. I kissed her mouth and caressed her breast. She pulled my hand away and backed up. "I'm tired. I'm going to bed," she said.

I went back to the living room and sat down on the orange couch. Despite the rejection, I thought our relationship was improving after a long decline. I felt relaxed and pleased about the lovely day we'd had as a family. I wanted to do it more often. I vowed that I would think of more things we could do together. We had taken nice vacations the previous three years—Mexico City, the Oregon Coast, and Austin, Texas. I thought we had enjoyed each other on those trips.

I didn't see that we were growing apart in many ways. I was an avid reader of politics and current events. Christie never even watched the news and had no interest. I read a wide variety of books and periodicals. Christie read *Vogue* and *Rolling Stone*. I had begun to enjoy fine food, stimulated by taking law firm recruits to some of the best Los Angeles restaurants. Christie was happy with hamburger and peanut butter sandwiches. I had a vague sense that we were growing apart, but I didn't focus on it deeply enough to see how far.

Christie told me recently that she longed to climb rocks and mountains and go backpacking, a passion she had mentioned during our courtship and engaged in after our divorce. She saw me as sedentary—interested in reading, watching movies, and television and such. She felt that as long as we were married she would not be able to pursue her passion. Back then it was uncommon for married couples to engage in separate activities, so apparently that alternative didn't occur to her. Had she done that, no doubt I would have protested vehemently, and in light of my long work hours, we would have rarely done anything together. Maybe it was impossible to resolve this issue, but Christie never brought it up, making the impossibility of resolution certain. Apparently, she believed, and she may have been correct, that trying to resolve issues by discussion with me was futile. Perhaps she was intimidated by my domination.

Around the time of Lisa's birthday I thought about my unhappiness with my job. What could I do? Maybe I could get a job as a staff attorney with the American Civil Liberties Union. I had worked on a couple of their cases as a volunteer lawyer and found it fulfilling. I remembered the pride I felt when the judge announced he was dismissing the case against a kid I had defended. The police had choked him until he vomited up the joint he had swallowed. I wouldn't make as much money with the ACLU, but now that we had paid off a lot of debt and had no car payments, we would be fine.

When my secretary came in Monday, she handed me the *Daily Journal,* the legal newspaper for southern California. I turned to the classified section. There was an ad for a staff attorney for the American Civil Liberties Union of Northern California. It would require a move to San Francisco, but what the hell. Maybe I should apply. I couldn't get the ACLU job out of my mind that week.

I don't remember Christie smiling or joking or acting like she was having fun during the last couple of years of our marriage. I guess she wasn't. She often went to bed at seven or eight o'clock. I didn't realize that she might have been depressed, or at least did not want to be with me.

I took care of Lisa the Saturday after her birthday, while Christie went for a guitar lesson with Dan. Lisa crawled down the hall after the cats, laughing and shouting, "kitty, kitty." I crawled after her and caught her. I picked her up and tossed her in the air a couple of times. We laughed together. I fed her applesauce and strained beef, then changed her and tucked her in her crib. I stood there a moment gazing at her pale face and wispy blond hair, as her eyes closed. I smiled and walked slowly back to the living room. I finally felt like a father.

The garage door hummed and banged, and Christie walked in. I was on the couch reading the paper. I thought I would talk to her about the ACLU position. She put down her guitar case and walked over to me with an awkward quickness to her step. She stopped abruptly and stood over me. "I want to talk to you," she said. I put the paper down. She paused for a moment. "I'm leaving you. I want a divorce. I'm moving to Tujunga Canyon to live with Dan."

An invisible boulder smashed into my stomach. I held my breath. I sat up on the edge of the couch and looked up at her, speechless for a moment. A breathy, "Why?" was all I could get out.

"I don't want to talk about it. I've made my decision. Don't try to talk me out of it. I won't change my mind. I'm just taking a few pieces of furniture. Dan is coming over with a truck to-night. It would be best if you weren't here. You can have what I don't take...and I don't want the house."

"I don't know what to say. Isn't there anything I can do?"

"No," she said. "Nothing. I've been very unhappy. I'm leaving. By the way, if you care, I have not been unfaithful to you." She looked down at the carpet. I sat in silence. I studied her face. It was calm, serious, and firm. She seemed more confident than I had ever seen her, though at the time I didn't appreciate her strength. My marriage was over. I was certain she wouldn't change her mind.

"What about Lisa?" I asked.

"Well, I'm taking her, of course," she said. "You have your work. That's what seems most important to you." She turned and walked into the kitchen.

I thought about following her and arguing but what good would it do? It was clear she'd made up her mind. I stayed on the couch, paralyzed, my brain frozen. Divorce didn't compute.

Finally, I got up. I heard Christie rummaging in the bedroom. I didn't want to be near her. I walked out back and paced, not knowing what to do.

I don't remember what I did the rest of the afternoon. Later, I went out to dinner to avoid Dan, and I drank a lot. When I returned, our home was empty of the orange couch, a few other pieces of furniture, Christie and Lisa and their things. Dirty dishes and Dan's beer bottles mocked me from the sink. Fitting that she didn't do the dishes before she left, I thought. I walked slowly back to the bedroom. The bed was unmade. I turned around and walked out.

I couldn't sleep that night. I had enough alcohol to sleep for about three hours the next night. I was tense all over, afraid of the unknown, being alone, a divorced man, a failure. Work distracted me for a while.

A few days later, when I opened my credit card bill, I found a charge for an expensive guitar from the guitar shop where Dan taught. The next weekend, when I picked up Lisa for visitation, Christie followed me to the car. "You should reimburse me for the guitar you bought," I said.

"I don't think so," she said quietly. "After all the financial support I gave you, I deserve a nice guitar." I didn't argue.

I felt humiliated telling friends and co-workers. I was terrified to tell my mother. I feared being a failure in her eyes. I showed up at her back door, nauseated, aching all over. We went in the kitchen, and I hugged her, then backed away.

"What's wrong?" She asked. I told her. Her lower lip dropped. Her eyes widened.

"I'm sorry," she said, and hugged me a long time. We finally separated, tears in our eyes.

People in my life didn't get divorced. Bad people got divorced, not us. The only person my parents and I had ever known who divorced was Ray, my dad's friend. My parents said he was wild. They talked about him as if he was trash.

That Monday at the office I stared at the wall opposite my desk. I was still incredulous. I faced a future of loneliness, without my daughter. She was only one year old. I had thought marriage was until death do us part. I wasn't so happy married to Christie, but I was willing to stick it out. Why wasn't she? I felt betrayed. I asked myself what I had done to cause Christie to leave me, but I didn't dig deep enough to understand. I reached the least painful conclusion—Christie was crazy.

I drove home from work sober, but when I got home I couldn't remember the trip. The house, like my life, was empty.

To write my final insights on my role in the failure of Christie's and my marriage, I schlep my computer to the Boston Museum of Fine Arts and sit on a bench facing Claude Monet's lily pads.

When we married, we entered into an unexpressed contract that was certain to be broken, because neither of us was aware of its existence or terms, and Christie could not have fulfilled mine, even if she had been aware.

I needed her to prove my manhood by having sex with me. I was drowning in sexual insecurities. Any hope of eliminating them, though it was a false hope, required marriage. I believed consciously that I was not attractive to women. That terrified me; I thought it might prevent me from proving my manhood. If I was not a man, I was nothing. I couldn't be anything else. I also wanted the status of marriage and children—what other men had. My expectation was that Christie would provide these needs. She was a sex object. Another expectation, part of being a man, I thought, based on my father's model, was that I would control the relationship as the benevolent dictator.

I didn't express these expectations. I wasn't conscious of them.

I had another expectation that we did express in our wedding ceremony—that no matter what, so long as I didn't abuse her, Christie would stay with me 'til death do us part, for as long as we both shall live. I believed it. Perhaps Christie didn't, or she might have thought I did abuse her. I think most of the millions in America in the last three generations who made that promise consciously or unconsciously never intended to keep it, but at the time I believed it was a sacred promise.

As for Christie's part of this unexpressed contract, I can only speculate. Perhaps, most important, was what she did not expect—another father figure. She said she hated her father. He helped make her the self-conscious, fearful person that she knew she was. She went to college to become a dental hygienist. She would not be dependent on a man for financial support. She didn't want or expect another father.

Maybe that's why it took her so long to decide to marry me. She feared another father figure who controlled her and made her feel inadequate and incompetent. It must have sent her into despair when that came to pass.

I feel confident in speculating that she expected a husband who cared about her enough to take the time and effort to understand her needs and make a reasonable effort to ful-fill them—trying to satisfy her sexually, spending a reasonable amount of time with her, showing that he cared about her and would not refuse to allow her to fulfill her own needs.

I broke the unexpressed contract repeatedly by not fulfilling those expectations. That, I believe, is why she left me. I don't think it was coincidence that when I asked her after our di-vorce why she left me, her first response was the Led Zeppelin concert.

While I was not happily married, Christie provided me with the status that came with marriage and a child. She allowed me to control her, and her passivity in allowing it lulled me into assuming that my control was acceptable to her. I don't think it was. She didn't eliminate my sexual insecurities, but that was impossible.

Lying in bed in my Cambridge apartment, though sad, I

take solace in the thought that I finally understand something about my role in the failure of my first marriage. I still want to understand why I had these unrealistic expectations, and if they were based on my parents' marriage, why I didn't realize, considering the time I lived in, that they were unrealistic and unfair. I suspect I carried these same attitudes into my second and third marriages. I'll just keep writing, and, hopefully, find out.

PART TWO
Stephanie:
In Sickness and in Health

Chapter Ten

"How are you holding up, Boyd?" Asked Pam, as I walked by her secretarial desk.

"I don't know, Pam," I said. "Sad and lonely, I guess." It was worse than that. My marriage to Christie was finished, and I didn't want to be a lawyer anymore, at least not the kind I was. My chest felt distended, my stomach like a cement mixer. I was like a plane that had lost power in both engines. I was scared. And I was scared of being scared.

"You should get out and date," she advised—*terrible advice, by the way.*

I was desperate to do anything that might relieve me. "You're right," I said. "I probably should, but who? I don't know anybody."

"How about Stephanie, the new receptionist? She's nice and really pretty." When she started with the firm six months before I had noticed that.

"Well, yeah," I said, "but she's too young. She wouldn't

go out with me."

"What do you mean? No she's not. I'll ask her," said Pam. "I bet she'll go out with you."

"Okay," I said.

Five minutes later Pam called and told me Stephanie said she would love to go out with me. I called Stephanie's extension, the earpiece in my hand trembling against my ear. Whatever it was I said, when I hung up I had a date with this hot chick for the next Friday night.

I'm on a plane to Norfolk, Virginia for my daughter Jennifer's wedding, but I'm thinking about Stephanie, her mother, not Jennifer. I'll see her for the first time in more than three years.

When I unlock the door to my room in Virginia Beach, at the hotel where the wedding will take place, I finally think about Jennifer. Tomorrow, October 18th, she will be married. I smile. She has hoped for this day for years.

I have often reminisced about my first few dates with Stephanie. It was a giddy, ego-gratifying experience. Remembering our lovemaking used to get me hard.

I see her walk into the dining room before the rehearsal dinner. She looks terribly old. I probably look that way to her too, I think. I go over. We hug and exchange pleasantries. The next day we walk Jennifer down the aisle and hand her over to Ron, her husband-to-be. I notice Stephanie standing alone during the reception and consider striking up a conversation, but I can't think of anything to say. I pass by her to get a glass of wine and smile and nod. She smiles back, but we say nothing. I feel awkward. We ignore each other after that. I feel a vague sadness.

I spend most of my time with my children and grandchildren and don't think about Stephanie. I have brought my notebook and computer, but I don't write about her either. On the flight home nobody is in the seat next to me, so I pull my computer from my backpack and write.

On the Friday of our date I walked out of my office toward Stephanie's desk. My legs felt wobbly, and something burrowed into my stomach. I hadn't dated anyone but Christie in eight years. Stephanie's beauty and youth scared me. What would I talk about to a girl barely out of high school? At least now I know where to put it, I thought, should the occasion arise.

"Ready?" I asked.

"Let's go," she said, smiling, and got up from her desk. Her make-up was fresh. Her dark hair hung neatly just above her shoulders, bangs straight and brushed. Brown eyeliner and mascara highlighted her brown eyes. She's really beautiful, I thought. I remember the dress she wore that Friday night nearly forty-one years ago. It was powder blue with brown trim and a conservative neckline, but it was fitted enough to show off her figure.

For dinner I took her to Chasen's, the trendiest restaurant in L.A. I ordered a Scotch, and she ordered a Coke.

"Some day I'll order Scotch," she said, "but I'm not old enough yet."

"How old are you?" I asked.

"Nineteen," she said.

I'm robbing the cradle, I thought. Well, twenty-eight and nineteen. That's not too bad. I don't remember what we talked about at dinner, only that she put me at ease. She asked me questions and listened to my answers, and she seemed relaxed. What a difference from my first date with Christie.

After dinner, we saw a play in Hollywood, *You're a Good Man, Charlie Brown.* At intermission, while we stood in the lobby, I screwed up my courage and put my arm around her. She leaned her head against my shoulder. I relaxed. Beneath her perfume and hairspray, she smelled freshly scrubbed.

"You smell good," I said.

"Thanks. It's *Charlie*," she replied.

A young guy in tight black pants walked by and nearly twisted his neck off staring at Stephanie. She ignored him. My pride swelled.

After the play, we walked back to my car. "Can you take me home, if you don't mind driving to Whittier? I'll get my roommate to take me Sunday to pick up my car from the office. She won't mind."

"I'll be glad to take you home," I said, amazed.

On the drive to her apartment, she told me she had left home when she graduated high school. She had started at Pasadena Community College, but quit after two weeks. She was hoping the Firm would train her to be a legal secretary.

"Do you know how to put license plates on a car?" She asked.

"Uh...yeah," I said.

"Would you put mine on my new car? I'm having a terrible time for some reason. I can bring them with me to the office on Monday."

"Okay," I said. "I'm not mechanically inclined, but I'm sure I can get your license plates on."

When I parked in front of her apartment, she said, "Would you like to come in?"

"Sure," I said. It looks like I'll at least get a make-out session out of this, I thought.

Her roommate wasn't around. We settled down on the couch and I kissed her. Our mouths fit together perfectly. What a great kisser, I thought. I wondered what she thought of my kissing.

I breathed in her sweet smell. Our intensity increased. My erection pushed tight against my pants, as I felt her warm breath around my lips. I caressed her breasts through her dress, and she sighed. I wondered what to do next. Unbuttoning the back of her dress seemed cumbersome. I'll just go for it, I thought. I put my hand under her skirt and caressed her thigh. She moaned. I edged my hand up, and she breathed harder.

When I touched her wetness, she whispered, "No," and pulled my hand away. I moved my hand back to her breasts, and we continued to kiss, my crotch aching.

I think she likes me, I thought, driving home. I remembered her wetness and imagined making love to her. My spirits soared like a hot air balloon in an updraft.

That weekend I couldn't think of anything but her. A Herculean force pulled me toward her. I wanted to be inside her, not just my penis, my whole body. It was as if Christie had never existed.

I plotted our second date. I would take her out to dinner near her apartment next weekend. Or maybe we could have a drink after work, say on Wednesday. Oh, but she's too young to drink. She could drink a coke, I guess.

My overall self-confidence had improved since I first dated Christie. I was more socially adept than I had been eight years earlier, but I still doubted my attractiveness to women. I doubt I would have asked out Pauline Newman, the woman lawyer in the Nossaman Firm, if she'd been available. I didn't think a peer would be interested in me. I still needed to feel superior. Stephanie filled that need. I saw myself as smarter, and I had more education and life experience.

The Monday after our first date, when Stephanie got off work, she led me down to her car, a powder-blue Volkswagen bug, just like mine. I preened my male feathers and installed her license plates, while she looked on. After I'd finished tightening the last nut, she said, "Oh, thank you so much. That was so nice of you. I really appreciate it." As if I had done something remarkable. She got into her car and rolled down the window.

"See you tomorrow," she said and started to roll up the window.

I blurted out, "Can we do something Wednesday after work?"

"I'd love to," she said. She rolled the window back down, stuck her head out and grabbed my arm. "Come here." I bent my head down, and she kissed me, a long delicious kiss.

"See you tomorrow," I said. I noticed my heartbeat as she started her car and pulled away. Adrenalin surged.

On Wednesday morning, Pam invited us to dinner that night. When we arrived at her apartment after work, Stephanie borrowed a red and orange shirtdress to replace her office outfit. She came out of the bedroom stuffing her bra and panty hose in her purse. Her breasts, braless, swayed slightly.

Bob and Pam left to buy groceries for dinner. As the door closed, Stephanie and I sat on the couch. She asked about my marriage. I told her about Christie and the shock of her telling me she was leaving.

"How awful," Stephanie said. "I can tell you were really hurt. I'm so sorry."

She patted, then caressed my thigh. My groin stirred. I kissed her. Soon my pants and underwear were down to my ankles, and I was pulling her panties off. I was about to enter her when we heard Bob and Pam returning, talking in the hall-way. We pulled our clothes on, and were decent just as the key turned in the lock.

At about midnight, after a pleasant evening of dinner, conversation and plenty of alcohol, Pam said, "Bob and I are going to bed. Neither of you can drive home. Sorry, I can only offer you the couch and some blankets."

Within moments after Pam closed their bedroom door, we were on the floor, clutching each other, kissing. When I entered her, she moved so vigorously I slipped out. Not much experience, I thought, but I can teach her. It didn't happen again.

After I lay down beside her and she caught her breath, she said, "That was fantastic. I hope it was okay for you."

"Yeah, it sure was," I said. "It was great."

"I'll do better next time. I've only done it twice before," she said. "But it was nothing like this. Wow." Pride surged up to my chest, though I wondered if she was sincere. We pulled a blanket over us and slept.

In the morning Bob and Pam woke us. We were tired and

hung over. Stephanie called in sick. I didn't have any work that couldn't wait another day. I called my secretary and told her I wouldn't be in. After Bob and Pam left for work, we made love again, then got up and showered together. As I soaped her breasts, her belly and between her legs, I was in awe. With no makeup, a few pale freckles peeked out from her light olive skin around her cheekbones. Similar freckles on her chest framed her breasts. I had never seen anything so beautiful. I held her and rubbed my body against hers.

"I'm famished," she said after our shower. "Let's get something to eat."

We ate pancakes, eggs, and sausage at the International House of Pancakes. We talked about our past lives. I thought I shouldn't talk more about Christie, but I did. Stephanie didn't seem to mind.

"Sounds like Christine didn't appreciate you," she said.

She said she had a boyfriend who went off to college in northern California. She hadn't heard from him since. He was the one she'd had sex with twice, once on prom night and once after that.

I told her I had a really cute one-year-old daughter. I pulled out my wallet and showed her a picture. "Lisa," I said.

Stephanie held the wallet and smiled. "Oh, so precious. When can I meet her?"

"Well, I have her this weekend."

"Bring her over then," she said. "My roommate's out of town. We'll have the place to ourselves."

"Great," I said. "Is Friday night okay?"

"Yeah. I can't wait."

That same day, we drove to my home in Granada Hills. "What a beautiful house," she said. "Christine must be crazy."

"Let's stay here tonight," I said.

"That would be nice, but I can't go to work tomorrow wearing the same clothes I wore yesterday, especially after calling in sick today. People would put two and two together. Besides

I need clean underwear."

"Don't worry. I'll buy you new clothes," I said.

We drove to a store in Encino. Stephanie picked out a dress, and I waited outside the dressing room until she came out to model it. It was green cotton with black fleur de lis, a scooped elastic neckline and gathered just below her breasts. It came to just above her knees. It was not as conservative as her other dress, but it was appropriate for the office. No buttons or zippers—easy to get off, I thought. She picked out new bra, panties, and pantyhose. I paid and we left.

We ate veal shank, sautéed spinach and roasted new potatoes in a dark little bistro on Ventura Boulevard. As we drove home I put my hand down the elastic front of her new dress and caressed her breasts. I liked that dress.

By the time we got home from the Ventura Boulevard bistro I was hard and she was wet. We tore our clothes off, rushed to the bed and made love. It occurred to me that I had last made love to Christie on this bed, but I quickly forgot about it.

I went down on her. "You taste so good," I said.

"Nobody's ever done that to me, Boyd," she said between heavy breaths. "It feels so good. I love it."

It was difficult to work the next day. All I could think about was Stephanie, and how nice she was, how beautiful, the sex. My sexual fantasies were all consuming. And although she hadn't been to college, I considered her intelligent. Finally, at about ten o'clock I focused. I had to.

Friday night, at Christie's, I dressed Lisa in a pale green dress and matching bonnet that tied around her chin. She slept during the hour drive to Stephanie's. We didn't get there until nine. Before I got out of the car, I brushed her blond hair and fluffed her bangs with a soft, miniature hairbrush and put on her white Mary Janes over green socks. She couldn't have looked cuter. She seemed to know this was something special. I carried her and her diaper bag, bulging with clothes, diapers, formula, and baby food for the weekend.

When Stephanie opened the door, she gasped. "Oh! She

is so cute I can't believe it. Hi, Lisa." Lisa smiled at her and cooed. This is great; the ultimate chick magnet, I thought. Stephanie held her arms out, and I handed her Lisa.

"I have to go get my bag and Lisa's Porta Crib," I said. "I'll be right back."

When I got back, Stephanie was rocking Lisa on her lap. "Could I feed her?" she asked.

"Christine fed her just before I left. It's way past her bed-time. You can give her a bottle, and she'll probably go to sleep."

"I would love that," she said. "I wish I could play with her. That'll have to wait until tomorrow, I guess. What a darling dress. You didn't dress her did you?"

"Yes, I did."

"Wow. I'm impressed."

True to my prediction, Lisa was asleep before she had finished the bottle. I set up her crib in the bedroom and put her down.

"We'll move her to the living room when we go to bed," I said.

After dinner Stephanie went to the bathroom and came out wearing blue striped pajama shorts and a matching pullover top. I stripped down to what I usually wore to bed, my underwear. She sat beside me on the bed, smiled, and looked at me passionately. I kissed her.

"I love you very much," I said.

"I love you too," she said, looking straight into my eyes. "I can't believe I'm so lucky."

"We're both lucky," I said. I was delirious with ego and lust.

"Let's go to bed," said Stephanie. We picked up Lisa's crib and put it in the living room. We embraced and kissed by the bed. Her pajamas didn't stay on long. As we made love, our bodies moving together, I wanted to melt inside her. I had never felt like this. I wanted to be part of her, united, and finally I was.

The clock said 3:05 when I woke up. I looked at Stephanie sleeping. It was a warm night, and the covers had slipped down to her waist. I gazed at her breasts, drew the covers down to her knees. I traced every centimeter of her body with my eyes and then with my fingers. She woke up and asked, "What are you doing?"

"Loving you," I said. She smiled. I kissed her cheek, her mouth, the rest of her down to her knees and back up to her mouth. We made love again. I thought I would never get my breath back. I couldn't get enough of her. I have relived that night in my mind many times. If I could only remember a few things from my life, that night is one memory I would want to keep.

At about eight o'clock I heard Lisa making crying noises, but not really crying. When I appeared beside her crib, she smiled and got up, holding on to the edge. I fixed her bottle, and we settled down on the couch. As I fed Lisa cereal and pears, Stephanie, looking sleepy-eyed, walked in.

"Oh, can I feed her? Will she let me? She asked.

"I think so. Let's see." I gave her the spoon and jar of baby food, then Lisa, who didn't seem to care who fed her.

"This is heaven," said Stephanie. "She's like a living doll."

Lisa demonstrated that she was finished by closing her mouth tightly when Stephanie offered her the spoon. We went out to breakfast and then to a park. Lisa crawled around on the grass with much chortling and grinning. Stephanie swung her ever so gently on a swing. I lifted her from the swing and took her over to a slide. I climbed the ladder and sat at the top. Down we slid, a wide-eyed look of terror on Lisa's face. I didn't slide with her again until she was older.

We went home and put Lisa down for her nap. Stephanie and I made love again and slept a little. She insisted on changing and feeding Lisa when she woke up. As time passed, when Lisa was with us, Stephanie gradually took over most of her care. I didn't resist. Feeding babies and changing poopy diapers was not my idea of fun.

For dinner that night I cooked chicken and corn on the cob on a little barbeque outside the front door, and Stephanie made salad. While we ate, Lisa alternated between playing on the floor and chortling in Stephanie's lap. Warmth embraced us. I had the feeling of a family that I never had with Christie. I forgot there was a world out there.

After we put Lisa to bed we made love and went to sleep early. Lisa awoke at seven. Sunday was a repeat of Saturday. I wanted it to last forever and thought it could. My lust was wild mind, overpowering loss of control.

I took Lisa back to Christie Sunday night. The next week I spent every night with Stephanie either at her apartment or my house. We had sex every day. I bought her a gold bracelet and more clothes. I took her out for meals in fancy restaurants. Lacking the confidence that being myself was enough, I was bribing her to be my girlfriend. I thought that was how to court a girl.

When Christie and I were in Mexico, Howard had talked to me about a dark-haired Mexican girl. She was the most beautiful girl he had ever seen, he said. I had been jealous of Howard ever since I noticed his knack for seducing pretty girls. In stark contrast to me, Howard seemed like a sex magnet. Stephanie was my beautiful, dark-haired girl. It was the first time in my life that I felt desirable. My jealousy of Howard evaporated.

I was in the infatuation stage. I was not seeing the real person, but, instead an idealized notion of somebody that a human being could never be. I perceived Stephanie as a virtual goddess. The problem with this stage is that it is a mirage. There is no perspective. Carl Jung said that the first six months of a typical romantic relationship are a period of pure projection. Goethe put it more cynically: "When two people are really happy about one another, one can generally assume they are mistaken." At twenty-eight, I didn't know then what I believe now—that "falling in love" initially is a sex-linked erotic experience. It has nothing to do with love, except as a possible catalyst. This infatuation I had was far from real love, but naively I didn't realize it.

In addition to sex and the feeling of superiority, Stephanie fulfilled another need I believe I had. She belonged to the new generation. She could pull me off the cusp into her generation—the generation of sex, drugs and rock and roll—instead of the boring, false "morality" of the old generation.

Two weeks after our first date, we were making out on the couch, while her roommate and her boyfriend had sex in the bedroom. I slipped off the couch, got on my knees and looked up at Stephanie.

"What are you doing? She asked.

I asked, "Will you marry me?"

"Yes, yes, yes!" she exclaimed. We agreed to marry in six months, when my divorce became final.

"I wish we could get married now," she said.

"Me too."

Stephanie had made me forget Christie. My angst had melted in her arms.

We went to the store and bought champagne. Back home I popped the cork and poured it into water glasses. We toasted to our future together.

I had introduced her to alcohol.

Chapter Eleven

After I return from a trip to California for dental and medical checkups, I walk to Harvard Square and sit down at the bar at Upstairs on the Square. A young couple sitting next to me look longingly at each other, talking quietly. He reaches into his pocket and pulls out a little box, the kind jewelry comes in. Her mouth springs open, her eyes wide. I watch as she opens the box, revealing an emerald necklace. After hugs and kisses, he clasps it around her neck. The scene reminds me that in courting Stephanie, I was extravagant and willing to do almost anything for her. When I get home, I sit down at my computer. The topic is how I tried to give Stephanie everything she could want.

About a week after we agreed to marry, Stephanie moved out of her apartment, giving only a few days' verbal notice to her landlord. He changed the locks before she could move some of her stuff out. She was outraged.

"I'll get your stuff out," said I, hero to the damsel in distress. After midnight, we drove to the apartment in a rented truck. We snuck up to the door. I was thankful it was ground level. I tried to jimmy the lock with a wire, and failed. I tried a screwdriver. No luck. I checked to be sure no one was around.

There was a window next to the door. I pulled up as hard as I could, grunting like a wrestler, but it was locked. There were no accessible windows that opened. I pulled the screwdriver out of my back pocket and jabbed it with all my strength into the bottom of the window. The glass splintered. Stephanie gasped. I jabbed again and again, making the hole bigger. I reached through the hole and unlocked the window, cutting my hand, then raised it and crawled in. I opened the front door to let Stephanie in.

"I can't believe you did that. My God!" she exclaimed.

We hurriedly carried Stephanie's stuff out in five or six trips, and drove away. I was breathing hard, and my hand was bleeding. Stephanie applied tissues to it and held it tight until the bleeding stopped.

I felt triumphantly masculine. I imagined she felt feminine. I had escaped the confines of my childhood into a wilderness of lust, risk and impulse. It wasn't until the next day, out of Stephanie's presence in the solitude of my office, that I thought through my folly. I had committed burglary, a felony. Our fingerprints were all over the doorknobs. If caught, I would be disbarred automatically. For the next week, I waited in terror for the police to knock or call. They never did.

I didn't use a condom, ignoring the possibility of Stephanie getting pregnant before I could marry her; abortion, even if we would have considered it, was still illegal, and it was still disgraceful for middle class unmarried women to have babies.

We were concerned that the firm would disapprove of our living together, and Stephanie didn't want to deal with her mother's wrath. My solution was to rent her an apartment in Mid-Wilshire, a few miles from the office, and another for me in Manhattan Beach, a half block from the beach. We lived in hers during the week and mine on weekends. Neither of us wanted to live in the house Christie and I shared. I sold it.

One Friday after work, I said, "Let's go downstairs and have a drink. If you're with me, I'll bet they serve you."

"Okay. I'm game," she said. "What should I order? I don't know what I'd like."

"Try a Tom Collins," I suggested.

When the waiter came to our table in the bar, I ordered a Scotch, "and the lady'll have a Tom Collins," I said.

Without hesitation, he said, "Thank you, sir."

We went to an ACLU garden party at a mansion in Beverly Hills that summer. About fifty people milled about the huge patio and the pool with a waterfall. Tall cypress trees bounded the yard. Tables with white tablecloths and cushy lounges and chairs adorned the pool area. Banquet tables bore shrimp, caviar, sliced salami, roast beef and turkey, numerous kinds of bread, crackers and chips, oysters and crab. Waiters in short white jackets and black bow ties mingled among the guests bearing trays of food, some of which I couldn't identify. We all stood around, cocktails and cigarettes in hand, lamenting the first eight months of the Nixon administration. Men flocked around Stephanie, and she charmed them. She is the kind of wife I should have if I'm going to be a partner in a big L.A. law firm, I thought.

We got in the car to leave. I slipped the key in the ignition and turned toward Stephanie. "Let's go to Vegas."

"Are you kidding?"

"No. I'm serious."

"Okay. Far out," she said. "Let's go."

I got on the I-10 and headed east. "What about clothes?" she asked.

"Who needs clothes?" I said. "When we're not in our room, we'll wear what we have. We can buy toothbrushes and toothpaste when we get there."

As we sat in traffic, I told her the doubts I had about my

job, "...helping rich people get richer. I think I would be happier working for some cause that I thought made the world a better place, or, at least, helped people who need it."

"Well, your clients need your help, Boyd," she said. "But you should do what makes you happy."

"The problem is that working to make the world a better place doesn't make much money."

"I'm sure that's true," she said. "You have to decide what you want, money or the reward of making the world a better place."

"I suppose doing what I'm doing now makes the world a better place, in the sense that it promotes our system of justice, instead of using violence to solve disputes. The problem is that the people who can afford to pay what the firm charges don't need more money. And what I do, if we're successful, only gets them more money. I don't know."

"Whatever you decide to do, I'll support you," she said.

"Thank you. I appreciate that." I patted her leg.

We poked along Interstate 10 in the early September heat, air-conditioning blasting. Stephanie lit two Herbert Tareytons and handed one to me. Eventually, we were in the clear on I-15, cruising along at seventy-five miles an hour. I had stopped and bought us little bottles of Scotch, the size they serve on airplanes. We drank them in the car. Stephanie grabbed my hand and put it between her legs. She was wet. She moaned as I fingered her. I unzipped my pants, and she fondled me.

Outside, the desert lay dark, silent, and empty. "I can't take this anymore. I have to be inside you."

"Oh, yes," she said.

I pulled off at the next exit, drove down a deserted frontage road, and parked at the side of the dark road. My sexual excitement blocked realization of any danger.

"Push your seatback all the way back," I said. I got out, ran around to her side and opened the door. Her panties were on the floor. I pulled my pants down and entered her. We came quickly. Just then I saw flashing red lights approaching behind our car. Terror struck. I pulled on and zipped up my pants and climbed out. "Good evening officer," I said, as he approached the car.

"Good evening. License, please." I handed him my license. "You can get in the car," he said. A few minutes after he had returned to his car, he walked back, and I rolled down the window. "It's not safe for you to be parked out here," he said. "Now go on your way, and don't pull off on these deserted roads anymore."

"Thank you, officer. I won't." I waited until I had rolled up the window to heave a big sigh.

Stephanie laughed. "What a trip," she said, as she wiped our juices off her seat with tissues.

I unlocked the door to our hotel room and opened it for Stephanie. She went in, pulled off her dress and jumped on the bed. I followed. After making love, we went down to the all-night buffet. We gobbled down salad, soup, shrimp, sour-dough bread, steak, mashed potatoes, green beans, and chocolate mousse.

"You know," said Stephanie, "I can't wear this dress and the same underwear the whole time."

"We'll buy you a new dress," I said, "but who needs underwear? I'm not wearing any."

"It'll feel weird," she said, "but kinda sexy. I guess you're right."

Holding hands, we walked down the hotel's long, deserted hall to a dress shop that was open at three in the morning—only in Las Vegas. I waited while Stephanie picked several things off the rack and went in the dressing room. In a few minutes, out she came in a silky red and orange jumpsuit with shorts. "They're all the rage now," she said. "They're called hot pants. What do you think?"

Her breasts swayed gently as she twirled around.

"Fantastic," I said, admiring her legs.

"They ain't cheap," she said.

"No matter. I'll buy them. Leave them on."

We drove home Monday afternoon, exhausted after a weekend of sex, eating, drinking, and a little gambling. "That was so much fun," said Stephanie. "I don't think I've ever had so much fun in my life."

I awoke one morning, Stephanie gone from our bed. The covers were pulled back, exposing two blood spots on the sheet. The toilet flushed, and Stephanie hobbled back to bed, pale and holding her back. She grunted and lay down on her stomach. "Boyd, please sit on my back."

"Huh?"

"You heard me. Sit on my back. I mean it," she said. "My period is killing me."

"Okay." I got up and gingerly sat on her back.

"Down, a little lower," she said. I moved. "Perfect. That helps. Thanks."

After a few minutes, she said, "This hurts so bad. I can't go to work like this. Stay home with me, please."

"I can't stay home, Stephanie. I have work to do on my cases that has to be done today."

"I guess I'm just not very important to you," she said. I felt bad, but I had to get a document out to court that day.

Melancholy, bordering on depression, creeps up on me as the days shorten in late fall and I begin to realize how I sabotaged my second marriage even before we married. One dark morning in my Cambridge apartment I remember not staying home when Stephanie was in pain from her period as the first time I refused to do something she wanted. I usually gave her control. I lived for my job and for her, but never for me. I couldn't have kept that up. How strange. It was the opposite of how I treated Christie. I had no awareness of either of these extremes. I was shy and insecure. It's possible that it was a relief to have strong direction from this beautiful woman.

The next time Stephanie started her period on a Sunday. I was determined to make up for not staying home with her the last time. "Let's do something that'll take your mind off your period," I said. "Come on out to the car."

"Nothing will take my mind off it, Boyd, but what do you want to do? I really don't feel like going anywhere."

"Let's go look at Porsches," I said.

"Well, that just might do it. Are you serious?"

"Yes," I said. "Come on."

We looked at two Porsches on display in the showroom. One was a red 911, the other a burgundy 912 Targa. The Targas had a removable hard roof. When the salesman left us for a moment, I said, "I like the burgundy Targa. What do you think?"

"Well, yeah," she said.

"We could trade in your Volkswagen, and I'll keep mine. The Porsche could be yours, but you'd let me drive it sometimes. Wouldn't you?"

"I don't know," she teased. "I don't know if I could part with it."

When I told the salesman we were considering the Targa, he hustled us off to the contract department. After pounding the keys of a calculator for a while, the finance guy handed me a sheet of paper. He explained his calculations, but I wasn't listening. I could see the bottom line showed a payment almost as much as our rent.

"Okay, we'll take it," I said.

Stephanie said, "I can't believe this, Boyd. Can we afford it?"

"Sure," I said. But I wasn't so sure. I would get a Christmas bonus. We could scrape by.

I didn't consciously realize the message I was sending

her when I bought it—and the two apartments, the expensive clothes, the weekend in Las Vegas, and countless other things: there would always be more. Unconsciously, I felt the need to bribe this beautiful woman. I was headed toward disaster. And I had no inkling.

I sit down at my computer to write about why I thought I had to bribe Stephanie, why I couldn't see that I wouldn't be able to keep it up. Nothing came to me. I go over to the couch and pick up my notebook and pen. I just sit there paralyzed.

A few days later I walk to the Central Square T Station—Boston's subway—to go to a concert at Symphony Hall to try to cheer myself up. My cell phone rings. It's Susan, my third wife. She has been calling me frequently. She repeats her wish that I come back to California to live with her. I tell her I have commitments in Boston.

When I get home from the concert, there's an email from her saying that Paso Robles has changed a lot since I lived there. She thinks I would enjoy it now. It has fine restaurants, over two hundred wineries in the area, and a much more cosmopolitan life–style than when I lived there in the nineties. I know all this. I like Paso Robles. I like Susan. But I have no reason to believe a new relationship with Susan would work better than the old one. Why did the old relationship fail? At this point, I don't know.

She calls the next morning. She says, "You should come and spend a week here at the ranch so you get a feel for what it would be like."

I tell her I have committed to be Kate's music business manager for two years, which requires me to live near her. I don't want to break that commitment.

"You're just running away to find yourself," Susan says. "You could find yourself in California."

Maybe she's right. Though I like living in Boston, I still don't understand fully my motivation for moving. I send Susan an email, "I plan to be in California over the holidays, and I'll come up to Paso Robles for four or five days."

I don't think I want to move back in with Susan, but maybe staying there for a few days will clarify things. I make a cup of pumpkin spice tea and return to writing about that first summer with Stephanie.

Stephanie had taken ballet lessons since she was four, and told me she had wanted to be a dancer. She started a ballet school and taught ballet to young girls while she went to high school. She applied to several ballet companies while still in high school, but they rejected her, telling her that at five feet, two inches she was too short. She showed me pictures of a recital and an article from the local Arcadia paper about her school. I was impressed by her drive.

"I would really love to open another ballet school some day," she said. "I think I could make money at what I love."

"How much would it cost to get one started?" I asked.

"Well, I would have to rent a studio. I rented a room in the Elks Club in Arcadia before. And then I did advertising. I would need clothes. And I'd run up a phone bill calling all my contacts in Arcadia. I probably could get some of the same students back. It's only been a little over a year."

"I'll finance it for you if it's within reason."

"Oh, Boyd. I can't tell you how grateful I would be. Teaching ballet is my dream."

She quit her job at Nossaman, and we gave up her Mid-Wilshire apartment. Two weeks later she began driving her Porsche to her ballet studio in Arcadia—forty-five miles each way. Within a month she had enough students to teach four days a week.

According to the budget I prepared, the ballet studio should have been close to breaking even after a month. But I had to keep putting more money in. One morning before I left for work I asked to see the studio checkbook. It showed multiple clothing purchases. "What are all these purchases?" I asked pointing to the lines on the check register.

"Those are ballet clothes for the girls who can't afford them, and for me."

"We can't afford it either," I said.

"It's a necessary expense. You said you'd finance the studio. Are you going to back out on your word?"

"I told you, 'within reason,'" I said.

"God damn it. I have to do this when I'm just getting started. Don't you trust me, Boyd?"

"Yeah, all right," I said. I turned around and left for work.

Complaining about Stephanie's ballet expenditures was my first attempt to shoot down the financial expectations in her that I had generated. I hadn't learned how to raise such an issue constructively. Anyone with a little sensitivity, or common sense, knows that it doesn't work to be accusatory, argumentative, or to whine about something you don't like.

As demonstrations against the Viet Nam War raged on college campuses across the country, and riots, rooted in the country's racism and the poverty it generated, erupted in city ghettos, my guilt deepened. I wanted to make a difference. In September 1969 I saw an ad in the *Daily Journal* for a position as Director of Litigation at Long Beach Legal Aid Foundation.

"If that interests you, go ahead and interview," said Stephanie.

"But the pay is thirty-five percent less than I make now."

"We'll get by," she said.

I interviewed and got the job. The Nossaman Firm agreed to a year's leave of absence. When I walked into my office my first day at Long Beach Legal Aid, everybody came by to greet me. All except George, the executive director, and two of the attorneys, were young. George told me five of the seven attorneys were just out of law school. It was my job to train them to be litigation lawyers. I'm going to be a teacher, I thought. Wow. After a few weeks I was high on work. We represented the poor of Long Beach in disputes with their landlords, spouses, predatory finance companies, and government agencies purportedly working for their benefit. In one case, I prepared a brief filed with the United States Supreme Court on behalf of welfare recipients, mostly single mothers. We won. The Court held that government agencies could not terminate a welfare recipient's benefits without a fair hearing in advance. I taught the bright young lawyers the practical ins and outs of litigation. I never knew work could be so much fun.

But problems lurked. Stephanie and I were falling deeper in debt, struggling to pay the minimum on our credit cards. We had the Porsche payment, and the ballet studio continued to lose money. Something had to give. The ballet studio was a big drain, but I couldn't summon the courage to tell Stephanie she had to close it.

Stephanie and I still made love every night. Afterwards, one Saturday night, she said, "It seems like the only time we see each other is in bed."

"Yeah, I know," I said.

"I miss you a lot. I feel us drifting apart, you doing your thing and I doing mine. I don't like that. We need to be a team," she said.

"I agree," I said.

"Maybe I should close the studio," she said. "I'm on the road three hours a day. That drive home in rush hour is a bitch after teaching all day. And I have to teach Saturdays, when you're usually home. That's the busiest day. I really don't want to close it, but...."

Soon, Stephanie told me she had decided to close the studio. "I think you'd better sell the Porsche too," she said.

I never gave Stephanie credit for her mature judgment in giving up the studio, neither expressly, nor even in my own mind. If I had, it might have encouraged her to be more frugal. I let her give up a dream without showing any empathy. Or, maybe it wasn't her dream anymore. Maybe the comfortable life I made with her squelched the passion she had. If I'd talked to her about it, I might have found out.

Perhaps, I should have considered and discussed with her

a way to keep her connected with her passion without going further into debt. And I could have adjusted my work hours at Legal Aid to do some paperwork on Saturday while she was teaching, and then I could take off early on one of her days off. But, apparently, I was not concerned with her dreams or needs.

George hired Stephanie as a legal secretary trainee at Legal Aid. We sold the Porsche and managed with one car. Even with her income and lower expenses, we were so far in debt I couldn't see much light. Stephanie's income made up only about half of the decrease in mine. We had spent beyond our means even before I went to Legal Aid, and we hadn't reduced our expenditures materially. I blamed it on Stephanie at the time and resented her for it. We were both at fault during that period. We just spent money on different things. Stephanie spent on clothes, parties and gifts to her friends and relatives. I spent on dining out and alcohol. I didn't see that. We didn't sit down and work out a budget, which I find astounding now. I can't blame that on Stephanie. I was older and more accustomed to money.

I believed that Stephanie loved me, so I expected her to put my needs ahead of hers—still my criterion for true love. I had been focused on doing for her everything she wanted, putting her needs ahead of mine. Or I thought I was. Maybe giving her everything I thought she wanted was a means to try to control her. Much of what I gave her was what I decided she wanted. Was the Porsche really for her, or was it for me, to impress her? Our apartment in Manhattan Beach was tiny. She wanted more space, while I dreamt of an ocean view. We moved to a two-bedroom apartment with an ocean view. Was it for her or me? My Legal Aid job was for me. Was the ballet studio for her? Originally, I thought it would make money.

She supported me in changing to a job that paid less. She took care of my daughter when she was with us. She kept a neat house and cooked most of our meals. She never said no to sex.

One day when I got home from work, she was standing at the kitchen sink crying. When I asked her what was the matter, she said she was addicted to diet pills. I knew she had been taking them, but I didn't know she was addicted. "I want to stay thin for you," she said. I told her she didn't need to be that thin—around a hundred pounds. Eventually, with medical help, she weaned herself off them.

We were each doing all we believed we could to please the other, but neither of us was taking care of our own needs. I was building resentment and, undoubtedly, she was too.

We continued the sexual adventures that fed my ego. One night we had two couples over. We had a lot to drink. Stephanie started to slow dance with me in the living room. She took her blouse off. I didn't stop her. "Let's go skinny-dipping," she shouted over the music.

"Yeah," yelled the guys. Eventually, they talked their wives into it. Stephanie stripped and grabbed a towel from the bathroom and wrapped herself in it. Everyone else left their clothes on, and we headed for the sand, two blocks away. When we got to the water, Stephanie was the first in. The rest of us stripped and ran in. I was drunk enough not to notice the cold. Nobody stayed in long. Stephanie and I were the last out. The others ran ahead. She laughed and ran naked through the sand. Even in the shadows of a slender moon, I noticed what a great body she had. I ran after her, grabbed her, and pushed her down. We made love in the sand.

In January 1970 we married in San Francisco in an old Methodist Church with Bob and Pam as our witnesses. About an hour before the ceremony, Stephanie came out of the bathroom smiling. She looked smashing. She had curled her long brown hair and made up her brown eyes. She wore a simple knitted white dress scooped at the neck and ending just above her knees. White heels finished it.

"You look absolutely beautiful," I said.

"Thank you," she said. "I'm glad you think so. It's for you."

Whatever the minister said, I remember kissing Stephanie, paying, signing the license and walking out of the church. After a cracked crab lunch on Fisherman's Wharf, we said good-bye to Bob and Pam.

We stayed at the Fairmont, then San Francisco's most famous and most fancy hotel. We drank champagne and dined on Chateaubriand, ending with baked Alaska. Then we had a cognac in the hotel bar. Stephanie still looked beautiful in her wedding dress. I noticed men looking at her.

When we got back to the room, we embraced and kissed. "Get in bed," she said. "I'll be there in a minute." In a few minutes she floated out wearing a black see-through teddy, thigh length, over the briefest of panties. She twirled around for me. I growled. Now, that's sexy, I thought. As she climbed into bed I smelled the fresh Charlie.

She burped. "Excuse me," she said. "My stomach is acting up."

I massaged her back. She turned over. I caressed her breasts under the teddy and pushed my hardness against her thigh. She pulled away. "Excuse me," she said, jumping out of bed and running to the bathroom, where I could hear her vomiting. She returned to bed. "I feel like shit. Could we consummate this marriage tomorrow?"

"Of course. It's not like this was going to be the first time," I said.

"I know," she said. "But I wanted to have a perfect wedding night."

"Sorry, but it's all right," I said. "We'll make up for it tomorrow." We did.

Chapter Twelve

I had arrived: a beautiful, young wife, a job I liked, a home near the beach with an ocean view. We partied a lot, usually with Stephanie's friends, often weekend-long, drunken, music-filled affairs. I barbecued, and Stephanie made salad and side dishes. She always cleaned up. Sometimes somebody would bring pot, and we smoked, but Stephanie and I preferred drinking. If Lisa was with us, Stephanie put her to bed early.

The hip media trumpeted wife swapping as one of the cool things to do. We never did that, but we did share sex in other ways. Once playing strip poker with another couple, I ended up naked. Stephanie gave me a blow job, the other couple cheering her on. We made love in the Gulf near San Felipe, Mexico and standing outside the front door of our apartment. One afternoon in West L.A., we spontaneously rented a hotel room and made love. Afterwards, driving home on the 405 Freeway, Stephanie gave me a blow job, as I struggled to keep the car between the lines in the fast lane. I loved the wildness of it all.

The dullness of my parents and the boredom of Alhambra appalled me. Nothing ever happened there. I wanted to live where something was happening, and there was plenty happening in the Manhattan Beach of the 1970s. We thought that was what an adult was all about. Never mind that what was happening didn't matter and didn't fulfill me. It was something. For a long time I looked at this first year with Stephanie as the happiest year of my life.

Stephanie and I started to argue at work. In my view, Stephanie didn't take her job seriously enough. One night she started to leave work at the same time I did, but she had a Complaint that needed to be finished. The client was coming in the next morning. I insisted she stay and finish it. "You're leaving," she said. "Why can't I?"

"Because that Complaint has to be finished."

She stayed and finished it, but when she came home she went to bed without speaking. That and our wedding night were the only nights we didn't make love that first year. The next morning at the office I read the Complaint she had typed. When she set my coffee down on my desk, I handed the Complaint to her. I was angry. "There are a lot of mistakes. Please fix them. The client's waiting." She looked at me as if I had murdered her newborn child, turned around without a word, and slammed my office door on the way out. I had a strong work ethic, instilled in me by my parents. I expected my employees to have the same; I was intolerant of those who didn't, although I was much more restrained with employees who were not my wife.

That night we apologized to each other. "I don't think I should continue working with you. It's not good for our marriage," she said.

"I agree," I said. "Why don't you go to college?"

"I'll think about that," she said. But she looked in the paper for jobs and never brought up college. She interviewed to be manager of an exclusive Beverly Hills candy shop. The next day she told me she got the job as co-manager with another girl. That Saturday I drove her to her first day of work. She was relieving her co-manager, Jennifer, who introduced herself. She was a blond, lanky hippie, as young as Stephanie. She said she had just moved here from Ohio. She had a smooth pale complexion, big grayish-blue eyes, and wore no make-up. She spoke so quietly I had trouble hearing her. She wore a multi-colored halter top, no bra, and a micro-mini skirt. Bending over to shelve candy, she exposed herself through transparent panties.

The next weekend she and her boyfriend John came over. We smoked the pot they brought, drank tequila, and got to know each other. They had been living together six months. John was a computer systems analyst, self-taught. Neither he nor Jennifer had gone to college. I liked John. Stephanie connected with Jennifer right away.

That summer, 1970, friends of mine, Alan and Carol, invited us to go water skiing and stay at his parents' cabin at Lake Arrowhead. Another couple joined us. Stephanie and I had never been water skiing, and everyone was patient trying to teach us. The lake was jammed with water skiers and boaters. Alan, in an uncharacteristically serious tone, explained that somebody must sit in the back of the boat to raise the yellow flag if one of our skiers went down, so the other boaters knew to stay out of the way. One time Stephanie sat in the back with the flag in her hand. She chatted with Carol. When our skier went down, she didn't notice and didn't raise the flag. Once we got the skier back in the boat Alan told Stephanie that it was important to raise the flag. "Downed skiers have lost limbs on this lake," he said.

Stephanie sulked and insisted on leaving early Sunday. "Alan was rude. That was uncalled for," she said. She told me she would never hang out with Alan and Carol again. I told her she was being overly sensitive, that Alan was right and that he was not rude to her.

"Thanks for taking his side," she said. We drove the

hundred and twenty miles home mostly in silence. Stephanie had accused other friends of mine, Mark and Stacy, of the same thing a few weeks before. They were rude to her, she claimed. I disagreed. Soon Stephanie refused to have anything to do with my friends. Howard was away working for the State Department Foreign Service in Viet Nam. He had R and R once that year. We saw him and his family often during his month of R and R. Stephanie said she didn't like him. I told her he was my best friend, and she would have to accept him. But except for Howard, I had no friends that were not Stephanie's.

The last autumn leaves float down from the trees like tiny loose kites. They crunch under my feet as I take my daily walk around Cambridge. I'll go to Inman Square for an early dinner. I have my notebook with me. I usually remember to take it with me wherever I go, unless I know I won't be able to write. It's a habit now. Sometimes nothing comes to me that I want to write down. But if something does, and I don't jot it down, I usually forget it. I don't know if that's old age messing with my memory or just normal. I sit down at the East Coast Grill bar and order a Diet Coke. I take out my notebook and lay it and the pen on the counter—just in case. In a few minutes I think about Stephanie's rejection of my friends and began to write.

I think Stephanie probably felt insecure and intimidated by my relatively well-educated, older friends. If I had discussed this with her and helped her to understand that they liked her and didn't intend to be rude, maybe over time she would have accepted them. If not, without accusation or criticizing Stephanie, I could go on seeing them without her. Instead, I resented her for "making" me give up my friends.

I know now that, similar to the old adage about real estate, the three most important things about marriage are communication, communication and communication. I had heard or read back then about the importance of communication in marriage, but I had not internalized it sufficiently to apply it. My desire to avoid confrontation was more powerful.

In September 1970 my year's leave of absence from the Nossaman Firm was about to expire. I loved working at Legal Aid, especially teaching the young lawyers. I felt for the first time since law school that I was doing something worthwhile. I was becoming known in the legal aid community statewide for the cases we had won. I wanted to stay. But we were deep in debt, still barely able to pay our bills. Increasingly, I blamed Stephanie and resented her for it. She gave expensive gifts for various occasions, and sometimes for no occasion, to her friends, sisters, nieces and nephews. Dresses and designer jeans that she never wore hung in our closet. When I took the trash out, I saw untouched fresh vegetables gone bad, spoiled cheese, fish and meat. She bought more food than we could eat and threw it away when it spoiled. She never served leftovers.

My third wife, Susan, took in stray dogs and cats. Stephanie took in stray people. A friend of hers named Gail and her baby showed up one weekend. Two weeks later they were still with us. When I asked Stephanie how long they were going to stay, she said, "I don't know. Gail has no money, no job and a baby. She can't find a safe place to rent on her welfare benefits."

She stayed several months, contributing nothing to her support. Stephanie even bought most of the baby's food and clothes. She told me later Gail was sending most of her welfare benefits to her mother, who was worse off than she. I complained a little, but, for the most part, I held in my resentment at having to support them.

I decided to go back to the Nossaman Firm. I thought I had no choice, and I blamed Stephanie. I didn't discuss my feelings with her. I just told her I had decided to go back. As I drove to the office the first day back, an overwhelming sadness enveloped me. By the end of the week I had convinced myself it was good to be back. We could get out of debt, and as a partner in a couple of years I'd be making the big bucks.

I sit at the East Coast Grill bar in Inman Square drinking mint tea after my meal of oysters and a surprisingly tasty bowl of Brussels sprouts. I'm sure it was the butter and bacon they were grilled in. I think about the money Stephanie spent on food, clothes and gifts. I pick up my pen. Writing helps to conquer my tendency to glide over the surface of things instead of digging deep to get to the bottom.

Perhaps I could have complimented Stephanie for her generosity and good cooking, and asked her how she thought we could save money on gifts and food. If Stephanie was unwilling, I could have discussed my ideas with her in a non-threatening way. But I didn't. I complained and accused Stephanie. It occurs to me that, in recent years, I have given and loaned a lot of money to dear friends and family. Have I changed my views, or did I feel that I had the sole right to decide who was worthy of our generosity? I knew the money I earned belonged to both of us as community property, but I think I looked on it as mine. I certainly acted that way.

I realize now that going back to the Nossaman Firm was a turning point. At the time I didn't see the alternatives, the choices. Stephanie and I had been together a little more than a year, married for about nine months. We could have tried to devise a plan to lower our standard of living, so that we could live on our two salaries and gradually pay off our debt. I don't know if we would have succeeded, but we didn't try. Instead, I felt helpless, trapped and resentful. I helped destroy our marriage by solidifying Stephanie's expectations of a high standard of living, then resented her spending. I thought I had no choice but to live a life I didn't want.

I hang my head and order a martini. I can't think about Stephanie anymore. When I finish my martini, I think, *this is not drinking to live more fully.* I drank last night too. I have to get back on track. I finish the martini and walk home. The cold air on my face seems to jar my consciousness. Loneliness creeps in. I think about how much time I spend alone. I see Kate once a week on average. Every couple of months I travel to California to see Lisa and my grandchildren and friends there. But I have no friends in Boston. Some of the writers that I correspond with all over the country have writing groups they meet with. I know there are a lot of writers in Boston. I should try to find or form a writing group. A few months later I do. We meet once a month; one of us brings a topic. We write for a half hour, then read aloud to each other. Of course, we have become friends.

One night not long after I had gone back to work at the Nossaman Firm, Stephanie talked about her father. He was a loving, patient man, she said. She wanted a baby boy, she said, and could we name him Jeffrey, after her father?

"Sure. I said. How about Jeffrey Boyd?"

"Okay. Jeffrey Boyd," she said. "That has a nice sound to it."

That wasn't the first time we had talked about having a baby. It had been a joint dream. I never considered not having another child. We talked of a boy and a girl and a nice house with a backyard for the children, trips to the zoo, playing catch with my son, as my father and I did, buying cute lavender dresses for our daughter.

Stephanie often spoke of her dreams—dancing, having a family, raising a son. Having dreams made a lasting impression on me somewhere down deep, but it didn't surface until years later. She also taught me, by example, to be generous with friends, to care more about them than I had; to think positively about the future in dark times—she often said that what was best would happen; and even a little about living in the moment, not always sacrificing for some goal. During our marriage I focused on her weaknesses and faults, and never appreciated these positive traits, and others, and how they contributed to a better life for me.

More than a year of almost daily, unprotected sex didn't get Stephanie pregnant. Her gynecologist told her she had severe endometriosis and a slightly tipped uterus. That most likely was the problem. She had a D & C to relieve the endometriosis. We hoped that would help.

I walked in the door one evening, work in my briefcase. Stephanie was playing on the floor with Lisa. Lisa's blond hair fell just above her shoulders, neatly brushed. Stephanie had dressed her in her Oshkosh short jeans and a shirt with pink giraffes. Lisa's bright blue eyes shined. She was laughing.

Stephanie got up and gave me a hug and a kiss. "Dinner'll be ready in ten minutes," she said.

"Could you hold it for a few more minutes so I can have a cocktail first?" I asked.

"I guess so," she said.

As usual, the house was clutter-free. When I changed clothes, I noticed my clothes had been washed, folded, and placed in the dresser. I went back in the kitchen and patted Stephanie on the butt. The kitchen was clean and neat. The table in the dining area was set. I poured a Scotch and waited at the table for dinner with Lisa chattering on my lap.

When I had picked up Lisa from her mother's the night before, she wore a stained onesie; her hair was matted against her head and her face bore food smears from who knows when. Stephanie had bathed her and washed her hair before we put her to bed in pajamas we kept for her. We had clothes for her at our house. With Stephanie's urging, I had talked

Christie into letting us have Lisa three days a week. Stephanie took care of her most of the time. When she had to work, she took Lisa to work at the candy shop or sometimes to daycare. I felt grateful to Stephanie for taking care of Lisa and playing with her, but I never expressed my gratitude. I still thought childcare was the wife's job, even though Stephanie worked outside the home, and Lisa wasn't her child.

A few weeks later, I came in from the office at ten. After looking in on Lisa asleep in the spare room, I undressed in our bedroom. Stephanie was in bed watching television. "This is three nights in a row you've been home late," she said. What's going on?"

"Just too much work," I said.

"You don't smell like work," she said, "unless you were making Scotch."

"We worked until eight, and then Bill asked me to go to the Jonathan Club for dinner. We had a few cocktails. I couldn't tell him no."

"But you can tell me three nights in a row you can't come home for dinner," she said.

Anger rose in my gut. "I'm trying to make partner," I said. "You think I wanna work this much? I'm doing it for us." I lay down in bed and turned away. "Turn the TV off. I can't sleep with it on, and I have to go in early."

We planned to drive up the coast to Washington in July 1971. Stephanie said she was looking forward to getting away. I needed a break too. In April I had told Bill the dates of our vacation. He didn't say anything. At the end of June, after a conference in his office, I reminded him.

"Vacation. You never told me about that," he said with a frown.

"Yeah, I did, Bill, almost three months ago." My stomach tensed. I struggled to remain calm.

"Oh...well, I don't remember," he said. "When did you say?"

"July 14th to July 28th."

"I can't let you go. I've got a lot going on. I might need you."

"Okay," I said and turned to leave. I didn't want to be around him.

"I'm not getting a vacation this year," he almost yelled, as I walked down the hall.

Stephanie will be livid, I thought, and I really need a vacation. I've been working a lot of nights and Saturdays for months.

"What? You're kidding me," said Stephanie, when I told her that night. "That asshole! He won't let you take a vacation just because he might need you. That's outrageous. You should quit that job."

"I know it is, Stephanie, but I can't quit now. I'm going to be a partner in a year and a half," I said.

"What good will that do if you still have to work as hard as you've been working," she said. "We hardly ever have any time together."

The ambition to be a partner was mine. I never discussed with Stephanie whether she thought it was worth it, or what alternatives were available. I assumed, without thinking about it, that the decision was solely mine. I didn't consider how the drive to partnership might affect her life.

That Sunday, as I walked down the stairs to the driveway to get the *L.A. Times*, I sighed--finally, a relaxing day. The morning sun, trying to pierce through the low clouds, cast a pale yellow on the eucalyptus trees. The eucalyptus scent reminded me of the oil my mother rubbed on my chest when I had a chest cold. *I'll have a cup of coffee and read the paper, and then we can go to the beach*, I thought. I picked up the paper and slipped off the string. I glanced at *Peanuts* before walking up the stairs. I love my Sunday mornings, I thought.

Stephanie was pouring my coffee. Lisa was sitting in her high chair eating cereal. I said good morning and kissed them both. I grabbed my coffee and sat at the kitchen table.

Stephanie sat down across from me. I pulled out the sports section. As I read about the Dodgers game, she grabbed the paper and pulled it down.

"Are you just going to stick your face in that paper and ignore me? I'm your wife. I am a living being, you know. I'm not just a piece of furniture."

"I know Stephanie. I'm just trying to relax and read the Sunday paper. We'll have all day together. I need time to myself too."

"I take care of your daughter. I keep your home clean and nice. But I need your companionship. We've hardly seen each other all week. I want to be with you, talk to you. I don't want to look at the back of a newspaper."

I slammed the Sports section down on the table. It slid to the floor. "All right. Fine. What do you want to talk about?" I asked.

She was already getting up. "Never mind. Read your fucking newspaper," she yelled. She stormed out to the living room. I sat there for a few minutes. I was feeling hemmed in, controlled. I did what my supervising partner and my clients told me to at work. I did what my wife told me to at home, I thought. This is no life. *But Stephanie is really pissed. I'd better do something to mollify her.*

I went into the living room and said, "I thought maybe we could go to the beach today and then go into West L.A. for dinner at that Italian restaurant we liked."

"That would be nice. I'm sorry I yelled at you. I just need you to be with me." She stood up and hugged me. We kissed. Stephanie lifted Lisa out of her high chair and put her on the floor in front of her dollhouse. We walked to the bedroom and started changing into our beach clothes. I kissed her as she was putting on her bikini top. "Wait," I said, grabbing it and throwing it on the floor. I ran over and closed the door. I kissed her breasts and pulled down her bottoms. We made love. Afterward, we lay side by side. The sun pierced the marine layer and lit up the bedroom.

"Now, we've got the day going in the right direction," she said. "Let's go to the beach."

Lisa banged on the door. Excellent timing. I got up and let her in.

I was happy we had made up. But we did nothing to resolve the issue. What could we have done about my long hours, my drinking with Bill and Bob after work instead of coming home, and Stephanie's feeling of abandonment? We chose to ignore these issues and soak up sunshine.

In October Stephanie told me she was two weeks late for her period. A week later, she said, "I don't feel well. I'm nauseous, and my breasts are tender. I might be pregnant, Boyd."

"Oh, wow," I said. "Wouldn't that be fabulous?" We hugged.

I was waiting in the reception room when Stephanie and Dr. Natale came out, smiling. "I'm pregnant," Stephanie said.

"Congratulations," said Dr. Natale, shaking my hand. The baby was due in June 1972.

Stephanie was increasingly unhappy working at the candy store. She was getting in arguments with her boss almost daily. When she came home crying one day, I told her since she was pregnant she could quit and stay at home. "You might consider starting college in the spring semester," I said. "The baby isn't due until June. You could get in a semester."

"No, I'm not interested in school right now. I just want to be a good wife and mother," she said.

We decided we should buy a house before the baby was born, but we had no money for a down payment. My mother's house had no mortgage. We visited her one Sunday and told her Stephanie was pregnant. She congratulated us. I told her we wanted to buy a house before we had the baby and asked if we could take out a mortgage on her house for the down payment. We would make the payments.

"Well, I don't know why not," she said. In February we moved into a house Stephanie picked out in the tree section of Manhattan Beach. It was beige with olive green trim, about two thousand square feet, three bedrooms, two bathrooms and a decent sized yard, big enough for a pool.

One evening about two weeks before Stephanie's due date, the phone rang. It was Dan, Christie's ex-boyfriend. He told me he was concerned about Lisa because Christie had boarded up the windows in her house and had not come out for two days. He didn't think they had any food. Lisa had just turned four.

I drove the forty-five minutes to Christie's house, apprehensive about what I would find. Plywood covered the windows. It looked abandoned. I walked up the wooden stairs to the front door. I knocked and waited, but nobody came. I turned the knob, and the door opened. I went in and looked across the darkened room. Christie sat on the floor staring blankly into the corner. Strewn about the living room were empty juice cans, wadded-up paper, Hare Krishna literature, burnt incense, clothes, books, old banana peels, apple cores and toys.

"Christie, what's wrong?" I asked. She kept staring at the corner. I heard whimpering and rushed into Lisa's room. She lay on her bed, face down, crying.

"Lisa," I said. She looked up.

"Daddy, I'm hungry," she cried. "There's no food here." Her hair was matted, her clothes filthy.

"Don't worry, honey. I'll take you to eat," I said. "Then we'll go to my house. Is there anything you want to take with you?"

"No, I don't want anything from here," she said. I picked her up and carried her. Christie still stared at the wall. We went to the nearest McDonalds drive-through and ate in the car. A few minutes later, Lisa finished the last bite of a quarter-pounder and fries and gulped down a Coke.

"That was good, Daddy," she said.

I walked into the house carrying Lisa. Stephanie looked at her, shook her head and hugged her. "Poor thing. I'll get her cleaned up."

Stephanie came out of the bathroom, leaving Lisa to play in the tub. I told her what I had found at Christie's house.

"You have to petition for custody," she said. We can't leave her with that woman. Lisa needs a real mother."

Christie didn't contest my custody petition.

Chapter Thirteen

On June 19, 1972 Stephanie called me at the office about ten in the morning. She said she had lost her mucus plug and felt mild contractions. "I can't tell if they're real," she said.

"I'll be there in a half hour," I said.

Adrenalin jolted my body as if I'd taken speed. I grabbed my coat and headed out. The elevator door was open. After practically diving in, I yelled to the receptionist that Stephanie was in labor.

We drove to Dr. Natale's office, my nerves clinging to my skin. Stephanie chattered away. Dr. Natale said she was in early labor, but because she had high blood pressure he wanted her in the hospital. We drove the few blocks to Queen of Angels Hospital. Pulling into the parking lot, I spotted a restaurant and bar next door.

"Do you see what I see," I said, pointing.

"Yeah," she said.

"How about a martini before we check in?"

She looked at me, eyes shining, and broke into a smile. "You're serious, aren't you?

"Yeah," I said. "You're not in pain, why not? Dr. Natale said you could have clear liquids."

Well, sure, why not?" She said.

We drank martinis and checked into the hospital around six. Twenty-four hours later nothing had changed—still early labor. At two in the morning her water broke. A nurse came in, cleaned her up and remade the bed. "Still only five centimeters dilated," said the nurse, after examining her.

"I can't believe I'm only half way there," Stephanie said. She grabbed her belly as the next contraction engulfed her.

Fifteen minutes later she said, "I have the urge to push. Get the nurse in here."

"Are you sure?" I said, touching her shoulder.

"Don't touch me," she yelled. "Get the nurse." I ran out the door. The nurse saw me and hurried in.

Dr. Natale appeared in the doorway at about three a.m. in green scrubs, the mask dangling from his neck. He bent over at the end of the bed, examined Stephanie and said she was fully dilated. He pulled the bed toward the door with help from a nurse, and told me to put on my scrubs and meet them in the delivery room. The nurse handed me a pile of clothes, and told me to put them on over my clothes. They wheeled Stephanie down the hall. I slipped the robe on. My hands shook as I tied the strings, then slapped on my hat, tugged on the booties, and finally, the mask. I looked down the hall. A nurse peeked out of the delivery room door and summoned me with her hand. I hurried in. They were strapping Stephanie onto the table. Her feet were in the stirrups.

After a lot of pushing, grunting, monitoring, and nurses scurrying around, Dr. Natale told us that the baby's heartbeat had dropped, and he would have to pull it out with forceps. He injected a foot-long needle in Stephanie's back—a saddle block. A nurse handed him something that looked like giant salad tongs. Another nurse painted Stephanie from navel to thighs with orange disinfectant. The mirror above and behind Dr. Natale gave me a perfect view of where the baby would emerge through the orange. Dr. Natale pushed the forceps in and braced his feet apart on the floor, like an Olympic weightlifter preparing. He began to pull. Out came the head—wet and bloody—then the shoulders and the rest followed. He held the baby up. The tiny penis protruded above an oversized scrotum.

"Three fifty-six a.m.," said a nurse, who notated a chart.

It was five in the morning when I drove out of the hospital parking lot. I had been up two nights in a row, but I felt as if I could climb a mountain or swim the English Channel, should the need arise. I wanted to proclaim to all that I saw my son being born, but there was nobody around to tell.

In a few weeks we took Jeffrey to meet my mother in the house where I had spent my childhood. She looked pale, and there was sadness in her eyes. Her shoulders were more hunched than usual. Although she was five foot six, she looked shorter. At seventy, she still didn't have much gray in her brown hair, but it had lost its auburn luster. I asked her how she was.

"Lonely," she said. "It's been nine years since Orville died, and I still miss him. And I'm sad because my eyesight is so bad I don't know if I'll be able to keep crocheting much longer. But I'm all right."

When my mother left to pour us fresh coffee, Stephanie leaned forward in her chair. "You should tell your mother to sell her house and move in with us. Jeff'll be in our room for a few months, and he and Lisa can share a room for a couple years before we need a bigger house."

"Are you sure?" I asked.

"Yeah. She'll be no trouble. She's such a sweet lady."

I was delighted with Stephanie's suggestion. Mom returned with the coffee. "We'd like you to come and live with us, Mom, if you want to," I said. Her face lit up. She asked if we were sure. We both said yes. She said she would think about it.

A few days later she called and said she would love to live with us. She asked me to make the arrangements to sell her house.

I soon developed misgivings about Stephanie and my mother living together. I had heard it was always difficult combining two adult generations in the same household, and the relationship between daughter-in-law and mother-in-law is often delicate. I also had a vague feeling that my mother might not be easy to get along with, though I couldn't think of anything specific. Maybe it was just intuition, but I didn't believe in intuition back then. Stephanie seemed so positive it would work that I went along. That was the easiest thing to do. Before we put my mother's house on the market I asked Stephanie one last time, "Are you sure you want my mother living with us?"

"I'm sure," she said. "It'll be fine."

A few months later, my mother's house sold. Stephanie took charge of the garage sale. I sat there feeling melancholy as things I had grown up with were carted away by strangers. My mother didn't seem to care. Stephanie set aside china and silverware, my baby book, old pictures, knick-knacks, and my mother's crocheted bedspreads, doilies, and tablecloths. An elderly lady ran her hand over the needlepoint cushions my mother had made by hand for the dining room chairs. She had worked on those for two years when I was a child. We can't sell those, I thought. I rushed over and told the lady they were not for sale.

"Oh, Boyd, that's silly. Those old things..." said my mother. She was ready to move on. She was thirty-two when she and my dad married in 1934, old for a woman to marry then. She had talked about her marriage as if it were a miracle that was bestowed on her. Then, another miracle: I was born. She was sure that there would be no others, but these two enabled her to slough off life's travails. She always moved on, her eyes always on her purpose in life, taking care of my father and me. Alone now, she had no purpose.

"You worked forever on those," I said. "They're beautiful. I can't let them go." I found an old screwdriver and removed the cushions.

When we got home, I helped my mother carry stuff to her room. She smiled at the flowers Stephanie had left for her. "Stephanie is so nice," she said. "She's queenly, the way she carries herself."

She reached into her purse. "Here," she said, handing me a check. "This is from the house sale. You take it."

"Are you sure, Mom?"

"Yeah," she said. "I don't need it. Your father's pension and Social Security are more than enough. I'm sure you and your family can use it."

"Thank you, Mom." I hugged her. "We can use it. I'll always provide you with a place to live."

We paid off debts and built a swimming pool in the backyard. Stephanie redecorated our bedroom with new window coverings, matching bedspread, and an upholstered bench at the foot of the bed, all in large blue, purple and yellow flowers. Then she bought a new couch for the family room and a new washer and dryer. In a few months the money was gone, and we were back in debt.

I feel like listening to music. I haven't been out all day, and the rain has stopped. Revisiting the traumatic years with Stephanie makes me melancholy, especially since I know what's coming. I walk ten blocks to the Clear Conscience Café. A young woman is playing the keyboard and singing folk music. She has a pleasant enough voice, so I go to the counter, order a cup of green tea and sit down. I listen for an hour, then go back home and write. I notice as I write that I see things more clearly than I did when I was just thinking. Memories slow down.

With my mother's money, we could have paid off our debts and had a savings account. This was another chance to live my life differently, to find work in line with my values. I could have gone into teaching or waited for a position to open up in legal aid or the ACLU or any number of organizations that hired lawyers to help those who needed it. With my B.A. and J.D. and six years experience as a lawyer, the opportunities were legion. Instead, I chose to spend the money on a swimming pool we would rarely use, and stuff that didn't improve our lives. Sure, there was pressure from Stephanie. I had taught her to live extravagantly. But rather than trying to work with her to establish a budget, I kept trying to live someone else's life. I squandered my opportunities before I'd even considered them.

I blamed Stephanie for her extravagant spending, but I was far from frugal. I wanted the swimming pool. I agreed to buy a house that stretched our ability to make the payments. I wanted nice furniture too. I bought another Porsche, an expensive camera, the best in alcohol and dinners at expensive restaurants. Stephanie may have spent more, but it was a joint extravagance that squandered my opportunities. And unconsciously I was still trying to impress Stephanie with an opulent lifestyle.

When I moved to Boston I lived in a single room for a year and a half; now I live in a small apartment. I don't own a car or have cable TV or an iPod. My furniture comes from Target or the Salvation Army, and my clothes are from Target or are hand-me-downs—more accurately, hand-me-ups—from David, my son-in-law. My dearest possessions are books and photographs of my loved ones. I don't miss a big house, expensive furniture or a fancy car—not one bit. I wouldn't have missed them forty years ago either. Why didn't I realize that back then? Perhaps because I knew of nothing else but trying to achieve, and what achievement in the law brought was status and money. Now, I have writing. It dominates my life. Though it hasn't brought me money or status, I don't care.

One night, when Jeff was an infant, I came home from work at about eight o'clock. The children were in bed, as usual. I wished that at least Lisa was up, so I asked Stephanie to keep her up at least until eight so I could see her and read her a story. "If I do that," she said, "we have no time together. By the time we have dinner it's time for us to go to bed. I'm stuck all day here with the children. I don't get to talk to another adult. Your mother stays in her room. She won't talk to me. We have nothing in common anyway."

"I can't help it that I have to work long hours, Stephanie. It's not that I want to. I'm doing it for us," I said.

"Yeah, yeah," she said. "You could spend more time with us on weekends, if that's what you wanted, but instead you read the paper or go to the office."

Just then Jeff, who had been asleep in his room, started to cry. I went in and picked him up. I paced the hall with him but he didn't stop. Stephanie came out of the bedroom.

"Give him to me," she said holding out her arms. I handed him over. She paced, and I went to bed. He stopped crying.

Stephanie got in bed and turned toward the wall. "Maybe you need a break," I said. "Let's go to New York City for a few days."

"That sounds like fun, Boyd."

"Mrs. Backer can take care of Jeff, and Lisa can stay with my mother," I said.

The night before we left for New York, I got home at nine. It had been a struggle to get things done so I could take the weekend and two extra days off work. I wolfed down a dinner Stephanie had heated.

"Everything is packed," she said. "You might check your suitcase and see if I got everything you want. I packed for Jeff and gave your mother instructions for Lisa. All we have to do in the morning is get Jeff up. I'll feed him while you pack the car."

I was grateful to Stephanie for preparing for the trip. It occurred to me that she had taken charge of my life. She made all social engagements, arranged what we would do during weekends when I didn't work and generally organized our lives. I took no part in our day-to-day existence, except to do what she had set up. I was like a political candidate who goes from event to event arranged by staff, goes to bed when he's told it's time, gets up when he's told he must and gives speeches written by someone else. At the office my days were dictated by partners of the firm and clients, the details by my secretary. I sometimes felt that I wasn't living most of the time, any more than a puppet lives.

After the long flight and cab ride, we arrived at our hotel in Manhattan at about nine. As I unpacked, Stephanie called Mrs. Backer. "I miss him already," she told Mrs. Backer. After she hung up, she said, "He's fine, Mrs. Backer said. He's asleep now, so I couldn't say anything to him."

"Of course, he's fine," I said. I was excited. "The next three days in the Big Apple!"

"Yeah," said Stephanie.

The next day we did tourist things—strolled along the paths in Central Park and down Broadway, rode the elevator that makes your belly sink to the top of the Empire State Building, lunched at a deli and gazed wide-eyed at paintings for a couple of hours in the Metropolitan Museum of Art. We planned to go to dinner and a show at the Waldorf Astoria. Before dinner we went back to our hotel to rest. Stephanie called Mrs. Backer for the third time that day.

She hung up and started to cry. "What's the matter?" I asked.

"Today was nice," she said, "but I miss my baby so much. I wanna go home."

"What!" I yelled. "We've only been here one day, and this trip cost a fortune. We have reservations for the boat trip to the

Statue of Liberty and a Broadway show tomorrow. We can't go home. Jesus Christ, Stephanie."

"I don't care. I'm miserable. I want to go home," she cried.

"No, absolutely not," I said. "This trip was for you in the first place. You said you needed a break."

"I did not. You said that. It was your idea," she said

"You didn't exactly protest," I said. "Anyway, we're not going home. It's time to get ready for dinner." I wanted to slap her, but of course never would have. She sobbed, then got up, undressed, and ran a bath.

Maybe if she has a drink she'll feel better, I thought. I ordered two tequila sunrises from room service, while she bathed. The drinks arrived as she was putting on her makeup.

"Here's a drink for you," I said. "I hope it makes you feel better."

"Thanks," she said.

We were silent during the taxi ride. I thought about how Stephanie was ruining our good time. She always did that, I thought. The last time we had expensive tickets to a concert at the Hollywood Bowl she claimed to be sick just before we were ready to leave, and we couldn't go.

We sat down at our table at the Waldorf Astoria for dinner and a show featuring Tony Bennett. The waiter came over. "Are you ready to order?" he said.

"No, not yet," said Stephanie. "I'll have another vodka and tonic."

"Yes, Madam. Another for you, sir?"

"Sure," I said.

After her third, she ordered a fourth and started to slur her words. Her eyes were drooping. She staggered getting up to go to the bathroom, so I helped her. We ordered dinner. It came, and I ate. Stephanie ordered her fifth drink. She ate practically nothing. When the waiter took away the plates, she put her head down on the table.

"Let's go, Stephanie," I said, putting down enough cash to pay the bill.

I helped her up. She passed out in the cab. One way or another she's determined to ruin this trip, I thought.

I woke her and nearly carried her to our room. I undressed her and helped her to bed. "Make love to me," she pleaded. I did, but I didn't see her plea as one for compassion. I didn't bother to try to understand her feelings.

We plowed through the next day. Stephanie didn't complain about her hangover, as we lounged on a bench in Central Park, eating hot dogs from a vendor. We didn't speak about the issue of going home, but it was present, like an invisible weight. Stephanie said she was tired and asked to go back to the hotel, then undressed and went to bed. So did I, snuggling up against her. I reached around and felt her breast. "Don't," she said.

I moved our flight up a day, and we left. I thought: I'll start doing things on my own, maybe take a photography class. She can just stay home with the kids.

Chapter Fourteen

At the end of October 2008 I arrive at Lisa's for another visit. She had told me when I called from the airport that she would be out doing errands. I use my key and carry my luggage upstairs to the guest room. I sit down at the desk and set up my computer. I'm going to write on what insights I have about the trip to New York.

Of all the insensitive things I did during my marriage to Stephanie, my conduct in New York may have been the most insensitive. The trip was my idea, not hers. Why couldn't I have understood that, as a new mother and hormonal from nursing, she might be miserable separated from her baby for the first time? Was my good time in New York City more important to me than my wife's well-being? Maybe that was the problem. I couldn't accept her feelings as legitimate.

I couldn't accept anybody's feelings as legitimate. I didn't think they should play a part in decision-making. Decisions should be based on logic and reason only. Only women made decisions based on feelings and something even more nebulous, intuition. I scoffed at both. That made me critical of many of Stephanie's decisions. I resented Stephanie without considering or discussing her feelings. Now, I understand that feelings are legitimate and important factors in making decisions, often more important than reason. Often reasons are recited for decisions that are based on feelings and are an after-the-fact rationalization. I couldn't ignore my wife's feelings and expect her not to care.

More than thirty years later I took Kate to Ireland. We planned two weeks. After we had been in Dublin two days, she asked to go home for personal reasons. She made it clear she felt strongly and wouldn't enjoy the trip if we continued. I immediately said, "Okay." I never considered saying no or even trying to talk her out of it. I was disappointed, but felt no resentment. I accepted her feelings as legitimate. I am proud of that evolution. I hadn't written about my marriages yet, but I had written about other aspects of my life. Writing about my feelings legitimized them in my mind and made me more aware of them in myself and others.

I was elected a partner of the Nossaman Firm in January 1973, but I continued to work long hours and often went drinking with Bill or Bob after work.

In August Stephanie came by my office after she had been to see Dr. Natale. She closed the door. She was smiling. "I'm pregnant. The baby's due in March."

"That's great news," I said, hugging her. "A little sooner than we wanted, but that's okay. Maybe we can have our girl, and our family will be complete."

"Yeah," she said.

One night a few months later, when I climbed into bed, Stephanie lay back staring at the ceiling. "Your mother has not come out of her room all week. I go in with her meals, ask her if she wants to eat at the table, and she says she'd rather eat in her room. I try to talk to her, but she won't talk. I don't know what's wrong. I've tried to do everything I can to be nice to her. She just doesn't respond."

"I'll talk to her," I said.

"It's depressing to have someone like that around," said Stephanie.

I went to my mother's room and asked her if something was wrong. "No, not really," she said.

"Stephanie told me you haven't been out of your room much lately," I said.

"I don't want to disturb her or get in her way. She has a lot to do with this big house and the kids, and all, and now she's pregnant again. And, Boyd, I know she really doesn't want me here."

"That's not true," I said. "She's always told me she's happy you're with us."

"Well, she doesn't act happy," she said. "There is one thing. She used my towel the other day, and I can't have somebody using my towel. I don't understand why she would do that."

"I don't either, Mom. I'll ask her about it."

I went to the kitchen and said to Stephanie, "My mother said you used her towel, and she doesn't want you to. Would you...."

"That's a lie. She's just trying to turn you against me. I never used her towel. Why would I? I use our bathroom. I never go in the other bathroom, except to clean and take the towels down to do laundry. That's ridiculous."

"Okay, well, I guess she was mistaken."

After dinner a couple of weeks later, Stephanie said, "Come into the living room. We have to talk about your mother." My stomach clenched. Stephanie sat in the rocker. She lit a cigarette and looked away for a moment. I sat on the couch. "She won't talk to me," said Stephanie. "She just stays in her room. She can't be happy here."

"I don't know what to do," I said. "I'll talk to her again."

"Boyd, she can't live here anymore. I want her out of here."

"We can't do that Stephanie. We took all the money from her house, and I promised her she could live with us. You approved. In fact, it was your idea. We can't just kick her out now."

"She has to go, Boyd. I can't stand her aloofness, her refusal to communicate."

"Why not? She doesn't bother you. If she wants to stay in her room the whole time, what's it to you?"

"Because it's just too depressing around here. It's not good for the children. Besides, when the new baby comes, there's no room for her. That has to be the new baby's room."

"The new baby'll be in our room for a few months," I said. "Then the crib can go in the kids' room. After a while, we'll get a bigger house. I'll be making more money by then."

"Boyd, I'm telling you. She has to go. That's all there is to it. It's either her or me."

"Oh for god's sake. How can I kick her out?"

"That's your problem," said Stephanie. "Just tell her she has to go. You can rent her an apartment. She'll be happier there anyway."

After I poured a drink and lit a cigarette, I sat down in my chair in our family room, sick to my stomach, thinking about kicking my mother out. How could I do it after taking the money from her house? I felt like a fraud. My strongest loyalty should lie with my wife, I thought, but I didn't feel loyal. I just didn't want to lose my family over my mother. A man can't do that.

At that moment I hated Stephanie. I should call her bluff and refuse to kick my mother out, I thought. I doubt Stephanie would leave me, with a child and another on the way. But it would be too unpleasant. I didn't think I had a choice. As usual, Stephanie would get what she wanted, and I would resent her for it.

On Saturday morning I was ready to tell my mother. It had

to be then. Jeff was down for his morning nap. Stephanie and Lisa were out shopping. I sat in my chair in the family room, rehearsing what I was going to say. I was sweating. This is the hardest thing I've ever had to do, I thought. *Waiting won't make it easier.* I got up and walked slowly to the door of my mother's room. I could hear the TV through the closed door. I knocked. She opened the door. "Oh, it's you," she said.

"Hi, Mom," I said. "I need to talk to you."

"Okay, can we go out to the living room? There's no place for you to sit in here," she said.

"Sure," I said, and we walked to the living room. She sat on the rocker, and I sat on the couch across from her. We looked straight at each other for a moment. She wore a quizzical expression. *She has not anticipated what is coming,* I thought. *Oh boy. Here goes.*

"Mom, I'm afraid I have to ask you to move out. I don't want it, but Stephanie insists." Her jaw dropped; her brow furrowed; her eyes scrunched. She looked as if I had just slugged her in the face. "She says it's either you or her. Don't worry. We'll rent an apartment for you here in Manhattan Beach. I'll pay the rent, always. I'll see to it that you always have a place to live." She cried, then sobbed. I went over and put my arms around her. "I'm so sorry, Mommy. I don't know what else I can do."

After a while she stopped crying. "Why? What have I done? I've tried my best to not interfere."

"I don't know," I said. "She says she can't stand you sulking in your room all the time.

"I'm not sulking. I'm just trying not to interfere in her activities. She has a lot to do. I was trying not to be in the way."

"I know. I know. But I don't know what else we can do. I don't think anything will change her mind."

"Is there anything I can do?" she asked.

"Not that I can think of," I said. "You could talk to Stephanie."

"No, I won't do that," she said.

My mother and Stephanie never spoke after that. The next Saturday we found a furnished apartment that Mom liked. I told her I would buy her kitchen stuff and linens and the things she needed, but she insisted on doing it herself. The apartment was within walking distance of the senior citizens' center that she had been active in since she first moved to Manhattan Beach. I drove her to the apartment with her clothes and things and helped her put them away. Neither of us spoke. When the last pair of pants was hung, I hugged her.

"I'm so sorry, Mommy," I said.

"Don't worry, son," she said. "I'll be fine." Her face bore no expression. I could tell she was just toughing it out. So was I, until I got back to the privacy of my car. I sat in the driver's seat and sobbed. I wasn't crying just for my mother; I knew my marriage was in trouble. If Stephanie could do this, what would be next? This was the first time I had cried for as long as I could remember. Stephanie and I didn't talk further about my mother.

I think Stephanie's insistence that my mother move out was an appalling betrayal, but I could have handled it better. Stephanie meant well when she asked my mother to live with us. Stephanie liked to help people, and she couldn't have foreseen how difficult it would be to have my mother living with us. Maybe I should have. I was older with more life experience. I knew my mother was judgmental, could play the martyr role, and although she wouldn't say anything to criticize Stephanie, she had a tendency to sulk in silence to let you know she was displeased. At best, the mother-in-law and daughter-in-law relationship is tricky. And I was home so little I couldn't know how my mother acted when just she and Stephanie and the kids were home.

When Stephanie suggested that my mother live with us, I anticipated it might be difficult, but I failed to express that to Stephanie. I should have trusted my intuition. But I couldn't do that then. And I should have made it clear to Stephanie that it was a no-going-back decision.

I didn't consider or discuss Stephanie's feelings. I thought she had made a commitment and she should stick to it, no matter what. I should have insisted that Stephanie and I discuss how her problems with my mother might be resolved short of kicking her out. I should have discussed these issues with my mother. The three of us should have sat down and discussed the issues at hand. What my mother was doing in trying to stay out of Stephanie's way apparently was having an unintended affect on Stephanie. There should have been a way to reach a middle ground between Mom shutting herself up in her room and being in the way. Stephanie may have anticipated my mother would be another adult to talk to during the day when she had only small children to talk to. It didn't work out that way. My mother thought talking to her would be interfering. I don't know if we could have resolved anything, but I didn't even try. I simply acquiesced and harbored more resentment.

Our baby girl was born March 14, 1974, and we named her Jennifer after Stephanie's friend from the candy shop. John and Jennifer Weil, who had married and had their own baby, had become our best friends. Our Jennifer lived in a bassinet in our room. My mother's old room remained empty. I knew it would.

The next day at Lisa's, I sit on my usual kitchen counter chair. Lisa and I have a cocktail and David puts the children to bed. In a few minutes Lisa gets up and begins dinner preparation. A little later David comes in. I hadn't seen him the night before. He got home from a business trip late.

"How've you been?" I ask.

"It's been kind of a tough month," he said, "especially for Lisa. I've been gone a lot on business, so she's had to take care of the kids alone. And they've been sick a lot. That always makes it harder."

"Yeah, she has a hard job," I said.

"Just one cold and ear infection after another, and then David and I catch it," says Lisa. "Seems like I haven't been anywhere but the doctor's office and grocery store for a month."

In a few minutes, Lisa and David talk, and my thoughts go back to Stephanie. Until I observed Lisa and talked to her about being a stay at home mom—a SAHM, as Lisa calls herself—I never appreciated what Stephanie did. She had two kids and my mother, and, like Lisa, a big house and complicated finances. David knows what Lisa does and expresses his appreciation. I didn't. Lisa is forty. Stephanie had two kids to care for at twenty-two, three at twenty-four. I was not aware of how difficult it was.

I remember one time I heard a commotion from the bathroom. Jeff stood and Jennifer, who couldn't walk yet, was on all fours. They were pounding on the downstairs bathroom door. Lisa stood behind them yelling, "Stop it, you guys." Stephanie came out without pants. "I can't even go to the bathroom," she cried.

I feasted on Stephanie's beauty, but gave her little back except material things and sex. I did support her financially and for a while, without complaint, gave her everything she asked for. But, as with Christie, I failed to appreciate her, or show appreciation. My third wife also complained that I didn't express appreciation for the work she did. Needy women or ungrateful husband? It's not as clear as I once thought.

As Ryan tears through the house pushing his locomotive on the tile floor and generally making a racket, David and Emily play with her little ponies on the floor, and Lisa makes salad. I am once again reminded that I didn't want to be involved in my household. I just wanted Stephanie to take care of it—children, house cleaning, laundry, grocery shopping, bill paying, taking and picking up my clothes from the dry cleaner—all of it. So, I paid no attention to it. My mother was part of the household. I avoided involvement in what she was doing and how she was integrating, even though I had my doubts about how it would work out.

I thought I had found something I was good at, practicing law, so I focused totally on it. I felt I had to or it would overwhelm me. I feared failure if I didn't give it my all. I didn't apply the same principle to marriage and family. I wanted marriage and family, but I didn't want to be bothered with it, wanted it to just run on its own. I shirked its responsibilities--and missed out on its joys.

Not long after I had become a partner, Bill and a partner in the corporate department, Dick, came into my office. "We just got a new matter in, Boyd, and I want you to handle it. You know I've got that S.P.I. trial coming up."

"Okay," I said. "What is it?"

"It's a contested tender offer for Frank Carp's company for thirty million dollars," Dick said. "We need to go in for a temporary restraining order to stop it. I've assigned Gary Rollins to help you with the corporate and securities law aspects of it. He should be in shortly. Frank is coming in this afternoon. We're looking for misleading statements in the offering memorandum as a basis for a restraining order to prevent them from continuing with the offer."

"All right, sounds good," I said. Wow, I thought, they trust me to be in charge of this big case for one of the firm's best clients.

Bill said, "You can use Fred for associate litigation help. This will be intense, Boyd. Good luck."

For the next three months, I worked almost every night— twice I worked all night— and every Saturday and all but one

Sunday. I was in court two or three days each week. Ultimately, we lost. The tender offer went through.

Two days after it was over I woke up with a headache. I took two aspirin and went to work. The headache got worse. I took four aspirin. As the day wore on the headache got so bad I couldn't concentrate on anything, and my vision was blurry. I rarely had headaches. I told Bill.

"Maybe it's a migraine from all the stress you've been under lately. You should go to the doctor," he said.

I called my doctor, and he said to come in right away. I took a taxi. After the examination, he said he thought it might be encephalitis, an inflammation of the lining of the brain. He gave me prescriptions for antibiotics and pain, and said I needed bed rest until the headaches subsided. I was scared. The fear of possible brain damage was worse than the pain. Painkillers relieved the headache. Stephanie took care of me, bringing me all my meals in bed for the first week. She wouldn't let me get out of bed, except to go to the bathroom. I slept most of the time. In two weeks I felt fine, and the doctor cleared me to go back to work. Some might dispute it, but apparently I did not suffer any brain damage. I don't remember, but I doubt if I thanked Stephanie for her care, or for undertaking the added burden while she was pregnant.

Despite my long hours of stressful work I have always enjoyed good health, but that case got me down. It has been thirty-seven years, and I didn't remember how scared I was until I wrote about it. Writing brings these memories back and sometimes as intensely as they were felt at the time. Writing brings perspective to my life—a chance to wonder, to figure out how I got where I am.

It's November in Cambridge—no snow yet, but it's getting colder—a fleece jacket will no longer suffice. I sit at a table at India Castle, waiting for Tandoori Chicken, writing. I think about those early days with Jennifer. Thankfully, she was an easy baby to care for, no colic, and she slept through the night after a few weeks. But the third child added more burden on Stephanie and another dimension to the complexities of family life.

I came home from work one evening when Jennifer was a few months old. The kids, as usual, were asleep. "I need to talk to you about something," said Stephanie.

"Stephanie, how many times have I told you? Don't confront me with problems when I first come home from work. All I want to do is fall into my recliner and have a drink. I'm stressed out and exhausted."

"Fine. But by the time you have a drink or two and finish dinner, it will be too late. You don't want to have any serious discussion just before bed either. On weekends, when you're home, the kids are around, and we don't find the time to talk. So we don't talk."

"Okay, what is it?" I sighed.

"Now that Jeff is walking, I'm worried about having that pool out there. He could get out without my knowing it. And in another year I'll have two toddlers to watch."

"Why didn't you think of that when you asked to have a pool?" I said. "You were already pregnant with Jeff. Did you think he would never walk?"

"Boyd, do you always have to criticize? You wanted the pool, too. Anyway, I want to buy a new house. We could get a four-bedroom house so the kids could each have their own room, and a yard for them to play in. This house has no yard. It's not good for them to be cooped up in the house all the time."

"This house had a yard until we put in the pool," I said.

"Will you at least look at houses with me, so we can see what's available?"

"I guess so, but I want to live by the beach. I miss the ocean."

"Those houses have no yards, and the beach is just a mile from here," she said. "We won't get a house farther from the beach than here, okay?"

"Yeah, yeah." I knew then we were going to buy a new house. I felt controlled and manipulated and helpless to do anything about it. Why? I didn't even bother to discuss the pros and cons or suggest alternatives to buying a new house, such as fencing off the pool. I was afraid to say no. I lived in fear of another divorce—or maybe I wanted a bigger house too. I don't know, but my resentment of Stephanie continued to accumulate like ice on an airplane's wings.

I loved the house Stephanie picked out. It was a beautiful Cape Cod, bigger than the old house, with large front and back yards, four bedrooms, three upstairs and the master bedroom downstairs, a huge kitchen and dining nook, a separate formal dining room, living room, and my favorite, a small, cedar-paneled den. The previous owners had an antique rustic, cherry wood dining table that Stephanie talked them into selling with the house.

The old house had increased a lot in value, so we used some of the proceeds to pay off credit card debt and buy a slightly used red Porsche for me. Stephanie had bought a new Ford station wagon. When we moved in, our only debt was for our cars and the mortgage, but we could barely qualify for the loan on the new house and would be hard pressed to make the payments.

Even after Robert Kennedy's death, although I was no longer active in politics, I kept up with the news. Stephanie didn't, and she expressed resentment about the time I spent reading newspapers and magazines. Her lack of interest in politics and current events, it seemed to me, reflected her lack of education. I didn't think about that during the sex-filled early years of our marriage, but after five years that difference between us surfaced in my mind and irritated me.

I was fascinated that Richard Nixon's conduct as President

was not nearly as conservative or anti-communist as his words. He established diplomatic relations with the People's Republic of China, which liberals had favored and conservatives had opposed for years. About the time we moved into our new house, after more than a year of media frenzy about Watergate, Nixon resigned the Presidency. News of Nixon had been at or near the center of our country's political life since I was a child—his vehement anti-communism, his dramatic rises and falls, his paranoia. I was glad to see him go. He diminished the Presidency and shattered the trust of the American people. I don't think American politics have ever been the same. His kind of drama, scandal, polarization and bitterness have plagued us ever since.

What little was left of the youth movement in politics and its vigorous advocacy of civil rights and pacifism died. We never saw it again until a watered-down version appeared thirty-five years later, during the Obama campaign, and petered out in less than a year. Nixon and Ford finally got us out of Viet Nam. "Peace with honor," they called it. What crap! At the time, I thought Viet Nam was so traumatic for the nation, we'd stay out of war for a while, and Jeff wouldn't have to go. Stephanie responded only to join me in expressing hope that Jeff would never have to go to war.

Politics was a sideline. My career consumed me. I pulled my red Porsche out of the office garage late one night. It was close to midnight when I got home. Stephanie, sitting up in bed, confronted me.

"Are you having an affair? I find it hard to believe you work as much as you claim."

"Hell, no!" I yelled. "My work pays for this fucking house and all the furniture you bought."

"I bought?" she yelled. "You wanted it too. Don't blame it on me."

I threw my suit coat and briefcase on the floor and headed out the door. "Where are you going?" she asked.

"To get a drink."

"Great! You won't come to bed with me. I never see you. The children never see you. I don't know why you ever wanted a family."

"Oh, fuck you," I said, slamming the door behind me. I felt just as I had when Christie made the same complaint. I was caught between two impossible choices: to make my boss mad or make my wife mad. Neither appreciated me for working hard. It didn't occur to me that because both Christie and Stephanie complained, maybe it was a problem I needed to address. Instead, I decided they were both selfish and needy. At the very least, I could have stopped going out drinking with Bill. Declining most of Bill's invitations would not have adversely affected my career.

After downing two Scotches, I went to bed. Stephanie was asleep. In the morning I grabbed a brown spotted banana from the burgundy bowl on the kitchen counter. Stephanie, sleepy-eyed, shuffled in. She avoided my eyes. "I'm sorry about last night," I said.

"Yeah, so am I," she said. "See ya tonight. Maybe we can do better."

I worked all day dictating documents. I got ahead of my secretary, who agreed to work late, so when Bill asked me if I wanted to go downstairs for a drink, I agreed. He downed three to my one, and I declined another, saying I had to go back to work. He ordered a fourth.

I walked back to the office overcome with dread. I can't work now, I thought. I'm too exhausted. I can't even remember what I have to do. I could get up at five and come in early tomorrow. Stephanie will bitch about that. It wakes her up.

I signed in with the guard and went up to my office. Looking at my to-do list, I could see I would be at the office late for the next few days and on Saturday. Maybe Sunday. I picked up my briefcase and headed out my office door. The phone rang. I went back to answer it. It was Stephanie. "Haven't you left yet?" she said.

"Obviously not, but I was just walking out the door."

"I'm glad I caught you," she said. "Stop by Pancho's and pick up dinner. I just didn't get a chance to go to the store today."

"Okay," I sighed. "What do you want?

"The usual," she said.

I walked in about nine o'clock. The house seemed cold. I handed Stephanie the food. Before I could sit down, she said, "The bank bounced a bunch of our checks. I can't figure out why. Would you see if you can figure it out? The checkbook is on the counter."

"It's just arithmetic, Stephanie. Can't you do that? I don't have time, and please, I have asked you before not to bring me these problems as soon as I walk in the door. I'm gonna have a drink. Leave me alone!" I yelled.

"Don't talk to me like that, Boyd," she said. "I demand to be treated with respect, even if you are in a bad mood."

"I'm not in a bad mood," I shouted. I poured myself a drink, turned around and stomped out to the den. I sat down and took a sip. As usual, the harsh, musky liquid burned all the way to my stomach. I walked up the stairs to Jeff's room and quietly opened the door. The nightlight illuminated his face, angelic as he slept. He was always asleep by the time I got home from work.

The tacos from Pancho's were still in the bag on the counter, where Stephanie had left them. I sat down in the breakfast nook and ate mine. I went to the bedroom and undressed. Stephanie was sitting up in bed, smoking and sipping a drink. A bottle of tequila sat on her nightstand. I got into bed and turned toward the wall.

A couple of weeks later on a Saturday night, we got a babysitter and went out to dinner in West L.A. We had a pleasant time, no arguing. As I drove back, after taking the babysitter home, I thought about not having had sex for two months. Since Jeff had been born two years before, we rarely had sex. I would make a move, and she would say no. She has no reason for rejecting me tonight. She doesn't seem tired. She's in a good mood. We've had a romantic dinner out. We'll see.

Stephanie went to bed while I locked the doors and closed the curtains. I quickly undressed. She was on her side faced away from me. Not a good sign. I moved up against her and massaged her neck and upper back. "How about a massage?" I asked.

"For you, that's just a prelude to sex, and I don't feel like having sex," she said.

"We haven't had sex in over two months. You're my wife. Why won't you have sex with me?"

"I don't know, Boyd. I just don't feel like it."

I continued to caress her, thinking I could get her in the mood.

"Leave me alone," she said, moving over farther.

"Fine," I said, and turned over and slid all the way to my side, my remaining confidence drained out of me. It left me empty. I couldn't understand: How could she have changed from wanting it every night the first three years we were together to not wanting it at all? Had she faked it before? I lay in bed feeling dried up, a wrinkled raisin of a man at thirty-four.

I was unhappy and down, as I drove to San Diego for a court hearing. It was more than just not getting any. I need time for myself, I thought. All I do is work and do things with Stephanie and the kids, whatever she has arranged. I need a hobby. I have been working on photography, but that often involves the kids. I need something just for myself. We went horseback riding last summer, and Stephanie didn't like it. I thought it was great fun. I would love to take a horse out by myself on a country trail.

When I got home I opened the Yellow Pages and found a horseback riding stable about a half-hour away. During dinner I told Stephanie I wanted to take lessons.

"Fine," she said. "I wish I could do something for myself like that."

"You said you didn't like horseback riding."

"Not horseback riding. Something else, just for me."

"You already get your hair done and a manicure every two weeks," I said.

"It's not the same," she said.

After my third Sunday of lessons, I came home feeling good. "I cantered really well today," I said to Stephanie.

"That's good," she said, spooning baby food into Jennifer's mouth. "You know, you told me a month ago you were going to fix the wheel on Jeff's wagon the next day, and you still haven't done it. That's his favorite toy. And you haven't played with him in I don't know how long. Don't you care about your children?"

"I have worked every Saturday for the last month, and you always have something you want to do on Sundays," I said. "I haven't had time."

"Yeah, you never have time for your children," she scowled.

I threw myself down in the recliner in the den. I realized that Stephanie had picked a fight every time I had come home from horseback riding. I thought about going out and confronting her. But what would be the point? I turned on the TV and watched part of a Dodgers game.

I have always thought it was outrageous of Stephanie to resent me for going horseback riding on Sundays. Kate and I sit in my living room. We talk about my memoir. I tell her about my horseback riding and Stephanie picking a fight when I got home. She says, "If I had been married to you under those circumstances, I would have been really pissed at you for working as much as you did, and then taking off on Sunday to go horseback riding, leaving me with the kids. Stephanie didn't have a time like that for herself, and she didn't have quality time with you."

"Really?" I say. "That surprises me."

"I would have handled it differently," she says, "but I would have been mad."

After Kate leaves, I think: She's a strong, independent woman who isn't overly needy. Yet, she would have been pissed off too. Maybe I should have given Stephanie the opportunity to do something for herself. I could have done something with the kids, and I should have spent more time with her and my whole family.

I hadn't learned. Love needs attention, and marriage takes work.

Chapter Fifteen

It's cold enough for gloves tonight. I slip them on and head out in the November chill to the Cantab Lounge to listen to some music, to try to lift my spirits out of the pit they've sunk into. Writing about my marriages forces me to look at my true self, and sometimes I don't like what I see. At the door I hand a huge man in a red jacket ten dollars for the cover charge, then I walk down the stairs and sit down. "Cash Only," it says on a tattered sign behind the bar. I pull my wallet out of my coat pocket—two dollars. That won't do it. Oh, well. I shouldn't drink anyway. Lately I've been drinking when it did not help me to live more fully. I would be embarrassed if Kate asked me about it.

Without alcohol, I couldn't avoid Stephanie.

"This house is so great, Boyd," said Stephanie, surveying our new home. "It's my dream house. Thank you."

"It is nice. I really like it," I said.

"But none of our furniture goes in this house. It's too modern. We need antiques."

"I know, but we can't afford it right now," I said.

"I'm so excited. I can't wait until our home is filled with antiques," she said. "We need chairs to go with our dining table."

One Sunday morning, not long afterwards, we sat in bed surrounded by children. Stephanie said, "They're having another antique auction....Jeff, no jumping on the bed.... at the Helm's Bakery. Let's....Lisa, please take Jeff to the living room and play with him. I'm trying to talk to your father....Let's go see what they have."

"Okay, but we can't buy anything," I said.

"I know," she said. "But I want to see what they have."

We bought a small round oak table for the kitchen at the auction. Two weeks later Stephanie bought chairs for it. I went to a securities law conference for a week in Washington, D.C. When I returned, an antique rocker graced our living room. Not long after, Stephanie bought chairs for the dining room table and charged a new couch from Bullock's Department Store on her credit card. A few weeks later I came home from work to an antique brass bed and nightstands. Before long, the house was fully furnished, mostly on credit. At times, I seethed, but I didn't confront her. I was trying to avoid a fight. Other times, I liked the sight of our home furnished in antiques. They were beautiful, and symbolic of my success as a partner in a prestigious law firm. Still, I resented Stephanie. I wouldn't have bought them. I had hoped we could save money by buying broken or beat-up antiques cheaply and fixing them up. I had bought a book on refinishing furniture. I was surprised at how much I enjoyed the process. But, as for saving money, it was a tiny, ineffective gesture.

I finally stopped spending extravagantly. I was worried, watching us go further into debt again. I never figured out what to do about Stephanie's overspending. In January the credit card bills from her Christmas spree came in. They came to over $3,000. She had bought so many toys for the kids they couldn't play with them all on Christmas day, and more clothes than they would ever wear before they outgrew them, as well as numerous gifts for me.

We had gone to visit her sister Donna on Christmas Eve. The pain of embarrassment showed on her sisters' faces, as they opened expensive gifts Stephanie had bought them and her niece and nephews. Their gifts to us were homemade or token. She also bought John and Jennifer Weil expensive Christmas gifts.

The previous summer when we moved to our new house she showed it off with dinner parties. One time we invited John and Jennifer and another couple. Stephanie came home from the market with thirty pieces of chicken, four pounds of green beans, four quarts of potato salad, a whole chocolate cake, a whole cheesecake, four loaves of garlic cheese bread, and two cases of Budweiser. She mixed, in advance, enough for thirty margaritas.

"God damn it, Stephanie," I said. "As usual, most of this is going to go to waste."

"I'm just trying to be a good hostess. I can't help it. My mother never had enough food for guests; they left hungry. It was embarrassing. I guess I overdo it. Tough shit!"

One day when we had been together about six years, I deposited my semimonthly paycheck. "Mr. Lemon, did you know you're overdrawn?" The teller asked me. "This seems to be a recurring problem. Would you like a check guarantee card? That way you won't be charged for the overdraft, just the interest, as long as your account is negative."

"Yeah, I guess I'd better," I said.

When I went home that night I confronted Stephanie. "Our checking account has been overdrawn three times in the last three months," I said. "Did you know that?"

"No, I didn't. Boyd, I don't have time to balance the checking account. I don't know how anyway. And I don't have time to discuss this right now. The kids need feeding and bathing."

"Oh for Christ sakes! You think I have the time? Fine," I said and pulled down a bottle of Scotch from the cupboard. "I guess I'll have to make time."

I lit a cigarette and studied the check register while I sipped on a Scotch in the den. Stephanie was spending more than I was depositing every month. I went to the drawer in the kitchen where I knew she kept unpaid bills. There were six past-due credit card bills. Four of them had large balances. I stormed into the kitchen where she was loading the dishwasher. "You're overdrawn and behind on credit card payments. You can't keep spending more than I make, Stephanie. It has to stop."

"You don't think I do anything right, do you?" she said.

I poured myself another drink. "Here's what we'll do. I'll take the checkbook and the credit cards. You calculate your reasonable household expenses for a month, and at the be-ginning of each month I'll give you the cash. You'll have to get along on that."

"Okay. That's fair. I'm sorry," she said. "I'll be good. I promise." She kissed me.

When we went to bed, she threw back the covers, came over to my side and pulled my shorts down. After a welcome but somewhat dispassionate blow job, she climbed on top and rode me until I came. That was the first sex we'd had in months. I knew she was using sex to manipulate me, but I wanted it so much I didn't care.

A week later she told me how much monthly cash she needed to run the house. I took the checkbook and her credit cards, and each month I gave her the cash she had estimated she needed for household expenses. A week or so before the end of the first month she said she was out of money. I gave her more. The same thing happened the next two months. I increased the monthly amount so she wouldn't run out.

During the first month of the increased amount she called the office one afternoon about four and told me she didn't feel like cooking dinner. She asked me if I could come home early and bring pizza for a family dinner. We rarely ate as a family on workdays.

I came in with the pizzas at about five-thirty. I grabbed the paper plates from the kitchen cupboard and slipped the pepperoni pizzas for the kids and me onto them. I held the box with Stephanie's sausage pizza in my hand. "Would you grab me a plate, honey, please?" I asked.

She went over to the cupboard. "I really need to talk to you before we call the kids in for dinner," said Stephanie.

"Okay, what is it?" I asked.

She stood holding the plate. "I'm out of money. And we have no food. That's why I asked you to get pizza." She winced.

I was outraged—beyond anything I had felt before. "What? There's a week left," I yelled. "Every fucking month you run out before the end, no matter how much I give you." My anger exploded. I wasn't aware of what I was doing.

I grabbed Stephanie's pizza out of the box and hurled it at her head. It missed and splattered against the kitchen wall. We both stood motionless for a moment, looking at each other. I turned to the sink and splashed cold water on my face. She left the kitchen.

I found her sitting in a chair in the bedroom, smoking. I said, "I'm really sorry. I owe you an apology. I don't know what came over me. I could have hurt you. We have to do something about your spending. But violence is not the answer. I'm sorry."

"I accept your apology, Boyd, but sometimes you scare me." I didn't ask her about any other time I'd scared her. I had never committed or threatened her with any violence before.

"Don't worry. It won't happen again," I said.

One night when I arrived home, Stephanie was in the kitchen preparing dinner. I heard Lisa yelling upstairs. Stephanie said, "Would you see what's going on up there? I'm trying to fix dinner. Lisa's supposed to be bathing the kids."

I went up to the kids' bathroom. Lisa was rinsing off Jennifer's hair and crying. Her clothes were soaked. Jeff, from the other end of the tub, was splashing them both.

"Stop it, Jeff," I yelled. Lisa finished rinsing Jennifer's hair, but she still cried.

"What's the matter, sweetie?" I asked. "I'll help you."

"I have a project due tomorrow, and it's not finished," she said. "Stephanie is going to make me go to bed in a half hour, and I have to put these brats to bed. I'm the babysitter around here."

"You go work on your project. I'll take care of Jeff and Jennifer," I said.

Just then, Stephanie yelled up the stairs, "Your dinner is ready, Boyd."

"Sorry, I'll have to eat it later," I yelled back. "I have to finish the kids' baths and put them to bed. Lisa has to finish a school project."

A moment later Stephanie walked into the bathroom. "She's had plenty of time to finish that project before tonight. Come and eat your dinner."

"I'll be down in a few minutes, after I put them to bed." She glowered and left. I heard a crash from the kitchen. A few minutes later, as I put Jennifer to bed, I heard our bedroom door slam. When I had the kids in bed, I looked in on Lisa. She was pasting a picture of a dinosaur onto a piece of yellow construction paper.

"How are you doing, honey?" I asked.

"Okay," she said. "Stephanie is going to kill me tomorrow."

"No, she won't," I said. "Go to bed when you finish that, okay?"

"Yeah," she said.

I walked down to the kitchen and looked around for my dinner—on the table, in the oven, the refrigerator. I couldn't find it. I went into our room. Stephanie was sitting up in bed, reading *Parents Magazine*. "Where's my dinner?" I asked.

"I threw it away," she said, calmly.

"That was a childish thing to do," I said.

"Don't talk to me about childish," she said. "Lisa has you wrapped around her little finger."

"I simply don't think you should use her as a babysitter," I said, "especially when she has school work to do. That comes first."

"She could have finished that yesterday. Besides, she does nothing around here. I do everything. She's seven years old. She's old enough to help."

"Yes, she should help some, but she's not the mom," I said.

"Oh, leave me alone, Boyd."

I did. She was asleep when I went back in.

Now, sitting on my couch trying to wind down, I remember that back then I believed Stephanie didn't care about Lisa after she had her own children. But I don't believe that was it. I believe she was taking out her anger at me on Lisa. When our relationship was good, Stephanie treated Lisa well.

I knew after six years that our marriage was in serious trouble. I tried one approach that could have been constructive. I suggested therapy, and Stephanie agreed. My principal motivation was that Stephanie was rejecting me sexually, and I wanted a cure. After several months of individual and couples therapy, the therapist told us that the sexual problems were symptoms of deeper issues in our marriage. She said if we addressed those issues, good sex might return. In individual therapy she told me two things I remember. She said that I was letting Stephanie control me and I needed to assert myself more; and while therapy would help me, it might not save the marriage. These memories, like all, are selective, and what I remember confirms notions I had that I was not responsible for our marital problems, and ultimately I was powerless.

I believe I did need to be more assertive, but I didn't know how to do it constructively. I simply ratcheted up my complaints and accusations, which made it worse. And, of course, the problems were more complex and numerous than simply a need for me to be more assertive.

Stephanie quit therapy first. She said that the therapist was attacking her unfairly. I continued for a few months and then stopped.

I think—*If I saw a therapist now it would help me to gain more insight into my marriages.*

Chapter Sixteen

In April 1975 I got home from the office on a Saturday around seven. Stephanie wasn't in the kitchen, the bedroom, or upstairs. The children were in bed. "Stephanie, where are you?" I yelled from the top of the stairs.

"Down here."

She was sitting on the couch in the living room, where neither of us ever sat except when we had company. She was in her short, beige nightgown and had a drink in one hand and a cigarette in the other. Her eyes were wet.

"We need to talk," she said. I sat down in the rocker, grasping the wooden arms tightly.

"Okay," I said.

She looked over at the window, almost expectantly, then back at me. "I want a temporary separation. I need to do some thinking about our marriage that I can't do while we're living together."

"What!" I gasped. "What's wrong?"

"I don't know what's wrong. I just need some space. I'm sure it'll just be temporary."

"When?" I asked.

"As soon as you can leave. Now, if possible," she said.

"I can't believe this."

"I'm sorry," she said. "This is important. I'm sure everything will be all right if you just give me this time and space. Please."

"All right," I said.

I called Barnaby's Hotel a few blocks away and reserved a room. I packed in a fog. I was teary-eyed as I looked in on Jeff, then Lisa and Jennifer. I stood outside Jennifer's room to regain my composure. *I'll give Stephanie time and space, for a while,* I thought, *but I can't let this marriage fail. I can't leave my family.* I sobbed and shook. My chest ached. My muscles tightened. I picked up my suitcase and walked to the garage in a mental fog. Stephanie followed me. We hugged.

"Keep in touch," she said. "I'll call you tomorrow to see how you're doing."

The short drive seemed funereal. I checked in at Barnaby's and went straight to the bar. As I sipped on Scotch and smoked a cigarette, I remembered our first heady days together, almost six years earlier. *How did things get this crazy?* I wondered. The chaos of living with Stephanie had me reeling much of the time anyway, and now this. Our marriage was like one of those stock market line graphs in a volatile bear market, where the line spikes up and down, but mostly down. After my fourth Scotch, I went up to my room and in an alcohol haze put my socks and shorts in the drawer and hung up my shirts, ties, suits, and pants. I flipped on the TV and punched the remote until I went through all the channels, but I was hardly looking. Suddenly, through the alcohol, my nerves tightened. I felt tied up like Houdini, but I couldn't escape. I undressed and climbed into bed, wide awake. What would I do if Stephanie wouldn't take me back? I'd be alone. I've never lived alone in my life, except for those two weeks between Christie and

Stephanie, and that was miserable, I thought. Around five I woke up, tense and exhausted.

Driving to work, my stomach cramped. My underarm moisture made my shirt cling, though the weather was cool. I turned on the air conditioning. What was she going to do with her newfound time and space? She had three children to take care of by herself. What could she do? Leave them with Mrs. Backer, I guess.

I immersed myself in my work from early morning to evening, then drank trying to block out Stephanie. It didn't work. Wednesday evening I called her. "How are you?" she asked.

"Fine," I lied. "How are you?"

"Okay. It's weird not having you here, but it's something I need."

I asked if I could take the kids to the beach Saturday, and she said it would be fine. After a few moments of awkward silence, I said, "Well, good bye. I'll be over to pick them up about eleven."

"Okay. See ya," she said.

I drove by our house late that night. There was a strange car in the driveway. I wondered whose it could be. I could see only one light on in the house, but I couldn't tell where it came from.

I drove by the next night. There were two unfamiliar cars in the driveway. My chest tightened. I had a drink at the hotel bar, but it didn't relax me. I had about six Scotches and a pack of cigarettes that night and awoke nauseous and hung over.

I had to hold back tears when I picked up the kids. We went to the beach. They acted normal. They didn't ask me any questions about where I had been. I went through the motions of building a sand castle, wading in the surf, and splashing water on the kids. I buried Jeff in sand up to his head. That's the way I feel, I thought, as he stumbled up with sand all over him, but I can't get up.

I took them back home and stopped to use the bathroom, passing our bedroom on the way. The bed was unmade, and there was an empty wine bottle on the nightstand. I felt sick to my stomach and almost vomited in the toilet, but I said nothing to Stephanie.

She went out of town the next weekend. I was sure she wouldn't go alone, but I couldn't guess who might go with her. I stayed with the kids. By Sunday evening I was exhausted, having taken care of them by myself all weekend. It didn't occur to me that this was Stephanie's constant routine.

She rolled in Sunday night about ten. I met her in the living room. "Sit down, please," she said. We sat. She lit a cigarette and looked away, then back at me. "I want you to know something. I slept with somebody the other night. You met him once when we had lunch at that chili place in Santa Monica. You probably don't remember. His name is Chris. He was a high school classmate. He came over. We had some wine. He kissed me, and before I knew it we were naked. He carried me into the bedroom, and we fucked."

My chest contracted as if something had knocked the wind out of me. I feel certain I gasped for air. Then a wave of nausea and the fire of anger struck me.

"I really don't need to hear this," I yelled. "Why are you telling me?" I said softer, my voice cracking, as the hurt settled in. "Why are you doing this?

"I don't know, Boyd. It has nothing to do with you. It's just something I have to do. That's why I asked for a separation. But I don't want to hide it. I can't go sneaking around. I think it's something you should know."

"Well, I just don't understand it, Stephanie. Why?

"I wish I could tell you. I don't know, Boyd."

I cried. She tried to hug me. "I can't," I said. "I have to leave."

"One more thing I have to tell you. Another time Chris and a friend came over. All three of us ended up in bed. There was a lot of action, but I have to say, it wasn't very satisfying."

"My God, Stephanie," was all I could say. I picked up my suitcase and walked out, slamming the door. I sobbed all the way to the hotel. I thought this only happened in soap operas. Back in my room, I kept reviewing in my mind what she said, picturing her naked with these men pleasuring her—my wife. Jealousy raged. I wanted to castrate those men, then kill them. I remembered meeting Chris, a lawyer. How could he do this with my wife? The pain of what I saw as Stephanie's betrayal penetrated to my core, wounded the deepest part of my being. My anger was overcome by hurt, and I sobbed again. One of my basic assumptions—that my wife would be loyal to me— had shattered, and scattered, invisible, over my world. I was scared too. I was losing my family, I thought. I finally flopped down on the bed, exhausted. I couldn't think anymore.

I drank myself to sleep again. The next day at the office I still pictured these men fucking Stephanie, her sucking their cocks, them going down on her. I finally realized I had to stop thinking about it, or I would go crazy.

Two days after Stephanie's revelation, I wanted revenge. I thought, I'll ask out Karen from work. She's hot, and maybe she'll sleep with me. At lunch the next day, Karen mentioned her boyfriend, who lived with her.

I rented an apartment, month to month, on Highland, near where we used to live. I imagined Stephanie still fucking her brains out with various men. I wallowed in the torture for another month. I have to do something, I kept thinking—this can't continue. Either my marriage is over and my family is gone, or it isn't. I'm being passive. I need to take action, assert myself, as the therapist had suggested.

I called Stephanie and told her we needed to talk and suggested we meet for dinner at Yamamoto's in Century City.

"Sure," she said. "I'm always willing to talk with you. I want to keep lines of communication open."

I planned and rehearsed what I was going to say to her, just as I did with my arguments in court. I rehearsed again driving to Yamamoto's. As I pulled into the parking garage, I couldn't remember how I'd gotten there. I walked into a rare spring rain. By the time I entered the restaurant, water was dripping from my hair down my face. In contrast, Stephanie, her dark hair perfectly coiffed, sat at a table near the entrance. She wore a blood orange dress with small yellow flowers and a scooped neckline that showed her cleavage. She smiled at me. When I got to the table, she stood up and hugged me. She wore panty hose. She never wore panties with them. My groin stirred.

I sat down and folded my hands on the table. She reached and held them briefly. "I miss you," she said, looking straight at me. I looked away. I didn't know what to say. "I really do," she said.

"I miss you too," I said, looking down at the table.

"I need this time, though," she said. She lowered her voice. "I think I had my last fling last weekend. Chris had a conference in Santa Barbara. I met him up there. When I walked into his hotel room, he grabbed me. He ripped my clothes off and fucked me on the floor."

I felt the heat in my face and the constriction of my chest, but compared to before, I was numb to her confessions of betrayal. "I see," I said. "Don't tell me about your sexual escapades, please. I don't want to know." I wondered: *Is she deliberately trying to hurt me, or does telling me assuage her guilt?*

"This separation is better for our marriage than you know," she said.

"It's a strange way of strengthening a marriage," I said.

The server came up and asked what we wanted to drink. I said I was ready to order food. I didn't want to be there with Stephanie any longer than necessary.

"You order for me, Boyd," she said.

"We'll both have the vegetable and shrimp tempura," I said. "And the salad with your sweet vinegar dressing."

"Very good," said the waiter.

I launched into my prepared speech. "We've been separated six weeks now. That should be enough time for you to find out whatever you needed to find out. I'm not willing to continue in this state of uncertainty. It's too hard on me. It has to be hard on the kids. Remember marriage is for better or for worse, in sickness and in health. You can't just decide to take a break whenever it gets hard or you feel stressed. If you want to stay married, then you have to let me come back now. Either you want to be married to me, or you don't. Which is it, Stephanie?"

Her eyes were moist. She shifted in her chair and looked down at the table. She lit a cigarette. "I don't know," she said softly.

I hadn't anticipated this. I ad-libbed. "Well, okay, Stephanie. I insist that you make up your mind by the end of tomorrow. And I suggest you consider the children and whether you really want to be alone. If you don't make up your mind by then, our marriage is over." I pounded the table with my closed fist on the final word, "over," like I'd seen aggressive lawyers do. That was being assertive, I thought.

"Okay, Boyd, if that is what you want, I'll decide and let you know tomorrow."

The waiter brought our food, and we ate in silence. Neither of us ate much. She said she had promised Mrs. Backer she would be back by nine, so she had to go. We hugged, and she left. I stayed and had two Scotches.

After work I returned to the hotel the next evening. I drank Scotch, smoked cigarettes and waited in my room. Sitting on the bed next to the phone, I forced myself not to think of Stephanie having sex with those other men. It finally rang. My hand shook as I picked up the receiver, even with all the Scotch I had drunk.

"I want you to come home tomorrow," she said. "Let's start over. I love you."

"I love you too. I'll be home tomorrow after work," I said. I imagined that she wanted the extra night so she could fuck Chris, or somebody. But I relaxed for the first time in six weeks.

After work I drove home. We kissed passionately. I still

felt nervous, but nothing like before. I read Jeff a story. He got up and pulled his wagon down the hall. Jennifer played nurse with Lisa. I shuddered imagining what Stephanie had told them and what they had seen. At seven-thirty I read them *Good Night Moon* in Lisa's room. I kissed Lisa, and led Jeff and Jennifer to their rooms and kissed them.

I went downstairs and poured drinks for Stephanie and me at the dining room table. "Sit down," I said. She sat across from me. "To our reunion." We clinked glasses.

"Yes," she said. "To the renewal of our marriage."

When we went to bed, she pulled me to her. We kissed with urgency and passion, her soft, wet tongue warming me all over. She kissed my chest and licked my belly button—all the way down, taking me in her mouth. She hadn't done that in a long time. She must have done it to Chris, or whoever. But it didn't matter so much. I was getting what I desperately wanted from her—sex.

The next workday sped by. As soon as the kids were in bed that night, Stephanie undressed me, pulled me onto the bed and mounted me.

The following night, I snuggled up against her and caressed her breast.

"Don't."

"What's the matter?" I asked.

"I don't know," she said. "I just don't feel like it."

I tried again in a few days and a week later. Each time she rejected me. I still didn't address with her the reasons she had asked for the separation, or the reasons she was rejecting sex with me again. I never asked her what I could do to better meet her needs, or how we could change our relationship to avoid another separation or divorce.

We renewed our wedding vows in front of our children and friends, but I worried about her sexual rejections. We took a second honeymoon to Hawaii with the children and a friend who helped take care of them. Even in Hawaii Stephanie rejected me sexually. She let me make love to her twice, but she was dry. That hurt, and I was angry with her. But at least we were a family again, I thought. Jennifer took her first step in Hawaii.

I didn't attempt the hard work of addressing what was wrong with our marriage. I blamed Stephanie for being dry, but I didn't consider what I should do to make her wet.

For the remainder of our marriage, images of Stephanie having sex with other men trooped relentlessly through my mind, each one setting off a sickening feeling that radiated from my stomach to the top of my head. I couldn't stop thinking about it. My anger rolled around us like thunder, sometimes striking like lightning.

The lecture on Beethoven's Piano Sonatas is over, and I turn off my DVD player. It's almost Thanksgiving. Soon I'll be on my way to Jennifer's for the holiday. I haven't had a drink in a week. I haven't slept much either, but I'm determined not to go to a bar. I need to get out, though. I walk down to the 1369 Café, order a green tea, and get out my notebook. Through writing, I want to digest Stephanie's demand for the separation and understand what it meant.

Although my marriage to Stephanie lasted three years after the separation, I think it was doomed when I failed to address the reasons for her need for a separation. Thirty-four years have passed. The pain has melted into a vague sadness. I recognize now that from Stephanie's perspective her affairs might not have been the betrayal I felt. She was unhappy with our marriage; that was clear to her. It should have been clear to me. She asked for a separation. She was a highly sexual twenty-five-year-old woman, who had been rejecting sex with me most of the time for three years. That alone was an indication that something was terribly wrong. I couldn't reasonably expect that she would be celibate during our separation. It should have been apparent that having sex with other men was a possibility for her, or perhaps her reason for asking for a separation, though she didn't say so. She could have cheated on me without a separation. From her perspective, she was not cheating, because she had no obligation to me while we were separated. I couldn't see it that way then. I don't know if her need to tell me about her sexual escapades came from guilt or anger, or if she thought it wasn't cheating if she told me.

During or after the six-week separation it never occurred to me that Stephanie was trying to send me a message by the means she unconsciously knew would create the biggest impact—sex. The message was that she needed me to be a husband, one who paid attention to her and showed he cared about her, as I had in the early years of our relationship. I didn't get it, and I never asked her for an explanation or what we could do to change things after we got back together. I just resumed the marriage, as before.

Neither of us had the courage to address the issues in our marriage—or to end the marriage. She probably couldn't face raising the children alone. I couldn't face another failed family, and I still was desperate for sex with her. We made each other suffer for three more years.

Chapter Seventeen

A few months after we ended our separation, I pulled the pile of bills out of the kitchen drawer and made some calculations. There was no way I could make these payments on my income from Nossaman. We were hemorrhaging financially. What could I do? I had three big cases I was working on. If I left the firm and opened my own office, most likely these clients would stay with me. I was the only lawyer who knew anything about their cases, and they seemed happy with me. If they did stay with me I would make more money. But what would happen when those cases concluded, or what if they settled quickly? Could I develop enough business to keep going?

I didn't discuss this move with Stephanie. I simply told her what I was going to do. I don't know how she felt about it. Once again, I didn't think I had a choice. The Law Offices of Boyd S. Lemon opened in October 1975. I bought an IBM Correcting Selectric Typewriter—state of the art then—and Stephanie worked for me until I got established. Nossaman paid me for my partnership interest in the firm, which got us by until clients began to pay.

I don't know if I was reasonable in dealing with Stephanie's overspending. I've always thought I did everything I could to stop it. I think one of the problems was lack of consistency. I complained after the money had been spent, but often I participated in spending, not on her clothes or the food she wasted, or toys for the children, but on other things—furniture, meals out, vacations. I wasn't making sacrifices either, and this may have impacted her failure to rein in her spending. I never prepared a budget. I didn't try to sit down with her and address the whole issue. I picked at her about individual expenditures and bounced checks and whined about the problem in general. I focused on what I excelled at—making more money, but I could never make enough. I don't know if anything would have quelled her overspending. It has been a lifelong problem for her.

Stephanie and I fought more than ever during the six months she worked for me, but I did make more money, and we began to make some headway on paying off our debts. Still, I felt enormous pressure, with a wife and three children to support and no guaranteed paycheck. My hands would often shake when I opened the office mail, hoping one of the envelopes contained a big check.

Stephanie had gotten tired of her station wagon and bought a VW camper van with a connecting tent. We took a family camping vacation in the gold rush region of California in the summer of 1975. Our relationship improved on that trip, and I was encouraged. I didn't realize that my encouragement might have been influenced by the absence of sexual rejection. I didn't ask for or expect sex in a tent with three children.

Now that I had my own practice and wasn't putting in as many hours as I had been with the Nossaman Firm, I tried to spend more time with the children. I took Jeff camping in Big Bear for a long weekend that summer. In October, shortly after

I opened my new law office, it was Lisa's turn for a weekend with Dad. She was seven. We left on a Friday morning for Oak Glen Campground near San Bernardino. It was cold when we arrived. I built a campfire, and we waited in the van for the chicken drumsticks and corn on the cob to cook on the grill. I asked Lisa how she was doing.

"Okay, Dad," she sighed, "But I hate Stephanie."

"I'm sorry. Why, honey?"

"She always makes me take care of Jeff and Jennifer, and every time Jeff does something bad, he tells her I did it, and she believes him. She's just mean. She hates me."

"No, she doesn't, dear. She loves you. She's loved you since you were a baby."

Lisa's voice shook. She had tears in her eyes. "You just don't know. You're not around to see what she does," she cried out.

"I'll see what I can do, honey. I'll talk to her."

"It won't do any good. She'll just be meaner."

"We'll see. You tell me when you feel you've been treated unfairly. I'll try to help. Okay?"

"All right," Lisa said. We hugged. Her thin little body seemed so frail. My heart ached. Maybe I should leave Stephanie and take Lisa with me, I thought.

The next Sunday afternoon, while Jeff and Jennifer napped and Lisa was with her mom for her monthly visitation, Stephanie and I sat at the kitchen table eating hot dogs. Again, I told Stephanie I didn't think she was treating Lisa fairly, and that she felt Stephanie hated her. "Please try not to use her as a babysitter or maid, and don't blame her for things unless you know she did them," I said.

"I can't believe you are so naïve," she said. "Lisa is using you. She's old enough to have chores. And I don't blame her for things she hasn't done."

"Stephanie, god damn it, I've seen you scream at her when she hasn't done anything wrong. Please stop it. Show a little love for her, like you used to."

"Go to hell, Boyd. I do love her, but she's a manipulative child, and I won't let her get away with it. Stop letting her manipulate you." Stephanie picked up her plate, threw it in the sink, where it crashed and broke, and went to the bedroom. I heard her crying. I left it at that.

My law practice was prospering. I enjoyed not having a boss. I took pride in my own successful business. I was working full time, but rarely nights and only an occasional Saturday. I had time to spend with my family and try to resolve the emotional junk that had accrued, but, at best, I made only a half-hearted effort, bound to be ineffectual.

By 1977, three years after we had pulled out of debt, Stephanie was spending more than ever, and we were back in debt, unable to make our monthly payments. The solution, I decided, was to buy a smaller, cheaper house. Once again our house had appreciated in value, and we used part of the proceeds to pay off debt. Our new house was small, but only three blocks from the beach. There was a room over the garage that we could rent out. It was on Tenth Street, a walk street—cars not allowed. The kids played out there with neighborhood kids. This time I had gotten my way—a house near the beach. Stephanie acquiesced, although I didn't see it that way.

Shortly after we moved, Stephanie called me at the office. She said that a friend of Jennifer Weil's, Anita, needed a place to live. She was two months pregnant and was going to have the baby, but she wasn't going to live with the father. We'd met Anita about a year before. Stephanie asked if she could live with us in the room over the garage rent-free. She could help with the kids. I grudgingly agreed.

Stephanie's friends all knew Anita. Parties started erupting at our house every weekend and sometimes during the week. They always involved booze and drugs, though Anita didn't indulge. One Thursday when I got home from work, people were in our living room: Pat, Bonny, John, Jennifer, Anita and several others I didn't recognize. Wine and tequila bottles were on the kitchen counter. Everybody had a glass.

"Hi, Boyd, welcome to the party," somebody said.

John pulled a little bottle and spoon from his pocket and handed it to me. "A little something for the hardworking man."

"I'll be back in a minute," I said. I went to the kids' rooms. Jeff and Jennifer were asleep. Lisa was in bed reading. I kissed her good night and told her to turn off the light. She scowled, threw down her book and shut off the light.

I went back to the party and snorted two spoons of John's cocaine—it wasn't my first—and poured myself a tequila. A couple more people arrived, and soon there were about ten of us sitting in a circle on our living room floor. At nine o'clock, the boisterous talk and laughter reverberated. The music blared—Jimmy Buffett, the Eagles, Fleetwood Mac, the Doors. I checked on the kids again. They were asleep. We drank and snorted. Somebody passed me a pipe. "What's this?" I asked.

"Hash," somebody said. I took a hit.

Later, I took a quarter of a Quaalude and snorted more cocaine. By one o'clock, everybody had left, earlier than usual. Stephanie said she was going to clean up the kitchen. I took two Valiums so I could sleep and went to bed. The next day was a workday.

I woke up. I glanced at the clock—a little after three. Stephanie stood over me, her eyes wide. "I've been raped," she whispered.

"What?" I thought I'd heard wrong.

"I've been raped." Her voice shook. Her head shook. I catapulted out of bed.

I held her. "You can't mean it," I said.

"Yes," she cried and held me tightly.

"My god. What happened? No, wait a minute. Where is he? Could he still be around?"

"He...he... could be," she said.

"I'll call the police," I said. "Make sure the doors are

locked." I ran to the kitchen phone.

"My wife has been raped," I said to the dispatcher.

"Where is your wife?" She asked.

"Here, at home," I said.

"Is the perpetrator still in the vicinity?" she asked.

"We don't know. He could be."

"Was he armed?"

I asked Stephanie. "Yes," she said.

My heart sank to my shoes. My hand shook on the phone. "Yes," I whispered.

After getting our address, she said, "Until the officer arrives, have your wife make sure all the doors and windows are locked. And tell her not to clean herself. You stay on the line, please." I repeated the instructions to Stephanie. She went to the bedroom.

I heard the dispatcher repeating what I had told her, on the police radio, I assumed. Then she spoke to me again. "There's a patrol car four blocks away. He'll check the perimeter of your house. Then he'll knock on the front door. If he does not identify himself as a police officer and display his badge, do not, I repeat, do not open the door," she said. "Now stay on the line until you hear the knock."

In what seemed like only a few seconds I heard the knock. I told the dispatcher. She said, "Don't hang up. Just put the phone down and find out if it's our officer."

I went to the front door, and with my hand shaking I pulled open the curtain that covered the top half. A heavyset, short man with a tan police uniform stood there, shining a flashlight on his badge. I opened the door. "Hello, Mr. Lemon," he said. "We looked around the area and didn't find anything suspicious. My partner is at the back door. May I let him in?"

"Oh, sure," I said, and went to tell the dispatcher they were here.

After determining that Stephanie didn't need immediate medical attention, the heavyset officer said that a female officer was on her way, and she would question Stephanie. In the meantime, he got basic identifying information from me, as Stephanie sat and waited. When Officer Gerry Williams arrived, the other officers left. Gerry asked Stephanie if she would like me to be present for the questioning. Stephanie, said, "Yes, unless you don't want to be, honey. It's not a pleasant story."

"I want to hear it," I said.

She had been washing dishes. She still wore her blue jumper—panties, but no bra, she said in answer to Gerry's question. Apparently, she had not locked the front door when the last guest left. I hadn't checked it before I went to bed. While she loaded the dishwasher she heard nothing, until a dirty, scruffy-looking, young guy—it turned out he was seventeen—appeared beside her brandishing a knife about eight inches long. He told her to be quiet, that he knew her husband and children were asleep, and if any of them woke up he would kill them all. He took a gun out of his jacket pocket to show her, then put it back. He ordered her into the living room and told her to undress. He pulled down his pants and told her to suck him. She did. She said she gagged, but had nothing in her stomach. He told her to lie down, and repeated that if she made a sound and woke anybody up, he would kill them all. He climbed on top of her, held the knife by her face and penetrated her.

After he came he ordered her to take him to her car. She led him to the garage, and they got in our VW Van. He told her where to drive. After a while he ordered her to stop. He raped her again in the back of the van. He then told her to drive back toward our house. Before she got there he ordered her to stop. He got out and told her to stay there for ten minutes. If she drove away, he would come and kill her and her family, he said. When he was out of sight, she left the van and ran home, terrified that she would run into him.

Stephanie didn't cry during the questioning. She's still in shock, I thought. So was I, but I felt a heavy ball deep in my stomach when I thought about not checking to see if the front door was locked before I went to bed. I slept through the whole rape, not much of a protector. Of course, if I had awakened, we might all be dead. When Officer Williams left, we held each other and cried. I felt so sorry. My anger at her receded deep under my consciousness—for a while.

Since our separation, my trust in her had been electron-thin. I wondered if she enjoyed sex with the rapist. I even doubted whether she had been raped. I wondered if the sperm the hospital had verified was her lover's. At first I didn't mention any of these doubts to Stephanie. I thought it would be too cruel. But my jealousy and anger had poisoned our marriage.

We went on with life. After a couple of weeks, when the kids were in bed and we were alone, we sat on the couch in front of the TV, neither of us really watching it. My doubts rose to the surface. I looked at Stephanie and cried. She hugged me and asked me what was the matter.

"I'm sorry, but I can't help wondering...if you enjoyed the sex with that guy," I blurted through the tears.

"Oh, god, no," she said and started to cry. "It was awful, and it hurt. I almost threw up. It was only my fear of making noise and waking you or the kids that stopped me. I was terrified somebody would wake up, and he would kill us all."

We held each other and cried. I finally believed she really was raped. I wanted the guy found and killed. Most of the time I suppressed my feelings. So did she, at least around me. Briefly, after the rape, we seemed closer. I felt so badly for her, but I didn't know how to express empathy.

About a month after the rape, Officer Williams came by and said she thought they had the guy in custody. We went to a police lineup that night. Stephanie leaned over and whispered in my ear. "That's him, the third guy from the right." Her whole body shook. I couldn't look at him. I have no memory of what he looked like. I wanted him sent to prison, immediately. On the way out, walking to the car, Stephanie stopped and held me, shaking, crying. "It was really hard to see him again," she said between sobs. "I'm sure he's the one."

"I hope so," I said, "Because he's going to prison." She never wavered in her identification. For a while, my strongest emotion was hatred of him and intense rage. Stephanie and I had marital problems, but he had committed the ultimate crime against my wife. Stephanie testified at the trial. I went with her and spent as much time with her as possible in the weeks before, during and after the trial. She held up, showing her strength. I was proud of her. Her weakness would come out later. The jury found him guilty, and he was sentenced to prison.

She didn't ask for, and I didn't suggest, psychotherapy to help her deal with the trauma. The drunken, drug-laced parties with John and Jennifer and their friends, who had become our friends, increased in frequency, length and intensity.

I came home from the office early one day—about four o'clock. Only Stephanie, Anita and the kids were home. Stephanie was drinking a glass of wine, the first time I had seen her drink before evening. After that, the sight of Stephanie drinking and snorting coke during the day became common. I didn't make any connection to the rape. I can't know if it would have been different if she hadn't been raped, but I didn't understand what a profound effect the rape had on her. Twenty-five years later, she still panicked when she found, during the day, that she had forgotten to lock the door to her apartment.

Jennifer was only three. Jeff was five. We didn't talk to them about the rape. Lisa was nine. I sat with Stephanie and Lisa while Stephanie explained to Lisa what happened. Lisa's eyes widened, and she cried. She has always kept her doors locked.

We replaced the van because Stephanie couldn't bear to be in it. A few months later she said she couldn't bear to live in the house where she'd been raped, so we bought a new one, the biggest, most expensive house we had ever owned— newly built, with every modern convenience, two stories, four bedrooms, and a family room upstairs that was bigger than the whole house on Tenth Street. It had a view of the planes on final approach to LAX, and a wet bar that could seat eight people. The master suite had a bathroom with a round Jacuzzi tub set in redwood. It was a party house. Stephanie picked it out. I didn't offer any input.

I'd hoped that the new house would put the rape behind us. How I could have thought it would be that simple, I don't know. We were to move a couple of weeks before Christmas.

When we signed the papers to buy the new house, Stephanie invited all our friends to a party to celebrate. It started on a Friday night in November. When I got home from work, the kids were in bed. The kitchen counter was full of food: honey-baked ham, a whole turkey from a deli, sliced roast beef, breads, cheeses, olives, chips, nuts, potato salad, macaroni salad, green salad; there were also bottles of wine, a trash can full of beer on ice, tequila, Scotch and cognac. In the master bathroom were two mirrors with a couple of grams of coke, ready to snort, with a razor blade and cut-off straws. I scraped some into lines and did two. By the time I changed and went out to the living room, five people were already there with Stephanie. She wore her sexiest dress, a white knit see-through, with no bra and thin panties that exposed a blur of pubic hair in the front and the crack in her ass in the back.

The party rocked on all night and all the next day. Anita took care of the kids and put them to bed early. None of us, except Anita, went to bed Friday night. Saturday night I went to bed, but Stephanie didn't. When I got up around seven on Sunday morning, she was sitting alone in the living room, in her nightgown, drinking cognac. Her face had the puffy, pale, and loose look it always had after she had been using drugs and drinking. She looked older than her twenty-seven years. Her boobs spilled out, and she wore no panties. I finally began to worry about her.

"I guess I never made it to bed again," she slurred.

"I guess not," I said. "Why don't you come to bed with

me now. You could take some Valium if you need it to get to sleep."

"No, Anita and the kids'll be down soon." I sighed and went back to shower.

By evening the party had resumed. The kids were with Anita in her room above the garage. Stephanie ordered more booze from Super Sam's. She disappeared for an hour, I guessed to buy more cocaine. I went to bed about eleven o'clock. Around midnight I woke up. Pat, Jennifer Weil, and Bonnie came out of the bathroom. Stephanie followed and went to the closet. Somebody said, "Sorry to wake you, but Stephanie wants to go to Cassidy's, and we had to have a little hit for the road." Stephanie came out in a dress I had never seen before. It clung to her like Saran Wrap.

I got out of bed, only partly conscious that I was standing in front of these women in my white Jockeys. "Stephanie, can I talk to you?"

"About what?" she asked.

"Oh, we'll leave," one of the women said.

"No, no, stay," Stephanie said. "These are my friends. You can say whatever you have to say."

"You have been up all night the last two nights," I said. "Please stay home and go to bed."

"No, I feel like dancing. I haven't been out all weekend. I'll be home later."

"Stephanie, I beg you, come to bed." I held out my hands, palms up. "Please."

"I'm going. I'll see ya later," she said. And they all traipsed out of the room, leaving me standing there in my underwear. Stephanie woke me up climbing into bed at about five.

The next week, as another all-night party at the Tenth Street house wound down, the grandfather clock chimed six. I headed upstairs to shower and go to work. Shit, I've done it again, I thought, stayed up all night with Stephanie, and John, Pat, Bonnie, tequila and a gram of cocaine. With a headache, a dry mouth and nose, red eyes and a dizzying exhaustion setting in, I had to go to work. The shower, two glasses of water, and brushing my teeth didn't help. Two more lines of coke did.

I picked up my briefcase from the living room floor. Stephanie sat on the couch, staring into space, hair stringy, face pale, and eyes puffy. She was sipping a glass of tequila. "See ya," I said.

"Yeah, see ya."

Anita, carrying Jennifer, walked in. "Good morning Anita. Bye, Jennifer," I said, kissing her on top of the head. "See you tonight."

"Bye Daddy," she said, waving her hand.

When I arrived at my office in Westwood, I realized I didn't remember anything about the half-hour drive from home. It was like "Beam me up, Scotty." I was able to focus enough to get my papers for the day organized and start on my sixteen-item to-do list. My secretary, Dora, brought me coffee and a folder with airline tickets and other documents for my business trip to Tokyo and Hong Kong.

A few more lines of coke kept me going all day, but I only finished six of the sixteen items. I was interrupted by a malfunctioning typewriter, client calls, and a long harangue from an opposing attorney that ended with her threat to schedule a court hearing while I was in Asia.

I left the office at about six and picked up Chinese food. I couldn't rely on Stephanie to cook or have any food in the house. I planned to go to bed immediately after I ate.

Only Anita was home. She was sitting on the brown, flowered couch in the family room, looking down at the coffee table, and didn't look up when I walked into the room. She wasn't crying, but her eyes were red. "What's the matter, Anita?" I asked. "Where are Stephanie and the kids?"

"I don't know, Boyd," she said. "They went out a couple hours ago, and Stephanie didn't say where they were going or when they'd be back. Boyd, I'm worried about you. Take care of yourself. I don't like what Stephanie is doing, and I don't understand it, but I'm her friend. I can't really talk to you about it."

"Anita, is she cheating on me?" I asked.

"I couldn't tell you, even if I knew, which I don't," she said. "But I will tell you, the other night when you weren't here, she and John were awfully friendly here on the couch." She shook her head. "I've really said too much. Please don't tell Stephanie what I said."

"Jesus Christ," I said. "No, I won't, Anita. I don't know what to do."

"I feel badly for you, Boyd, but I really grieve for the kids."

"I do too, Anita. I do too." I knew my life was insane, out of control, but—*I'll deal with it when I get back from Asia*, I thought.

I was still sitting on the couch when Stephanie and the kids showed up with John, Pat and Bonnie, who immediately went to the kitchen and poured themselves and Stephanie shots of tequila. John looked at me. "What's the matter, Boyd? You look so glum—hard day at the office? Join the party." He held out his little amber bottle of cocaine.

"No, thanks," I said. "I have a big day tomorrow."

I followed Stephanie to check on the kids. "There's Chinese in the kitchen," I said.

"Thanks," she said. We looked in at the sleeping children. Then she headed down the hall. In our room she pulled out of the nightstand a mirror with coke on it. She looked sexy in her white satin dress. She wore no bra, and, looking closely, I could see her nipples and the outline of her breasts, firm and full. She still had a near-perfect figure, even after two children. "I'm leaving for Asia day after tomorrow, you know. We need to talk tomorrow. I'll try to get home early."

"Okay," she said, frowning.

She went back to the living room. I drank a shot of tequila, ate some shrimp with lobster sauce and rice in the kitchen and went to bed. I awoke to the alarm at six. Stephanie was not in bed. I walked around the house. She wasn't home. Neither were the kids. I assumed they were with Anita.

I went to court that morning. Back at the office, I frantically did the ten remaining items on my list. At home that night, the kids were in bed, and a party was in progress. I had to leave for my trip the next day. I tossed down two shots of tequila and banged a fork on the glass to get everyone's attention.

"I'm sorry, but you all will have to go. Stephanie and I need to have a family meeting," I said. I wanted to talk to her about changing this crazy life style.

"Oh sure, sure," I heard several people say simultaneously.

When the last person left, Stephanie yelled, "That was really rude. You humiliated me in front of my friends. I'm going out. We're not having any god damned family meeting." She grabbed her purse and walked out the door.

I followed her to her car, yelling, "Stephanie, stay here. We really have to talk."

"Fuck you!" she said, and slammed the door to her car. She drove off. I was yelling as she drove off. The neighbors stared at me out their window.

When I cooled off, I thought, *somehow we have to stop this. It's no way to live and it's a horrible environment for the kids.*

Three hours later Stephanie came back, drunk, and woke me up by turning on the lamp next to her side of the bed. "Boyd, I don't know what to do. I'm so sorry." She sat up in bed, looking haggard and despondent. She left and came back with a glass of brandy. She put it on the nightstand and undressed. I snuggled up against her thigh. She got up, picked up her brandy, and left without saying anything.

Sitting in my seat for the seventeen-hour flight to Tokyo (I had made the flight about two minutes before the plane's doors closed), I thought about my marriage. Could it be saved? Did I want to save it? Tears flooded my eyes when I thought about leaving the kids. I fantasized that Stephanie had been killed. Then I could live in peace with my children and take control of my life. I wondered if other husbands daydreamed about their wives being dead. I thought I must be a terrible person to wish my kids' mother were dead.

I took a deposition in Tokyo and repacked for the trip to Hong Kong. I put my little amber bottle of cocaine deep in the suitcase. After checking into the posh Imperial Hotel in downtown Hong Kong, I opened the mini-bar and took out two little bottles of Scotch. I wondered what Stephanie was doing. She's probably having sex with somebody, I thought. After finishing the Scotches, I walked down the street a few blocks, entered a bar and ordered a double Scotch and then another. As I sipped my drink, I eyed the bartender, a woman probably in her early thirties, a kindly, attractive face, good figure and a friendly smile. She carried herself with a confidence that was lacking in most Chinese women I had observed, and spoke English fluently with only a slight accent. I asked her if she had been to the United States. "Yes, I went to NYU for two years," she said. "Do you have plans for the evening, sir?"

"My name is Boyd, and no, I don't," I said.

"Would you like me to come to your hotel room for a little fun?" she asked. I was shocked at first, but then remembered Hong Kong was supposed to be a wild place. She's probably a hooker, I thought.

"Well, maybe. How about another drink first?"

"Sure," she said. "I charge $500 in advance for an hour, and my boss follows us and waits for me downstairs," she said.

Hmm. It might be fun, I thought. I've never been with a hooker. I didn't feel any loyalty to Stephanie.

"Okay," I said. "When do you want the money?"

"Now, please," she said. I pulled my wallet out and gave her five hundred. "I'm Cheryl," she said, as she held out her hand. "Nice to meet you, Boyd."

"My pleasure, Cheryl," I said.

When we walked in the door of my hotel room, Cheryl shook off her sandals, pulled off her T-shirt, shorts and panties, and went into the bathroom. I heard her peeing. My knees shook. *What the fuck am I doing? I can't do this*, I thought. Cheryl came back into the room and smiled at me, apparently waiting for me to do something.

"Cheryl, I can't do this," I said.

Without hesitation, she said, "I wondered, Boyd. I noticed you were nervous, and, frankly, you don't seem like the type. Well, you paid for an hour, and I can't give you your money back. Would you like to talk?"

"Sure," I said.

As she put her clothes back on. I said, "I think I just decided to have sex with you to get back at my wife. She cheated on me. She's drinking too much, partying, using cocaine. And we have three young children. It's a terrible environment for them."

"What have you done about it?" she asked.

"Nothing, really," I said.

"Have you given her any ultimatums?"

"No, not really."

"It seems like you might be drinking too much too," she said.

"Yeah, I sure am. And I'm using cocaine too, just not as much as she is."

"How long have the two of you been using?" she asked.

"About a year."

"And I bet you haven't cheated on her, right?"

"Right," I said.

Cheryl was quiet for a few moments. "Well, I'm nobody to tell someone how to live their life," she said. "But I'd say you should get out of this relationship."

"Maybe," I said. "Thanks for listening."

"Sure," she said. "And if you need to talk more, come back to the bar. If you come before eight in the evening on a weekday, there's usually nobody around, except me." She got up, gave me a hug and walked out the door.

I arrived home about seven on the Saturday night before Thanksgiving, tired and hungry. Nobody was home. After carrying my suitcase to the bedroom, I looked in the refrigerator: milk, bread, cheese, butter, baby food, and beer. I grabbed my keys, opened the garage door, and got into my Mustang GT. A beer bottle lay on the floor of the passenger side next to an empty pack of Camels. Stephanie did not drink beer or smoke Camels. None of her girlfriends smoked Camels.

I picked up Enchiladas Suizas from Pancho's, and when I got back home, the kids were watching TV in the family room. Stephanie and Anita sat in the living room. Stephanie wore a tight white shirt that showed off her bare, flat midriff and the outline of her breasts, and soft red cotton shorts that clung to her. She stood up without saying anything. No panty lines. Her eyes were bloodshot, her nose red. She picked up her purse and a sweater and headed for the garage.

"See ya later," she said, as she opened the door.

"Stephanie, wait," I yelled, but she walked out.

Anita said, "I'm going up to my room, Boyd. I'll be back down to put the kids to bed a little later." She hurried out the back door.

I talked to the kids a bit and ate the enchiladas. I went to bed when Anita came down to put the kids to bed. I couldn't sleep, agonizing about leaving Stephanie, trying to imagine not living with the children, and worrying that they would be in jeopardy if I left them with Stephanie. I wanted out of this crazy life.

I couldn't sleep, but I didn't want to take drugs, so I went to the office to get my work organized for the week. I got home about three in the morning and went to bed.

Stephanie didn't come home. When I got home from work the next day, she stood in front of the bedroom mirror in a new black dress, with black heels, the kind that click loudly on a hardwood floor. Without saying anything she turned around and went into the bathroom. I could hear her snorting coke. She came out. "I'm going to Cassidy's," she said.

"Where were you last night?" I asked.

She looked down. "At Jake's," she said.

"Is that who drove my car while I was in Asia?" I asked.

"Yeah, we went to Catalina last weekend," she said. Her voice was as calm and emotionless as if she had told me they had gone to the liquor store to pick up some beer.

I felt like I had been hit by lightning. How could she tell me this so casually? She's drunk, I thought. She usually is these days. I have to get out of here.

"I'm going to leave you," I said. "I can't take this."

"Okay, if that's what you want, but please stay until after Thanksgiving. My mom and stepdad and Anita's parents are coming over for Thanksgiving. I don't want to have to explain to everybody why you're not here on Thanksgiving. It's only a few days away."

The thought of leaving was scary. I didn't understand what I was afraid of. I just wished there was something I could do to save my marriage. I wasn't thinking clearly. I was hurt and angry, and I felt hopeless, like it really didn't matter what I did. My life was chaos. What would a few more days matter, I thought.

"All right. I'll stay for Thanksgiving," I said.

I went to bed about eleven and woke up when Stephanie got into bed, landing hard on her side. I could smell the tequila and perspiration mixed with her *Charlie*. It was a little after three. She pressed her naked body against me and slipped her hand down my briefs. We fondled each other. She was wet—from Jake, I figured. With my erection throbbing, I convinced myself for a few moments that I didn't care anymore. We fucked until I came. She climbed off, and I went to sleep.

I trudge down Harvard Street in early December as the first winter storm wanes. Snow is piled on both sides of the sidewalk, leaving just enough room for one person to walk. The snowflakes meander down silently and settle on the white ground. I wonder why it always seems so quiet when it's snowing. It's below freezing as the unseen sun sets, so ice is forming. I walk with chicken-like steps to avoid slipping. My whole attention is focused on getting to the Renaissance Restaurant without slipping on the ice. After I sit down at a table and exchange pleasantries with the server, I think more about that emotionally wrenching and drug-and-alcohol-drenched second half of 1977. I've thought about it a lot since then, so I know it won't make me cry now. I'm done with the crying. In that week before Thanksgiving I think Stephanie was close to a breakdown. So was I. If I had been thinking more clearly I might have made my staying for Thanksgiving conditional upon her going in for rehab. I felt too sorry for myself and was too unstable to consider help for Stephanie.

I couldn't look myself in the mirror and see what I had become. Had I been rational, I would have left Stephanie before I went to Asia and avoided some of the pain I suffered on my return. I had numbed myself with drugs and alcohol, and couldn't feel much but general malaise. I couldn't see that staying with her was worse than any loneliness I would suffer if I left. Before I went to Asia, I had the false hope that somehow something would happen to change things, but I did nothing to make anything happen. It probably was too late anyway.

Chapter Eighteen

I checked in at Barnaby's the day after Thanksgiving. If I had been serious about leaving Stephanie, I would have looked for an apartment that weekend. She called me at the office Monday.

"Please move to the new house with us, Boyd. Everything will be different there. I promise. The children need you. I need you. We'll be a family again, and we'll get our sex life back on track." She knew what would get me back.

"I'll think about it," I said.

"Anita is moving to Washington with Dan and the baby," she said. *That's why she needs me,* I thought.

I really wanted to move back. I was lonely. I couldn't face failure again. I didn't want to live apart from my children. What would I do with Lisa? I couldn't leave her with Stephanie. We would have to sell the new house right away if I didn't move in. I couldn't afford two places. We would lose all the money we put into it. There were a lot of reasons I thought of. I believed what I wanted to believe—that Stephanie would come to her senses. I moved into the new house. If I had understood my motivation better, I might have realized that it probably was Stephanie's promise of sex that I really couldn't resist. Without realizing it, I was desperate to allay my sexual insecurity.

The first night at the new house, with boxes all around us, Stephanie made good on her promise of sex. We had good sex several times that week. My spirits rose. The house was as peaceful as it could be with three children. No parties. No cocaine, as far as I knew, and a moderate amount of alcohol. Stephanie cooked dinner for the family every night.

A week before Christmas I came home from work to Pat, Bonnie, Jennifer and her boyfriend, Rich—she and John had divorced—and a girl I didn't know playing gin on the family room floor. A mirror with lines of coke sat beside Pat. "Merry Christmas," somebody said. Oh, god, no, I thought. I walked into the bedroom. There was no door between the master bedroom and bathroom where the Jacuzzi hummed. Stephanie was in the Jacuzzi with a glass of cognac.

"Where are the kids?" I asked.

"Jeff and Jennifer are at Mrs. Backer's. Lisa's sleeping over with a girlfriend," she said. "Come on in."

Well, I suppose I shouldn't deny her a party once in a while, I thought. It is Christmas season. I undressed and joined her. I could feel my muscles relax from the warmth of the churning water. "It feels really good," I said.

"Yeah," she said, "This is the best feature of the house. Her breasts floated on top of the water. I imagined the rest of her body below and got hard. I moved toward her and massaged her breasts.

"I'm too warm," she said. "I'm getting out."

I got out too, pulled on my shorts, and went out to the family room. Richard asked if I wanted to take his place in the gin game. I did a couple of lines of coke, sat down, and picked up my hand, a good one, mostly hearts. Richard stood and watched. Stephanie did a couple of lines, her breasts spilling from her robe as she bent over. I also caught a glimpse of her ass under the short robe. So did Richard, I thought. Oh, well. In a few minutes Stephanie got up and went into the bedroom. I didn't notice Richard leave. I played my winning hand, and then another.

"Hold on just a minute. I have to pee," I said. I hurried through the bedroom door and into the bathroom to the toilet. As I peed, I looked over toward the tub. I had to stare a few seconds to realize what was happening. Richard was sitting on the edge of the Jacuzzi, naked, his feet in the water. Stephanie was in the water, kneeling between his legs, sucking his cock. Neither noticed me. I stood speechless for a moment, as I finished peeing.

"What is going on?" I finally said, as if I didn't know; rage, but no other words popped into my mind. They broke apart, but said nothing. Richard pulled on his pants, grabbed his shirt and, with head down, left with a faint, "Sorry."

Stephanie said nothing for a moment. She looked down at the water. "I'm sorry. I didn't mean to. He came in and grabbed my head and shoved his cock in."

"Oh, bullshit, Stephanie. From what I saw, you weren't re-sisting in the slightest." *If I hadn't come in, they would have been fucking by now*, I thought.

I felt about to burst from the pressure of anger and hate, as I walked downstairs and out the door, turning right at the side-walk, going nowhere. *I have to leave her*, I thought. I walked around the block. My anger turned to sorrow. When I went back in and up the stairs, everyone had left, and Stephanie was sitting up in bed, sipping on a drink.

I pulled my large suitcase down from the closet shelf and began packing. "What are you doing?" she asked.

"What does it look like?"

"I'm sorry, Boyd. I really didn't mean to. I was drunk."

"I can't accept that, Stephanie. I don't do anything like that when I'm drunk."

She looked away.

I checked back in at Barnaby's. The vision of Stephanie and Richard stayed with me. But when she called a few days later and asked me to come over, I went. She initiated sex, then told me she was going to have surgery for possible cervical cancer. I agreed to stay until she recovered. The parties and her abuse of drugs and alcohol continued, and so did sex until her surgery. She knew what she had to do to keep me there; she knew that she was a sex object for me. I wasn't aware of it at the time. I thought I loved her, but I avoided spending time with her. I didn't consider her needs. I didn't want a relationship. I just wanted sex from her and the comfort of thinking I had a family, nothing much more.

After writing about Stephanie as a sex object, I realize that until recently I always looked upon women I met as sex objects. When I saw a woman, her physical appearance was all I considered at first. Looking back, I avoided women that were not physically attractive to me, when it was practical. It has only been since I became close to Kate and to Howard's daughter, Carla, in non-romantic relationships that I have been able to look at them and other women as whole human beings. I believe that they, unknowingly, changed my view of women. Both were uninterested in sex with me, but we connected platonically. I got to know them well and appreciate their strengths, intelligence and humanity. We became like family to each other. Of course, they are sexual beings, as we all are in part, but I did not look at them in that way. I was finally able to accept women as whole human beings.

Three months after Stephanie's surgery, I was still with her. I finally drove around Manhattan Beach looking for signs for apartments for rent. I found a dinghy one-bedroom. I couldn't live there. Our nice houses had spoiled me. I felt overwhelmingly sad. I didn't want to leave my family. I sat in my car and cried. I drove to a bar near where Christie and I had lived in Granada Hills. I drank four rusty nails, my first since Christie had gotten sick in Colorado. I fell asleep in the car. It was dark when I woke up—eight o'clock when I got home. I walked into the kitchen. Stephanie was washing dishes.

"Hi, where've you been?" she asked.

"Oh, just driving around," I said. "I'm depressed. I don't want to leave. I'll see how it goes."

"Okay," was all she said.

A week or so later, after work, my secretary, Dora, and I went down to the Greek restaurant on the first floor for a drink. "Order a glass of wine for me, please, something sweet," she said. "I don't drink much." What a relief that would be, I thought.

She took her glasses off, and we looked at each other for a moment and smiled. She had blue eyes and medium blond hair with natural loose curls and that creamy pale skin that blonds have.

When we finished our wine, I walked her to her car. "Thanks for the wine," she said. "I know you're going through tough times. If you need to talk, you know how to find me."

I smiled and moved closer. "Thanks," I said. I put my hand on her shoulder and kissed her. She kissed me back, and I pushed my tongue into her mouth.

She didn't resist, but when we ended the kiss, she said, "That was nice, but if we're going to do that any more, you'll have to leave Stephanie. I don't fool around with married men."

"I understand," I said.

I guess she really likes me, I thought, as I waived to her. *She's a really nice girl. She doesn't drink much. She's quiet and conservative. It would be peaceful with her as a girlfriend, and I wouldn't be alone.*

I went home early that Friday to pack for Stephanie's ten-year high school reunion in Pasadena. I wondered if she'd take cocaine to the reunion. She was in the bedroom packing.

I started to pack. "Oh, Boyd. I'm afraid you can't go to the reunion. I'm sorry. I couldn't get a babysitter."

"What about Mrs. Backer?"

"She can't. She has some family obligation this weekend. And Amy is out of town. I couldn't find anyone. Doug is going with me as my date. You don't mind, do you?"

"I suppose not," I said. Doug was African-American, and Stephanie had told me she was not attracted to African-American men. But I knew her not being able to get a babysitter was a ruse. She could always get a babysitter, and she had known about the reunion for months. She just didn't want me around. *She probably wants to fuck somebody.* Visions of the men she'd been with filled my head.

An hour later, she carried her suitcase out the door and set it down. "See you Sunday," she said. "It should be around mid-afternoon. There's a brunch Sunday at the hotel."

"Okay," I said. "See ya Sunday." I went up to her expecting a kiss or a hug, but she turned around, grabbed her suitcase and headed for the garage.

That Sunday was Father's Day. I had a hangover: dry mouth, churning stomach and pounding head. I wondered how many guys Stephanie had slept with the night before. I took two Tylenol and went to make coffee. The kids' cereal bowls and puddles of milk were on the kitchen table. I heard their voices outside. I gulped down a large glass of orange juice and started the coffee maker. I sat down heavily in front of the only clean place on the table. *I really should leave Stephanie,* I thought. *This is no way to live.*

After I had two pieces of toast, my stomach felt a little better, and the Tylenol quelled my headache. I still had that wrung-out hangover feeling. *Will I ever stop drinking so much?* I wondered.

About eleven o'clock Jennifer Weil called and invited the kids to go with her and her son, Ezra, to the carnival at Old Town Mall. I really didn't want to owe her any favors, but I said yes. Having them out of my hair would be a relief. I drove the kids to Jennifer's house and went back to bed. I woke up in an hour feeling worse.

At about two I heard Stephanie's car in the driveway. She strolled in, Doug behind, carrying her suitcase. Her eyes were bloodshot and her nose red. She patted it with a tissue. Slimy white stuff clung to the corners of her mouth.

"Looks like you had a rough night," I said.

"Yeah, it was pretty wild. I don't remember much."

I followed them upstairs. Doug took a bottle of coke out of his pocket and handed it to Stephanie. "This is yours," he said.

"Have some," she said.

He took a snort in each nostril, as did she. She offered me some. I declined. Doug left.

"Where are the kids?" asked Stephanie.

"Jennifer took them and Ezra to the carnival at Old Town," I said.

"That's nice," she said.

"So, tell me about the reunion," I said.

"Oh, it was fun seeing all those people. I got to dance a lot. The food wasn't very good. I have some pictures. I'll get them."

She went into the bedroom and returned with some Polaroid pictures. I glanced at the first two. The third picture I stared at. It showed Stephanie and Chris, one of the guys she'd slept with when we were separated, with their arms around each other. Stephanie's eyes were glazed over, her drunk look. In the background was an unmade bed.

"So, you were with Chris, I see—in a hotel room."

"Well, yeah, he was there. We didn't do anything, if that's what you're thinking."

"That you can remember?"

I threw the photos on the floor and walked out. Then I turned around and came right back in. Stephanie was changing into her nightgown.

"I've had enough, Stephanie. I'm leaving you, and this time I won't come back."

"Do what you have to do," she said. She turned away.

As I write about leaving Stephanie, I think about how phony my gesture was. I didn't leave because of the photo. I didn't suddenly summon the courage. I was finally able to leave because I thought I wouldn't be alone. Dora was waiting in the wings.

I went to the closet and for the last time pulled down the large suitcase. Stephanie walked out of the room without looking at me or saying anything. I heard the kids laughing and shouting downstairs. Jennifer must have brought them back. I focused on packing. When I had packed everything I needed I closed the suitcase, picked it up and walked slowly down the stairs. I grabbed my briefcase from the kitchen floor and walked out to the garage. The kids were playing in the back yard. Stephanie didn't come out. When I dropped the suitcase into the trunk of my car I had a sense I was doing something momentous that would change the rest of my life. I knew at a deep level I had finally made a decision that would improve—no, save—my life. It felt uplifting. The pressure cooker that had been my body all this time felt like it was expelling the steam.

As I drove down Manhattan Avenue, I passed Becker's Bakery, where we always bought the kids' birthday cakes. I turned up Manhattan Beach Boulevard past Highland Avenue, where we lived before we bought our first house, past the Safeway, where we had shopped for nine years. I turned left on Ardmore, by the walking path next to the abandoned railroad tracks. A dozen or so people were jogging down the path. My feelings turned to a mellow sadness. I wasn't scared anymore. I left my car with the valet and checked into Barnaby's. I hadn't taken any cocaine with me, and I didn't buy any afterwards. I drank less.

It starts to snow again. In my apartment I pull off my clothes, except my shorts, and put on a sweatshirt. I light a stick of incense, Nag Champa. I turn off the lights and sit on my couch, tucking a leg under me, like girls sit. I gaze at the flakes swirling outside my window like pillow feathers descending from above. I think about what I might have done to save my marriage with Stephanie. A while later, I write. Since then I have rewritten the conclusion of this part many times. Now, another winter has come. I sit down at the computer and delete the conclusion and start over. I think I am finally ready to write the truth—at least my truth.

I carried my failure with Christie to my relationship with Stephanie. Given that failure, my need to prove that I was a man and my fear of loneliness were even stronger. My quick sexual successes with Stephanie and her demonstrated adoration, generated in me powerful feelings of confidence, pride and manhood secured. For years I looked upon the early period with Stephanie as the happiest years of my life. I didn't realize it, but that was because I finally felt like a man, physically and emotionally adored by a woman I saw as exceedingly beautiful and sexy. My sexual insecurities were at bay, temporarily.

As I had with Christie, I looked on Stephanie as a sex object, inferior to me in every other way. With Stephanie, at first, I was inflated with male ego from her physical and emotional adoration—much more than I was with Christie because I saw Stephanie as much sexier and more beautiful. I was so grateful that I was willing to give up control of my own life to give her whatever she wanted. That was our unexpressed, unconscious contract. My expectations are clear to me now. I thought that I had to give her everything she wanted to keep her sex and adoration. I believe she came to expect that, but what she expected initially I must speculate about.

She had been neglected by her mother, who gave greater attention to her younger sister. Her father had given her a taste of the security of male adoration, but he died when she was sixteen. To feel secure she needed the love and attention of a man. She needed to be noticed, and there is a lot of noticing in sex. I think she also wanted material security and status. Since she was unwilling to go to college, she needed a man to provide those.

Our contract was that she would give me all the sex and adoration I needed to make me feel like a man and the prestige of a beautiful wife, and I would give her the notice and attention through sex and adoration, and also the status and material security that she needed. The early sex was so good because it drove away my sexual insecurity and gave her some of the noticing that she needed.

She demonstrated her needs and insecurities by demanding and acquiring more and more material things that satisfied that need and her need for status. When I stopped noticing her by withholding my attention, except for sex, and tried to withhold material things, she felt betrayed, and responded by denying me what I needed—sex.

I demonstrated my needs and insecurities by an almost singular focus on sex. I was happy only when we had regular sex. I was devastated when she withheld it and almost destroyed when she betrayed me. I kept going back to her when she promised or provided sex, even in the face of the pain and humiliation she had made me suffer. I left for good only when I had another potential sex partner available—Dora.

Neither Stephanie nor I could perform our end of the contract. She couldn't eliminate all my male insecurities, and I couldn't give her everything she wanted—for long. Once we both broke the contract, failing to fulfill the other's expectations, it would have taken a monumental, perhaps superhuman, effort to repair the damage and enter into a different contract. Neither of us was up to it.

Why couldn't I leave, despite my suffering? Why did I keep coming back? For the sexual goodies, and because I couldn't face another failed marriage. My life had been driven by achievement. Good people didn't fail at marriage—certainly not twice. I had let my love affair with Stephanie define who I was. I didn't realize that fulfillment had to be based on myself, on who I was, not on the love of someone else.

My expectations of both Christie and Stephanie were similar: sex to ameliorate my insecurities and status by way of marriage. Although the result was the same, it played out differently because Stephanie's needs and expectations were different from Christie's.

Maybe Kate was right—Stephanie was the love of my life, and I hers. I don't know. It must remain one of those mysteries of the human heart. But I know now that the marriage couldn't work with the unconscious contract we entered into and could not possibly perform.

Understanding something about my role in the destruction of my marriage with Stephanie and the similarities to my marriage with Christie brings, not the jolt of an epiphany, but the melancholy peace that comes with some understanding of myself and what drove me. Digging up what was buried within me is bringing it to the surface. Writing is letting me dig deep; it is healing me.

PART THREE
Susan:
"For Better or For Worse"

Chapter Nineteen

I'm on an AMTRAK train from Jacksonville to Boston, a journey of twenty-five hours. I gaze out the window at the passing browns of bare limbs and scattered red and orange foliage of late fall along the southeast coast, barely visible as the sky darkens. I'm ready to write about my marriage to Susan. *This will be the hardest*, I think. I have always believed that marriage had the best chance of working out, and I like Susan a lot.

She told me after our divorce and repeated again recently that three years after our marriage I withdrew from her emotionally and never returned. She's probably right.

I know I stopped wanting sex with her. I'm puzzled. *Why did I pull away from her?*

I don't want to get back together with her now, but I just agreed to stay at her house for a few days during the holidays—why?

Three years and six years seem to be the hex, I think, as

the train stops in Savannah. After three years of marriage with Christie, she began to complain about my working long hours, and sex with her was infrequent and no longer interesting. She told me after the divorce that she questioned the marriage after three years. After about six years she left me. Stephanie started rejecting me sexually after we lived together three years. After six years, she asked for a separation and emotionally left me. Susan told me I withdrew from her after three years of marriage, and after six years she asked for a separation, though I talked her out of it. This was the pattern. It was as if I wanted to be married; I wanted somebody in my life; but I didn't want the relationship to interfere with my life. Three years was as long as I could stay motivated.

During the four years between Stephanie and Susan I made no effort to understand what I had contributed to the destruction of the marriages. I believed I got divorced because Christie and Stephanie were crazy. It was that simple.

When I left Stephanie I had been using cocaine for over a year and abusing alcohol for longer. Except for a couple of times with lawyer friends three or four years later, I didn't use cocaine again. I didn't miss it. I significantly reduced my drinking. I moved into an apartment near the beach in Venice. What a relief to escape from the drama of life with Stephanie. The civil rights activists' cry of the sixties came to mind, "Free at last."

I wasn't worried about loneliness anymore. I asked Dora out to dinner a few nights after I left Stephanie. She wore a satin flowered dress that tucked under her breasts, contacts, instead of the glasses she usually wore in the office, and a little makeup. She was twenty-five; I was thirty-seven. I wanted her. As I looked at her across the table sipping a glass of white Zinfandel, I was excited, but at ease. I saw her as quiet, conservative, not histrionic—the opposite of Stephanie. This was our first date, but we had become friends during the two years she had worked for me.

After we ordered, I went to the men's room and called my office, as I usually did in the evening. There was a call from Stephanie on the answering machine: "Call me right away, Boyd. Lisa ran away. She didn't come home for dinner. I called the police. Come home and look for her. I can't. I have to stay with Jeff and Jennifer."

My back and chest tensed up. Gone four days, and Stephanie already has generated a crisis. I wasn't going to let her ruin my date with Dora.

I didn't call her back. I just hoped somebody would find Lisa, and that she would be okay. I called the machine again before we left the restaurant. "Maybe you don't care," Stephanie said on the second recording, "but the police found Lisa a few blocks from home. She's back now, safe and sound." Stephanie had cried wolf so many times that I was numbed by her reports of crisis, but later I felt guilty about putting my date with Dora ahead of my daughter's well-being.

I hadn't talked to my children about my leaving. Although I was close to the edge of some sort of emotional collapse, I have always had trouble viewing that as an acceptable reason. When I recovered from the alcohol and cocaine haze a few days after I left, and life seemed normal for the first time in years, I felt ashamed. I worried about my children's welfare. I had no reason to believe that Stephanie would stop abusing alcohol and using cocaine. I knew Stephanie would never agree to my having custody. I thought about petitioning the court, but my use of drugs and alcohol would come out, which would not only prevent me from getting custody, but would threaten my license to practice law. I tried to assuage my guilt by religiously visiting them.

A week after I left Stephanie, I went over to the house for Jeff's sixth birthday. I had to figure out what to do with Lisa. I couldn't leave her to be Stephanie's Cinderella. I asked Lisa to come to her room with me. "I'll figure out something so you won't have to live with Stephanie, Lisa. Don't worry."

"Please, Daddy, I can't live with her," she said.

"Just be patient," I said. "I'll make sure you don't have to live with her."

The next day, I asked Dora to dinner at my new apartment. I said, "I'll cook."

"I'm impressed," she said.

I cooked steak, artichokes, and baked potatoes. "This is delicious," she said. I beamed. As she chewed her filet mignon, she said that in about five weeks she and her friend Nancy were going to Europe for three or four months. That hit me like a blow to my abdomen. I tried not to show my sadness or fear of being alone.

When I got up to put the dirty dishes on the kitchen counter, she said, "What, no dessert?"

"No, sorry. I don't usually eat dessert."

I came back to the table and kissed her. "I guess I'm dessert," she said. We went to the couch and made out. When I suggested going to the bedroom, she said, "Not tonight. I'm on my period. But there'll be other opportunities." There were.

In about a month Stephanie called and said that she and Jeff and Jennifer were moving to San Clemente, to be near her friend Yolanda. She said she couldn't live in Manhattan Beach anymore. I was sad that the kids would be eighty miles away, but I figured that the environment would be better for them.

I went to move my stuff back to the house the day after Stephanie and the kids left. I couldn't afford rent in Venice and the house payment indefinitely. Lisa was visiting her mother. I unlocked the front door to an empty living room, devoid of furniture or wall hangings. The dining table and chairs were gone. I opened a cupboard—nothing. I flung open one cupboard after another, then pulled open every drawer. They were all empty. Even the trashcan under the sink was gone. Dust balls lingered where the refrigerator had been. I ran upstairs—no bed, no furniture; no towels, sheets or blankets in the linen closet. Nothing on any of the walls. She'd cleaned out the house completely. I was stranded in a big, extravagant house—which was completely unlivable.

I couldn't furnish it. I was a successful lawyer, but I had no money to buy towels and sheets and blankets, not to mention a bed. My credit was so bad because of the unpaid credit card bills Stephanie had run up, I couldn't get credit. I had a home, but I felt homeless. I slept on the floor the first night, and then rented a bed. Until Dora loaned me her furniture while she was in Europe, I ate off of and sat on boxes. By the time the house sold, a year later, I had paid off the debt and had enough money to rent an apartment, but I couldn't afford movers. I moved what I had acquired during the year in a dozen trips in a friend's sixteen-year-old white Cadillac convertible.

The day after I moved back to the house, Lisa, back from the weekend with her mother, told me she wanted to live with her mother. I told her I would think about it. I held back tears. When I was alone in my bedroom, a river of remorse flowed through me. Lisa didn't want to live with me. She preferred to live with the woman who had abandoned her. Then I realized that she had no memory of living with her mother, and until a couple of months earlier, she saw her mother only a few hours a month. Naturally, she wanted to know what it would be like, and I had no appealing alternative to offer her. My mother was taking care of her temporarily while I worked, but Mom told me she wouldn't be able to do it indefinitely. She was seventy-six, and it was too hard on her, she said. Lisa would spend more time with a nanny than with me. Her mother only worked eight hours a day, four days a week.

Gradually, over the next couple of days, the shock and remorse subsided. Lisa was ten. She should have a say in deciding which parent to live with. Her mother wasn't worse than the stepmother I had provided her. I believed Christie had been mentally stable since I had obtained custody of Lisa six years before. I met with Christie at the Charthouse in Sherman Oaks for dinner and told her it was okay with me for Lisa to live with her. She thanked me and cried. We hugged. When I told her dinner was on me, she ordered two entrees and ate everything. She might be mentally stable, but she was still odd. That night I told Lisa. A few days later she was gone.

I met Dora and her girlfriend Nancy in Munich in September, and we toured Germany, Austria and Italy for two weeks, my first trip to Europe. We resumed dating when she returned in November. On December 30th, after we made love on the yellow couch she had loaned me, we talked about what to do on New Year's Eve. I suggested Disneyland. "That would be fun," she said.

As we sailed down I-10, I told her I loved her. Impulsive and terrified of being alone, I asked her to marry me when my divorce from Stephanie became final in February.

Without much pause, she said, "No. I'm not ready for that kind of commitment." In January she moved to Santa Rosa, five hundred miles away.

The morning after Dora left for Santa Rosa, I waited for depression to blow in with the winter Santa Ana winds. I was alone, but it never came. I blunted my loneliness by working long hours and visiting my friends and children. Compared to the trauma of the previous three years, I felt at peace.

My mother died later that year. As the few people who attended her funeral began to leave, Lisa and I watched the workmen toss the first shovels of dirt on top of her coffin. She had few relatives that she was close to, and most of her friends in Manhattan Beach were too old to have convenient transportation to Rose Hills Cemetery fifty miles away. A woman like her should have known more people willing to come to her funeral, I thought. I wondered how many people would come to my funeral.

I felt cold. The warmth of the September afternoon sun was not reaching me. I couldn't watch them shovel dirt on Mommy anymore – at the age of thirty-eight, I still thought of her as Mommy— so I turned and walked to my car, holding Lisa's hand. Mommy dominated my thoughts during the hour and a half drive home in rush hour traffic. I thought about her dream to go to Hawaii—Hawiah, as she called it—and felt guilty for never taking her.

I remembered Mommy a few days before in the hospital. As I held her hand, she whispered, "I want to die." I didn't want her to see me cry, but when she cried, I couldn't help it. I put my head down on the pillow next to hers and kissed her on the cheek. Holding my face next to hers, wet from her tears, I let mine fall on the pillow. After awhile, her rhythmical breathing told me she was asleep.

After a court hearing the next morning, my secretary, in a hesitant tone, told me the hospital called and gave me a number to call back. I called. When I was put through to the head nurse in the ICU, she said, "I'm sorry to tell you, Mr. Lemon: Your mother passed away this morning."

When I got home from the funeral, after taking Lisa to her mother's, I turned on the Dodgers game and plopped down on the couch. I was hungry, but didn't feel like doing anything about it. Now the fearsome loneliness that I had expected months before, flowed through me like the late afternoon fog from the ocean flowing up the hill, wave after wave. I had no parents. I was nobody's son or husband. I had always been one or both. I lived alone. I didn't even have a girlfriend. If I died, nobody would know about it for days, maybe weeks. Nobody cared. I felt empty. It wasn't that I didn't want to live any longer; I felt as if I was wandering in an open, desolate field that stretched infinitely in all directions, like I imagined the desolation after a nuclear war. Nothing; no one there.

In 1980, after five years practicing by myself, I missed the camaraderie of other lawyers. I was invited to join a large law firm in Century City, and I accepted. The firm was in the same block where Ronald Reagan, who was running for President, had an office. A few months later he was elected. The conservative Republicans would have their chance. I expected the rich would get richer and the poor poorer. I was right. At least early in 1981 the American hostages in Iran were released, and the world seemed a little safer, though Reagan ratcheted up the Cold War with the Soviet Union. Still, we had not been involved in a major war since Viet Nam.

The fog of desolation and loneliness soon lifted, replaced by new friends and co-workers in the law firm. By 1980, I had paid off all the old debt and bought a small two-bedroom house on a walk street near the beach. I enlisted the help of Bob Schumann, a friend and real estate broker who agreed to be a co-borrower on the loan, because my credit was still no good.

I continued to pursue the American dream, though I had yet another opportunity to escape the burden of the private practice of law. I didn't need the income that working in a large law firm brought. By 1982 I was Litigation Department Chair of the 125-lawyer firm. Though it was not my dream, I blindly sought the prestige and the money with no realization that it wasn't me. At forty-one, I was still living someone else's life.

Although I didn't feel unhappy, something was missing— a woman? But only if the right one came along. This time I would be careful, I thought.

After Dora, I dated two other women. One was Mary, the woman I had pined over in college. She called me one day, and we dated for a year or so. She wanted to marry me, but I knew she wasn't the right one. I felt proud of myself for turning her down. The other woman, Liz, was a secretary at the law firm. She dumped me after a few dates.

Howard invited a woman from Mexico, Rosa, to stay with me on her vacation in California. Although I hadn't talked to him about the issues between Stephanie and me, apparently he thought it was a struggle for control. He wasn't far off. Howard had married a Latin American woman. He said he hoped that Rosa and I would hit it off, and I could marry a Latin American woman who would be more submissive than American women. I wouldn't have to worry about a "women's libber," he said. I never intended to marry a woman simply because she was submissive, but I saw no harm in Rosa staying in my house for a week. I picked her up at the airport, and she told me about her plans. She had cousins and friends in L.A. that she was going to visit. I don't think she knew Howard was setting her up. We went to dinner a couple of times. We joined Howard and one of his sons at a Dodgers game at Howard's invitation, though I don't think she had any interest in baseball. By the end of the week I felt awkward. I don't know if she did. She was a nice woman, but there was no chemistry. Rosa went home without even a kiss. Howard was trying to help. He needed married life, and he thought I did.

Lisa had been living with Christie for about two years. On New Year's Eve 1980 their next-door neighbor Barbara called. She told me Lisa had been staying with her and her boyfriend for three weeks—I had picked Lisa up there recently, but thought nothing of it. "Christie has disappeared," she said, "and I don't know where she is. I thought you should know."

I drove to Barbara's house and picked up Lisa, who, at the time, was twelve. Christie had another psychotic episode, but eventually was prescribed a medication that has kept her stable ever since. Lisa remained in my custody until she went away to college.

In April 1982 Susan came to work for the Firm as a secretary in the Litigation Department. She was blond, young—thirty-one, I found out later—pretty. My secretary told me a few weeks later that Susan had already gone out with two of my associates. This looks like an opportunity to get laid for the first time in over a year, I thought. I called her on the intercom and asked if she would like to go out to dinner the next night.

"Sure," she said.

When her workday was done, I walked down to her desk. She gathered her stuff, and we went down the elevator and out to the street. I was nervous, but she seemed fully at ease as she chatted on our walk down to Harry's Bar, an upscale Italian restaurant a block away. She told me she was taking acting lessons and wanted to be an actress. *You and every other secretary and waitress in L.A.,* I thought. At dinner she was a great conversationalist. She spoke about herself, and also asked questions about me and seemed genuinely interested. She told me she had a degree in psychology from the University of Hawaii. She had gone to law school at Villanova for a year, but couldn't hack it.

After dinner I ordered a cappuccino and asked her if she would like one.

"Sure," she said. "You're not quite as conservative as you seem in the office."

"I know I project that image. But let me tell you about my liberal credentials."

I proceeded to itemize my work for the ACLU, Long Beach Legal Aid, Robert Kennedy, and Hubert Humphrey, my representing anti-Viet Nam War and civil rights demonstrators, and even my experimentation with pot and cocaine. I was still trying to get off the cusp and into the younger generation.

"Okay, okay, you're not conservative," she said, laughing. She told me, after we married, that my monologue was one of the funniest things she had ever heard.

We talked on, during the second cappuccino, the third, the fourth and the fifth.

"I'm feeling kinda woozy," I said.

"Me too," she said. "It's no wonder; we've had five cappuccinos."

"So?"

"I don't know about you," she said, "but five alcoholic drinks after two glasses of wine are enough to make me woozy."

"You mean there's alcohol in here?" I said, pointing at the cup.

"Yeah," she laughed. "Didn't you know that?"

"God, no!" The only other time I'd had cappuccino was in Italy, and there had never been alcohol in it.

"You know, it's after one o'clock," she said. "Tomorrow's a workday. I'd better be getting home."

I arrived at the office the next morning at nine-thirty with a hangover. Susan was at her desk typing. I went into my office and closed the door, which I usually left open. I called my secretary and asked her to bring me a cup of coffee, a glass of water, and two Tylenol.

"Hard night last night?" she said.

"Yeah," I said.

"You'd better be careful. Everybody knows who you were with."

So I was going to be the star of the office gossip now? Well, that should do something to reform my conservative image.

Susan asked me Friday at about 4:00 if I would join her and some others from the firm at Hamburger Hamlet's bar across the street. I joined the group a little after five and sat next to Susan. To catch her attention, I put my hand on her knee, prominently displayed below a short skirt. She jumped.

"Next week," I said, "I'm leaving to try a case in Washington D.C. for three weeks."

"Call me while you're there, if you have a chance," she said.

Chapter Twenty

At the trial in Washington D.C. I had co-counsel and two younger attorneys to assist us. After dinner my evenings were mostly free. One evening in the first week Susan called me on business. We chatted a little after we took care of business. The next evening I thought of her and decided to call her. The second week of the trial, Susan called me nearly every night. She told me she liked smart, articulate men. I saw myself as smart and articulate. *This is going well*, I thought. One night at the end of the second week, after we chatted for a while, she asked me what I was doing.

"Just lying here in bed naked," I said.

"Ooo," she said. "You're turning me on."

When I told her I needed to go to sleep, she said, "Is this just a telephone affair, or am I going to see you after this trial is over?"

"I want to see you," I said. "Why don't you pick me up at the airport?"

"Okay, I can do that," she said.

While I was in D.C., Lisa stayed with Liz, the secretary I had dated. I called to check in one night. Liz said that Lisa's mother was in Hawaii and wasn't going to attend Lisa's middle school graduation. "Neither of her parents will be there. Sad," she said.

I felt guilty for the lack of attention I had given my children, especially Lisa, my first-born. On graduation day, after court was over, I boarded a flight to LAX. I didn't tell Lisa. I arrived just before the graduates were to march to the stage, and sat down in the audience, excited with anticipation of what Lisa would do when she saw me.

The traditional music started. The graduates marched up the aisle. Lisa was near the front. She didn't see me as she walked up to the stage to her chair. She turned around facing the audience, expressionless, as the rest of the graduates marched up. She looked down, then out at the audience, right at me. She put her hands to her mouth—first tears, then a huge smile through the tears. When the ceremony was over, we rushed toward each other in the foyer. We hugged for a long time. We both cried.

Thursday of the third week, I knew the trial would conclude the next day. I booked a flight to arrive at LAX at nine o'clock Friday night and called Susan.

"I'll be at the gate with bells on," she said. "I have a question. I hope I'm not being presumptuous, but should I bring my overnight bag with me when I pick you up?"

"Well...yeah," I said.

As I emerged from the gate, I saw her standing in a crowd— a flash of blond hair, a bright blue terrycloth strapless dress that hugged her breasts. She smiled widely when she saw me. I walked up and kissed her.

We drove to my house. Lisa was with her mother that weekend. We sat on the bed and talked until nearly midnight. She got up and grabbed her overnight case. "I'll be back in a minute," she said. I undressed, except for my briefs, and got into bed.

She came out in a short beige nightgown. "I can't believe I'm doing this on the second date," she said, climbing into bed.

"I'm very glad you are," I said, kissing her, "and I hope you will be, too."

"Why are you wearing these?" She said, as she pulled off my briefs, almost knocking me out of bed.

"I don't know," I said. "I won't anymore."

I pulled her nightgown off over her head. We held each other close and made love. I was nervous, so I didn't feel much passion. I worried that she didn't either.

I awoke early, as I always had since having children. At eight I walked over to Safeway and bought a box of fresh raspberries, cream and bread.

Susan walked into the kitchen in her nightgown, sleepy-eyed. "What is this? Oh my god—raspberries, my favorite. You sure know the quickest way to my heart."

We ate breakfast, took a shower together, and made love again—no nerves this time. Originally, my only interest was getting laid, but there is more to this girl than that, I thought. She was also smart and articulate, though again, I was after a woman I could feel superior to, a secretary eleven years younger than I, who had flunked out of law school. I hadn't tried to date any of the many women lawyers I regularly saw.

For the next month Susan and I went out to dinner a lot, watched movies and talked and talked. She was the easiest person to talk to I had ever known. My shyness didn't matter. And unlike Stephanie she didn't try to control me and didn't complain about my reading the Sunday paper. She read it with me. She also understood I worked long hours, and she didn't complain. The sex got better and better.

Her father came to visit for a week at the end of July, and the three of us had dinner. I liked him right away. One Saturday while her father was visiting, she came to my house to pick up a dress she had left in my closet. Lisa was in her room.

Susan and I walked over to my bedroom closet. She kissed

me. "You are so delicious," she said. "I have to get back to Daddy, but I'm turned on. I can't leave without making love."

She closed the door, kicked off her sandals and pulled her shorts and panties off. I started to untie my shoes. "Never mind your shoes. This has to be fast." She undid my pants and pulled them and my underwear down. She pushed me down on the bed and kissed me until I got hard, then climbed on top. Thirty seconds after we came, she was fully dressed and out the door. I lay on the bed laughing.

I heard a knock on the door. I pulled up my pants, sat up, and said, "Come in."

Lisa said, "What was going on in here?"

"Never mind," I said. "You don't want to know."

"Oh, my god," she said. "Daddy!" She was fourteen and curious about sex, but like most children was shocked at her dad's sexual side.

Though the thought scared me, I began to think Susan might be wife number three. She didn't seem to have any of the issues Stephanie had, and although I wasn't as wildly passionate about her as I had been about Stephanie, I thought that was good. I'd be more rational. I wouldn't marry impulsively again. I didn't think about whether I should marry at all.

In early August Susan went to Portland, Oregon, and I agreed to feed her cats twice a day. The first time I walked into her apartment I saw papers piled on every surface—the couch, end tables, coffee table and the floor—bills, receipts, magazines, letters, envelopes, books, ads, a diary, junk mail of every kind. I wondered where she ate. The cats sashayed around my legs, making it difficult to walk. I fed them, and they were no longer interested in me. I went into the bedroom—same thing—papers piled everywhere, including the bed. How did she live this way, I wondered. I didn't think about how someday it would drive me crazy.

I wanted to take a test drive. One warm summer night at Harry's Bar we were sharing a dessert Susan had ordered—no cappuccinos this time. I said, "Why don't you move in with me? I'd like to live with you so we can see if marriage would work."

"Oh, my," she said. "I wasn't expecting this. I don't know. I'll have to think about it. My parents won't approve. I've never lived with any guy before. I like my independence. I'll think about it."

I'm sitting in Atomic Bean Café in Cambridge with my computer and a cup of green tea. I decide to do writing practice on the topic: "Why Did I Think I Had to Marry Susan?" "Go for ten minutes," I can hear Natalie Goldberg saying, as if I were at a workshop.

I was happier having Susan as a companion and sex partner than I had been single. Susan was almost thirty-two. She had said she wanted to have a family and that she wasn't happy being single. I knew in time she would stop dating me if I hadn't proposed. Having her live with me might delay that confrontation, and it would give me a better basis to decide if we should marry.

I still hadn't tried to understand my role in my divorces so that I could try to avoid a third one. I continued to think Christie and Stephanie were crazy. Naturally, Howard and my other friends supported that view. Before I dated Susan I still felt lonely at times, and I thought marriage would eliminate that. I continued to think that loneliness was something to avoid. Although Susan was the fourth woman I had dated in the four years I had been single, I still feared I might not get another chance to marry. Two of the previous three had dumped me. I liked Susan, and I didn't want to lose her.

A few days after I brought up living together, she told me she was concerned because she wanted to have a baby, and I already had three children. I was not opposed to having another child. I wanted the chance to help raise a child to adulthood, to be more involved than I had been with my other children. I told her if we married she could have one child. She said that was fine.

I also told her I did not want a stay-at-home wife to support. "I had enough of that with Stephanie," I said. I had talked to her about the travails of my marriage to Stephanie.

"I'm not Stephanie," she snapped. "I want to work."

The next evening we were both working late. She came into my office and said, "May I interrupt you?"

"Sure," I said.

She sat down in one of my client chairs. "I'm doing this with great trepidation," she said. "I'll try living with you and Lisa on one condition."

"What's that?" I asked.

"I'll live with you for six months. Then we'll either set a wedding date, or I move out."

"Couldn't we make it a year?" I asked.

"No," she said. "It's hard enough for me to agree to six months, but I think that's fair. That should be enough time."

"Okay, I'll go along with that," I said. I smiled. She didn't.

"I'll move in over Labor Day weekend."

"That's fine," I said, "but you know Lisa and I will be in Guatemala visiting Howard. We'll be back the next weekend."

"That's okay," she said. "It'll give me and the cats time to get settled."

When Lisa and I returned from Guatemala, Susan and her two cats, Klutzy and Blaze, were ensconced. After Susan and I hugged and kissed, I walked around the little house. Only a few things had changed. Her hair and skin care products and hair dryer were in the bathroom. The closet and dresser were more densely packed. There was a new couch in the living room.

Susan was kind and loving toward Lisa and didn't unduly control her. She let Lisa continue doing the chores she had been doing—laundry and dishes—no more, no less. To impress on Lisa that Susan and I were both parent figures, one night we sat down with Lisa and proposed a curfew. Lisa agreed it was reasonable. Having been subjected to her mother and Stephanie for comparison, Lisa respected Susan.

Once when I came home I found them in Lisa's room deep in conversation. That was a frequent occurrence. I explained to Susan Lisa's tumultuous relationship with Stephanie. I appreciated Susan showing Lisa love and kindness, and I told her so.

"Some day you'll really believe that I'm not Stephanie, I hope," Susan said.

One night during dinner, Lisa, said, "Daddy likes your big boobs."

"Boyd, you said that to your daughter!" Susan said.

"Well, I guess so."

"I hope you've noticed other things," she said.

"Of course, I have," and I leaned over and kissed her on the cheek. She pulled her face away, shaking her head back and forth.

"Thanks, Lisa," I said, as she headed for her room.

My life was better. Susan was easy to get along with. I had somebody to talk to, to cook dinner for Lisa and me, and Susan and I had regular sex. It didn't occur to me that I should have stronger feelings if I was going to consider marrying her.

One night Susan told me she had returned from the market and smelled the unmistakable aroma of marijuana burning. Lisa ran from her bedroom, and pulled out a bowl from the microwave. She was drying it, she explained to Susan. Susan told Lisa she didn't approve, but waited for me to come home to let me decide what to do. We had a talk with Lisa about the risks and dangers of pot, realistically, I think, and told her we didn't want it in our house. If she continued to smoke pot, we didn't know about it.

Before Susan came to live with us, Lisa had been out of

control. I came home one night to find a bottle of tequila almost empty. I woke her up, and she was so drunk she couldn't stand. A few weeks later, I came home to find my closet and dresser drawers ransacked. The window was broken. I looked around the house. Nothing valuable was missing, just my Manhattan Beach Hometown Fair T-shirt and portable radio. It seemed more like a prank than a burglary—teenagers, I thought. I yelled for Lisa to come in. "Considering what's missing, I would say this was done by your friends. Wouldn't you?"

She hung her head. "I think I know who did it," she said.

"This has got to stop," I said.

"I know, Dad."

After Susan moved in, Lisa settled down except for one curfew violation, though we wrung our hands over her loser boyfriends. That problem resolved itself when she went away to college.

Susan and I went to a party one Friday after work. I had broken my left ankle jumping from one deck to another on my sailboat. My leg was in a cast. I was supposed to keep it elevated, so I sat down with my left leg draped across a couch and my right foot on the floor. Liz sat down between my legs, and we chatted. In my peripheral vision I saw Susan look our way with her eyes burning. Then she turned around and left the room. I told Liz I needed to get up. I walked on crutches after Susan.

"Would you come into the bedroom, please," said Susan. I did. She continued, "You're humiliating me, the way you're carrying on with that woman."

"Wha'd'ya mean," I said. "I have no romantic interest in Liz any more. We were just talking."

"Yeah, with her sitting between your legs? Why do you think she did that?"

"I don't know. Where would she sit? I was taking up the whole couch."

"She didn't have to sit there," said Susan. "She's trying to humiliate me. And you let her."

"I'm sorry you feel that way, but she's a friend of mine, and I'm going to talk to her."

"Fine," said Susan. "I'm leaving. You just stay here with Liz and talk to her all you want. I'll see you at home later."

I stayed a few minutes longer and went home.

"Did you have fun with Liz?" Susan asked when I walked in.

"No, I didn't talk to her anymore," I said.

"I know you're not cheating on me, Boyd," she said. "It's not that. It's that Liz is your ex-girlfriend, and she's trying to get you back. Everybody knows it. And you let her sit there making goo-goo eyes at you, and let her humiliate me. I don't understand why you would do that."

"I'm sorry," I said. "I didn't see it that way."

A couple of weeks later, Susan came into my office and closed the door. "Lynn just reassigned me. I have to work upstairs. She says since you and I are living together it's not appropriate for us to work on the same floor. Please talk to her. I don't want to change bosses, and it's silly to reassign me because of that. You're the Department Chair. You can overrule her."

"I'm not sure I could if I wanted to," I said. "I don't have authority over secretaries, just lawyers. Besides, it wouldn't be appropriate for me to intervene. I want to keep personal and business affairs separated."

"Are you saying you won't stand up for me?" she said.

"It's not a matter of standing up for you," I said. "It's not appropriate for me to use my influence to help you. I wouldn't intervene for any other secretary, so I won't do it for you, Susan."

"Okay, Boyd," she said, and walked out the door.

Susan's reaction to Liz at the party and to her reassignment, I thought, displayed insecurities that concerned me. She was not secure in my love and loyalty. She was too clingy, I thought. She couldn't bear my having female friends. I had doubts about marrying her. Paradoxically, I wanted to be needed, but I didn't want the burden.

I needed to think through this issue, but I soon forgot about it. I thought Susan would feel more secure if we were married, but she wasn't. Early in our marriage she told me she didn't want me seeing Dora platonically, because Lisa told her that I had asked Dora to marry me. Lisa strikes again!

Chapter Twenty-One

One Friday night after dinner I was watching TV. Susan came in and said, "Turn the TV off please. I need to talk to you."

"Okay, what's up?" I turned off the TV. Klutzy climbed onto Susan's lap, purring.

"I'm not comfortable living with you and not having a marriage commitment," she said.

"The deal was I had six months. It's been less than three," I said. Anger filled my belly.

"I know. I'm sorry, but it really bothers my parents, and you know how close I am to them. And I love you. I want to marry you. It makes me feel bad that you can't decide if you want to marry me. I think about that every day. I told my father when he was here last July, before you ever asked me to move in, that you were the man I was going to marry. I knew then."

"I love you too," I said, "but marriage is a huge commitment, and I've made two mistakes already."

"I'm not Stephanie. I'm not Christie," she said. "You know that, don't you?"

"Yes, I know you're not, but I asked for a year and agreed to six months, because I needed at least that much time, and you agreed."

"Well, I think if you're going to marry me you can decide now," she said. "I just can't go on like this. I sure don't want to leave you, but I'm prepared to do that, if you can't commit to marry me."

"Okay," I said. "Let me think about it tonight, and I'll let you know."

"Okay, she said. "I'm going to bed."

Anger still churned in my belly, as I slowly walked into the kitchen and got a tall glass down from the cupboard. I opened the freezer, took out a handful of ice, and put it in the glass. I poured Scotch over the ice. It cracked and settled. I took a sip before any ice melted. The strong, musty taste made me grimace.

I walked back to the living room and sat down on the couch. Klutzy stood by my feet. He was a big gray and white tabby, sixteen pounds, not a friendly cat, but he had warmed up to me after a couple of months and even let me pet him on my lap. I picked him up and he started to purr. I put him on my lap and petted his soft, warm fur.

Klutzy probably knows whether I should marry Susan, I thought. I'll discuss it with him. He purred louder. My anger dissipated. I think I just needed to convince myself that this time I was not making an impulsive decision.

"Let's see Klutzy," I said. "She's not a drama queen. She doesn't drink much. She doesn't take drugs. She has never said anything mean to me. She's got a job, and she's willing to keep it. She's good with money; she doesn't overspend. She doesn't complain much. She's easy to get along with. She's sexy and she likes sex with me. She's easy to talk to. She's intelligent. She's liberal. We both like baseball and basketball and love to talk about politics, religion and philosophy. She's pretty enough. Right, Klutzy?

"What's bad about her? Well, she's messy. She never throws anything away and leaves stuff all over the house—old magazines, newspapers, junk mail, bills, everything. She's not that great a cook, but she's okay. She's possessive and has a jealous nature. I probably couldn't have any female friends. She just reneged on our agreement. I would have to have another child, but that wouldn't be so bad.

"But, you know, Klutzy, I don't feel the passion that I felt for Stephanie, or even for Dora. Not that I don't enjoy sex with her. I do. But passion is missing.

"On the other hand, look where passion got me with Stephanie. Less passion may make things more peaceful. I want peace, a calm, steady relationship. I had enough passion with Stephanie to last me a lifetime."

I put my hand on Klutzy's belly and looked into his eyes. He looked back. "I think I should marry her. What do you think, Klutzy?" His purring went up several decibels. "I'll wait another half hour, Klutzy, and see if any other major negatives come to mind." I went to the kitchen and poured another Scotch.

A half hour later I took the last sip of Scotch and put the glass down on the end table. I thought: *OK, I guess I'll go for the marriage triple crown.*

I opened the bedroom door. When I walked in, Susan opened her eyes.

"Hi," she said. I sat down on the bed next to her.

"I've decided to marry you," I said.

"Oh, Boyd," she said as she sat up and hugged me. "I had given up. I thought I'd be moving tomorrow. I love you."

"I love you too," I said.

"You smell like Scotch. You're not drunk, are you?" she asked.

I laughed. "Not that drunk."

As I write about this incident, I realize Susan's question

should have shaken me up. Making a decision to propose after two Scotches—large ones—is lunacy. But this wisdom didn't penetrate.

I married Susan to escape loneliness, rather than learn to deal with it, to learn to enjoy being by myself. To do that you have to be yourself. You can't be trying to be somebody else.

Susan is gregarious, at ease with other people. I am shy. When we commit to a relationship, we often see something in the other person that we don't have, but wish we did. We imagine the other person will give it to us or relieve us of the need for it.

I only thought about whether I should marry Susan—not whether I should marry again, period. I had learned that marriage requires more attention than I had given my first two, that I needed to share control with my wife and that marriage is a partnership. But I didn't consider whether I was willing to be a partner, rather than a dictator. I assumed the absence of passion for Susan was not a problem. It would result in a more stable relationship, I thought.

It would have been a good idea to think about all this before I made the decision. Depression sinks deep in my chest. How terribly sad that I thought I was making a rational decision. I had learned something, but I hadn't dug deep enough into my previous marriages and myself to fully understand my role in their failure, and I didn't consider whether I was willing to do what was necessary in a marriage—with Susan or anyone.

As we planned our wedding, Susan suggested we buy a larger house. "Three people sharing one bathroom is a little cramped, and in the not-too-distant future, there will be four of us, I hope." I agreed, and we bought a big, newly built house five blocks from the beach—a modern four-bedroom, three-bath, with a huge living room overlooking a park.

She told me she wanted a wedding with a white dress and

the works. I didn't care. I was willing to do that for her. Her parents shared the cost.

I asked Susan to handle the household finances, confident that she would keep track of them and not overspend. Whoopee! I had learned from my marriage with Christie, that insisting on control of the finances could create unnecessary conflict. I grew more confident that I had made the right decision to marry Susan. I had peace living with her, and I saw no reason it would change when we married.

Susan's parents, Jane and Mike, arrived a few days before the wedding. Susan and Mike were chatting in the kitchen while she prepared dinner. I sat down with her mother in the living room. Jane had retained some of the accent and Southern belle ways from her native Louisiana, though she had lived in Hawaii for nearly forty years. She had tight gray curls and a round, pale face. She hunched over a little. If you were going to cast someone for the movie role of a little old lady, based on looks she would have been perfect, I thought.

I asked if she wanted a drink, expecting her to ask for iced tea.

"I'd love a drink," she said.

"What would you like?"

"What are you having?" She asked.

"Well, I'm having a Martini, but we have wine, red and white, iced tea or just about anything you'd like."

"I'll have a Martini," she said. No indecision, I thought.

She took short, tentative steps over to the bar and watched me make the Martinis. We walked back to the chairs. She sat down, and I handed her a Martini.

When I sat down with mine, she raised her glass, "To you and Susan—a long and happy life together."

"Thank you," I said. "I'm a slow learner, but I think I've finally chosen the right woman," I said.

"You'll find that Susan has a lot of love to give," she said.

I look at that sentence. Jane's observation that Susan had a lot of love to give was true. What I didn't think about at the time was that she needed a lot of love too, and I wasn't willing to give it to her. My shoulders slump. The sadness of that realization penetrates. Writing the truth can be tough.

I had never met Jane before that night. She and Mike lived in Honolulu, and she hadn't visited before. I was a bit apprehensive. I wanted to make a good impression, especially because Susan was close to her mother. Jane's soft, friendly demeanor melted that apprehension away. I see where Susan got her personality, I thought.

I finished my Martini and got up to get another one. To be polite I asked Jane if she would like another.

"Sure," she said.

When we finished the second one, she asked, "Are you going to have another?"

"Well, I guess so," I said. "Why not? I'm not driving tonight."

"Good. I'll have another also," she said.

After finishing the third Martini, I felt like going to bed. I steadied myself as I rose from my chair. Jane got up, handed me her glass and walked toward the kitchen as steadily as if she'd been drinking iced tea.

That evening endeared Jane to me, and I suspect me to her, for the rest of her life, even long after Susan and I were divorced. She and her husband Mike were the first in-laws I liked. I had read somewhere that it is important to like your mother-in-law, because her daughter eventually would turn into her. I thought that if Susan were like her role model, she would make a fine wife, and she was like her mother. But Mike knew better than I did how to make a marriage work; they had been married more than sixty years when Jane died.

Howard, my best man once again, the other groomsmen and I stood at the church's left aisle by the side door, waiting for the cue to walk to the altar of the Episcopal church in Beverly Hills where the stars married, though at that moment, I couldn't remember which ones. I was sweating and nervous. A rock rolled around in the pit of my stomach, a hangover from the celebrations of the night before. I looked at the door. Howard touched my arm. "Wanna go out that door, Big B? This is your last chance." A part of me wanted to.

The ceremony started at twelve-thirty, and the reception at a Marina Del Rey hotel went on into the evening. Then I took Jeff and Jennifer to the airport. Susan and I ate dinner at ten o'clock and went to bed, exhausted. For the third time I didn't have sex on my wedding night.

We drove across the country and back in the three weeks of vacation I had. When I suggested it Susan agreed enthusiastically. Near the end of our marriage she raised my ire when she told me that she had always wanted to go to Paris on her honeymoon, and she was upset because I ignored her wishes and took her on the driving trip across the country. She mentioned it again recently, saying that she felt especially bad when, after our divorce, I took my daughters to Paris. She had never told me she wanted to go to Paris. How was I supposed to know?

My friend and associate, Jim and I had bought an old wooden sailboat, the *Fleur de Mer*. Jim loved sailing, and I wanted to learn. About a month after our honeymoon, Susan and I joined Jim and his girlfriend, Sarah, on a short cruise up to Point Mugu. We anchored just before dark, and Sarah cooked dinner. Susan and I went to bed across from the galley. The boat rocked back and forth and up and down—boats do that. The stuff in the galley—cans, bottles, jars and whatnot—slammed and banged against each other all night. We didn't sleep much. That was Susan's first and last trip on the boat.

When we got home the next afternoon, we lay down on our bed and slept. When we woke up, we made love. Mark was born nine months later, April 7, 1984—my second son—a little sooner than we had hoped, but oh how glad I am now.

From almost the beginning, Susan felt the pregnancy in her back. When she was almost five months pregnant, she came into my office and said she was going to the doctor. "I got stuck in the elevator," she said, "and it fell about a half floor. It was really scary, and I felt it in my back. I wanna make sure the baby and I are okay."

A week later she told me she was going to have to stop working. She couldn't sit at her desk all day. It was just too painful. I wasn't happy about it. "If that's the way it is, that's the way it is," I said.

Once again I watched in awe - the wonder, the miracle of the emergence of my child from my wife's body. I held his frail, warm little body a few minutes later, this time with confidence that he wouldn't break. It had been ten years since I had last held a newborn, Jennifer. Knowing that Mark would be my last made it incomparable.

Susan wouldn't let me smoke around the baby, so I quit. It was hard when I was having a cocktail, but I haven't had a cigarette in twenty-five years now.

I remember walking Mark up and down the hall. He often suffered from colic. I was determined to play a greater role in caring for this child.

Although I consciously helped Susan with Mark more than I had helped Stephanie with Jeff and Jennifer, I rarely played with him. I don't play with babies or toddlers. I don't know what to do with them. I never roughhoused or played trains with my sons, like most fathers do. I didn't play dolls or draw with my daughters, like David does. I like to watch babies and toddlers as they discover the world. I like to take them places to discover new things. I just don't want to play with them. I don't play with my grandchildren much. Is there something wrong with me? After writing about it, I decide that's just the way I am. I'm finally learning about myself and accepting who I am.

I did not curtail my evening cocktails with Jim across the street from the office, while Susan waited at home with the baby. Once, Jim had to drive me home. I had drunk even more Martinis than he had, and he was about twice my weight—I had switched from Scotch to Martinis. When we pulled into the driveway, Susan, carrying Mark, came down to greet us. I reached for the baby. She backed up and clutched him tighter. "No way will I let you hold my baby in your condition," she said.

Although Susan reminded me later of this incident, I never saw the red flag. I didn't see that I was still drinking after work too often, instead of going home to my family. Susan didn't complain about my drinking with Jim or the long hours I worked during the first two years of our marriage, but I suspect she resented both.

One day in early 1985 I had lunch in Marina Del Rey with an old colleague, Art Chenen. He told me he had just formed a law firm with a fellow named Steve Hirschtick and a few other attorneys. Their philosophy was that there was more to life than practicing law; they worked full-time, but not the long hours that he and I had been used to. He said that, except in unusual circumstances, they went home by six at the latest, and did not work on weekends. Their office was only fifteen minutes from our house.

This appealed to me. I was mindful of my previous wives' complaints about my long hours, and I didn't like them either. I could make plenty of money working at a more leisurely pace.

I joined Hirschtick, Chenen, Cavanaugh & Lemon. I liked being in the firm's name. I started a week after Mark's first birthday. Susan sometimes brought Mark in at lunch time, or we met at a restaurant for lunch. Occasionally, they hung out at the office for an hour or so. Mark crawled down the main hallway, gaining lots of fans. I was almost always home for dinner and on weekends.

By this time, my dream of teaching or working in something

other than a private practice had been buried so deep that I had quit thinking about it. The practice of law was no more fulfilling than it had ever been, but with rare and temporary exceptions, I never again worked sixty- to eighty-hour weeks. At least, at forty-four, I realized that lifestyle was not what I wanted, but I trudged on, making more money than we needed, still living someone else's life.

One balmy 1985 Summer evening at sunset, I pushed Mark in his stroller down the strand next to the sand. Susan walked beside me. We gazed out at the setting sun's orange light on white-capped waves over the dark blue water.

"Thank you for Mark," said Susan. "It's a dream come true for me—what I've always wanted."

"Thank you," I said. "I'm thrilled to have a child I can help raise to adulthood. And a marriage that makes me truly happy. I've never been happier."

The peace of that moment comes back to me when I think of Mark or Susan. There were many moments like that during the first few years. I thought I finally had it right.

There were signs of trouble though. Although our house, like most near the beach, had no yard, just the minimum three-foot setback around the house and a patio about ten by ten, we bought two Golden Retrievers, one named Red for me, the other named Artie for Susan. I walked them fairly often, but otherwise they were confined to the house. Susan didn't even walk Artie much. She rarely wanted to go outside, an inheritance from her southern mom. Ladies keep the house and sit in the parlor drinking iced tea. Men work and play outside—that sort of thing. I had grown to love hiking, horseback riding and other outdoor activities. This was a difference I didn't consciously recognize. We never discussed it.

I received a call one day near Christmas 1984 from Susan. She said Artie had bitten eight-month-old Mark on the face. He was bleeding profusely, and she was taking him to the emergency room. The bite missed his eye by less than an inch, and he bears a permanent scar. I didn't see it until the wound had been repaired and stitched. I was horrified when I saw how close the bite had come to his eye. After that, the dogs were confined to the setback and patio outside the house most of the time.

They did their business in that small area, most of it behind a gate that was a few feet from the front door. Since Susan didn't work outside the home, and I did, we agreed it was her job to clean up the dog poop. Most of the time she didn't do it, and outside the house, it reeked of dog poop. I only smelled it when I left or came home or barbequed on the patio. I still remember answering the door when Lisa's boyfriend came to visit. He stood with his head down, his sweatshirt pulled up over his nose and mouth, muttering something that I could only guess had something to do with Lisa, and I let him in. I complained to Susan about cleaning up. So did Lisa. But it had no effect. Lisa complained to me. "The sweet smell of success," I said. I didn't like Susan leaving papers and junk all over the house either, but I knew that was her habit before I married her. I had to accept it. After Stephanie, I was happy not to have any major crises.

We had been married about two years. Life was too comfortable to consider any change in lifestyle, to figure out what I really wanted to do and get out of the practice of law. I was contentedly unaware that soon Susan would feel that I was withdrawing from her emotionally. I believe she was right, but I don't yet understand why.

Chapter Twenty-Two

My office was two miles from Hollywood Park Racetrack. The Firm had a day at the races for lawyers and staff, and we had a grand time. I decided to go by myself one afternoon. I got out of my car and smelled the salty ocean breeze sweetened slightly with horse manure. The sight of the emerald green grandstand adorned with flags took me back—going to the races with my father. We sometimes went to Hollywood Park or Del Mar, but more often to Santa Anita. It was closer to home, and my dad said he liked the ambiance—he didn't use that word—of purple, white, and yellow pansies by the entrance and in the infield, the towering fountain by the entrance, and the resplendent San Gabriel Mountains in the background.

The afternoon that I went to Hollywood Park, I paid admission, walked through the grandstand and stood in line for a hot dog. At the condiments counter, as I squeezed the little packets of mustard and relish, I remembered eating hot dogs with my father at Santa Anita. Some of the mustard usually ended up on my shirt or pants.

I was astounded how much better a hot dog tasted at the races. The one at Hollywood Park tasted just as good, and even better with a beer. "Shit," I said out loud as I took a bite, and from the corner of my eye saw a blob of mustard fall on my shirt. Some things never change.

I had only been to the races a few times in the past twenty-five years. As I drove home, I realized they brought back the old excitement I felt as a child. I loved the grace of the horses, the escape from everyday life and the anticipation of winning that gambling brought.

That weekend I asked Susan if she would like to go to the races. "Sure," she said. She told me she had read about Affirmed winning the Triple Crown a few years before, and was fascinated. She had gone to Hollywood Park to see him race. He won. That was the only horse race she had ever seen. We took Mark and sat on a blanket on the infield grass. I won $80.00.

We went to the races almost every weekend that spring. The only time Susan complained was when I took her on Mother's Day, and she didn't say anything until after we got home. During one of those outings I sat on our blanket reading the ads in the Racing Form. A small ad offered classes on the business of racehorse ownership given by a horse trainer. "Wouldn't it be fun to own a racehorse?" I said, showing her the ad. "I'd like to go to that class. Would you be interested?"

"Yeah, I would," she said. "I need to get out of the house more, anyway."

One Saturday morning we went to the horse ranch east of Los Angeles where the class met. From one of the stalls emerged a little guy, small enough to be a jockey. We introduced ourselves. Gary Spinelli had long sideburns and wore an orange baseball cap with "Spinelli Stables" printed in white. He spoke with a Midwest accent, though we later learned he was a California native of Italian descent. He had wanted to be a jockey but hurt his back exercising horses.

Now he trained them.

We learned a lot from Gary—how a healthy, mentally and physically fit racehorse looks and acts; the typical training regimen; how to keep a horse physically fit, without breaking it down; and the details of the expenses to train and maintain a race horse: about $2,000 a month. We also learned how to handle a racehorse: how to walk it safely, pet it without being bitten, clean its feet and stand near it without getting kicked. What Gary didn't tell us was that few, if any, owners made money or even broke even.

Susan and I agreed that all we wanted to do was break even. I remember telling her I didn't want to go into debt again, but I would be willing to use the increasing equity in our house to finance horse ownership.

When the class was over, we told Gary we wanted to buy a horse for him to train. He called one afternoon and said he had bought us, in partnership with two classmates, a filly named Tradition of Hope. When I got home from work that evening, Susan and I ate hurriedly and left for Hollywood Park. Lisa stayed with Mark. We showed our credentials to enter the barn area—called the backstretch—and walked up and down looking for Gary's barn. The cool February night air, heavy with the sweet aroma of horse manure, made me shiver. In my excitement I'd forgotten to bring a jacket.

We asked a guy sitting on a rickety chair outside one of the barns where Gary Spinelli's barn was. He pointed across the way. We walked in through the wide opening. The stalls were dark. We made our way by the light of one bare light bulb. Then we saw the orange "S" on Gary's four stalls. Three of the horses were lying down, sleeping. The other was pacing.

From around the corner came a heavyset Hispanic man. "Hello, are you the new owners?" he asked. We said yes. "I'm Raphael, Tradition of Hope's groom. That's her there." He pointed to the pacing horse. "She's a little nervous."

Susan walked up and tried to pet her, talking softly. At first, the horse threw her head around, but after a while settled down, and we were both able to pet her. "What a beautiful horse you are," I almost whispered. My hand warmed on her velvet soft face.

She stopped pacing. The groom smiled. "She likes you guys," he said.

I was exhilarated. Wow, I thought, I actually own this racehorse. My father would be proud. I don't think he ever dreamed of owning a racehorse. It was far beyond his financial means. But maybe he dreamed it for me. I never did until that day at Hollywood Park. I was so excited that it took me hours to get to sleep that night.

Susan called Gary and reported to me every day about how Hopie, as we called her, was doing. We watched her gallop Saturday morning. Afterwards, we walked over to the backstretch kitchen. I shoveled in a greasy omelet with hash browns and bacon, feeling like a real horseman, smelling the mud and manure the grooms and exercise riders brought in on their shoes, blended with the smell of the grease from the kitchen.

Susan called me at work about a week later. "Hopie's entered in the fourth race day after tomorrow," she said.

After the third race we went to the paddock grassy area, where the owners wait for the horses to be saddled. As we stood with a dozen or so others, Susan whispered, "There's David Cassidy over there to your left." I glanced over and recognized him from the TV show *The Partridge Family*. He owned a horse in Hopie's race.

Horse number one came out from under the grandstand to where we stood, followed by horses two through five. Then came Hopie, led by Raphael on her left side, and Gary on her right.

I was nervous, but my stomach didn't start to churn until the announcer said, "The horses have reached the starting gate." They would start a few feet to our left and race around the track once—a mile and a sixteenth.

Hopie was trotting around in a circle. An assistant starter

grabbed a rein and led her to the number six stall in the starting gate. Another ran up and pushed her in from the rear, and
closed the back of the stall. In a minute all ten horses were
in the gate. The bell rang, and the doors on the stalls flashed
open. The horses sprang forward as if tied together—zero to
thirty-five miles an hour in three strides. Hopie fell quickly to
the rear of the pack. She stayed there as they raced out of the
first turn. She was five lengths behind the last horse down the
straightaway. By the time they reached the final turn, she was
even farther behind. She picked up a little ground down the
stretch and passed several horses, but she finished eighth or
ninth.

Neither Gary nor Hopie's jockey offered any explanation
for why she ran so poorly. My excitement escaped like air in
a blown out tire. Disappointment took its place. Susan had
no expression. Hopie raced ten times that year and finished
in the money only once, a second. We ended up owning one
hundred percent of her. The other owners didn't want her anymore. The following year we retired her. She never won a race
for us.

About a month after we bought Hopie, Gary told us there
was an auction sale of two-year-olds in training at Hollywood
Park on March 7th. They already had three to six months of
training, and could be ready to race in two or three months.
He asked Susan if we were interested in bidding on one.

"I'd love to," I said to Susan. "I've read in *The Blood Horse*
that some of the horses sold at that auction became major
winners."

"That's great, Boyd," she said, "but we don't have any
money to buy another horse."

"I know a loan officer at a small bank named Marathon
Bank in West L.A. I bet they would loan us the money, and we
can pay it back at the end of the year when I get my bonus."
So much for not going into debt.

"Let me get this straight," she said. "You want to borrow
money to buy a racehorse?"

"Sure. We can pay it back. Why not?"

"It's up to you," she said. In the early years of our marriage Susan usually acquiesced in spending money as I wanted to spend it, as if she believed it was my money. That would change.

At the time, I didn't consider why I wanted to go into debt to buy another racehorse. I knew that Hopie's prospects were limited. I dreamed of a horse that could be a champion. My drive to achieve wasn't limited to law.

Susan, Lisa, Mark and I went to the auction. By eleven o'clock Gary hadn't bid on any of the horses. I told him I had to go to work the next day and Lisa had to go to school. I asked him to call us in the morning if he bought a horse.

Gary called early in the morning. Susan talked to him. "He bought a filly by Flying Paster out of a winning mare for $17,000. Her name's Flying Shopper," she said. "I'm so excited."

"Wow, Flying Paster. He's California's leading stallion. How did he get her for $17,000?" I said.

"I don't know," she said. "He said she'd be ready for her first race in three months, if there are no setbacks. I told him I'd be right over to see her."

"Let's go. I can't believe we got a Flying Paster filly."

When I saw Flying Shopper, my heart pounded. She was beautiful, big, and strong looking, with a shiny chocolate brown coat and intelligent eyes. I repeated, "I can't believe we got a Flying Paster filly." That became a mantra during the next few months.

Three months seemed like a long time. We went to the track every Saturday and Sunday at six in the morning to see Flying Shopper train. After thirty days of galloping two miles a day, she began to breeze—a workout close to race speed—every five to seven days. As the weeks went by, her breezes, starting at a quarter mile, became longer and faster. Her second half mile breeze was the best of the day for any two-year old, male or female, and Gary said she was going to breeze five-eighths next. He called the day before it was scheduled. Shopper had a cold and would have to take time off from training.

Two weeks later, she started galloping again. Her first breeze was back to three-eighths of a mile, then a half mile, then five-eighths. Finally, she was back to where she was five weeks before.

The next week at six-thirty in the morning we watched her second five-eighths breeze through binoculars. The rider crouched low on her back, loosened his hold on the reins and grabbed her mane with his other hand. She took off flying right at the five-eighths pole and finished in 59.2 seconds. The winner in her first race wouldn't run much faster.

We arrived at the track on race day morning and hung around Shopper's stall until Gary said we were making her nervous. We certainly were nervous. I went out to the grandstand and suffered through the pre-race rituals.

As the horses approached the starting gate, my stomach felt like it was in my throat. It was a cool afternoon, but I was sweating. I wanted it over.

Shopper was number four. She entered the starting gate. A minute later, the announcer bellowed, "They're all in, and there they go!"

Shopper broke from the gate with the first flight of horses, but then began to drop back until she was seventh. I slumped with disappointment. The horses straightened out in the stretch with less than a quarter mile to go, and Shopper was still seventh. Her jockey pulled her to the outside to give her clear racing room. He tapped her once on the rump with his whip. She started passing horses. With about a hundred yards to go she was fourth, and it looked like she would finish no worse than third. Not bad for her first race. But she flew in those last hundred yards. Through the shouting of the crowd, the announcer yelled, "And it's Flying Shopper flying on the outside and winning by a neck." Twenty-three years later, I still get shivers up my sides when I relive that race in my mind.

We ran down the stairway for the winner's circle, almost

falling down. Susan was yahooing. I had never seen her so excited. Shopper trotted halfway around the track and back to us. We followed her and her groom to the winner's circle. The photographer lifted up his camera. We smiled. The camera flashed. That night we bought Champagne. Shopper had earned $9,000.

We had a winning racehorse, a daughter about to graduate from high school and go to the University of California, and a home by the beach. Life was good. I had no awareness that, around that time, I started to emotionally withdraw from Susan and shift my attention to the horse business.

The following week, Gary entered Shopper in Hollywood Park's most prestigious race for two-year-old fillies. For the next two weeks I daydreamed of her winning major races and making us rich. But Shopper finished ninth out of twelve.

Two weeks later we went to Del Mar and watched her in a workout with a colt. Down the stretch, in the last few strides, she passed the colt. I was excited. Female horses usually don't beat males. Again I daydreamed of glory.

After a few minutes of her cool-down walk, she started to limp on her right front leg. "That don't look good," Gary said. He grabbed the lead shank and walked her to her stall. He called the vet, who came within ten minutes and x-rayed her leg. Shopper had broken her right knee.

Susan and I discussed what to do with Shopper. There was no disagreement. We both wanted to keep her and try to race her again after her year-long rehabilitation. We went to see her at a ranch east of Los Angeles almost every weekend.

About a year after her injury, the vet approved Shopper's return to training. We wouldn't know for several months if she could race. We sent her to a new trainer, Jude Feld. We felt Gary had pushed her too hard too soon. She needed to come back slowly to avoid re-injuring her knee. She trained well. By the middle of October, she was ready to race. Jude shipped her to trainer Allen Severinsen in San Francisco for an easier race.

On race day our flight was delayed by weather. The taxi dropped us off in front of the grandstand and we ran to the track. The race had just ended. The board showed that Shopper finished third.

We hurried over to a TV monitor and watched the replay. The starting gate opened. "Terrible start," I said, shaking my head. She spotted the lead horse five lengths. Around the turn she caught the last horse, and barreled down the stretch, passing every horse but the first two.

She raced once more—poorly—before the vet found a bone spur on the injured knee and recommended retirement from racing. Twenty-five thousand dollars since she broke her knee—gone.

My sexual desire for Susan waned that year, and we made love infrequently. I remember a night she caressed my thigh, and I turned away. That even surprised me. I didn't remember ever rejecting sex.

I want to know when and why I seemed to fall out of love with Susan, or if I ever loved her. I stare at the blank MS Word page for a long time before I start writing. Was my emotional withdrawal, which coincided with our involvement in horseracing, related or was the timing just a coincidence? I'm stuck. I don't know what to write. I loved horseracing. It was exciting and I always was a gambler, I think. I don't believe it was compulsive though. I don't know. I can't write.

I always thought our marriage might have lasted if we hadn't suffered the conflicts and stress of the horse business. But all relationships—certainly marriages—have conflict. It's how you resolve the conflict—or don't—that determines the course of the relationship. And there wasn't much conflict when Susan says I started to withdraw.

I think that when we started buying racehorses I was in love with Susan—not the passionate, consuming love I felt in the early years with Stephanie, but a solid, stable love, based on respect, tempered with my feeling of superiority. I thought love based on respect would last. I felt closer to Susan, a stronger bond than when we were first married.

Stephanie had broken into something inside me. I let her all the way in. I depended on her for my emotional wellbeing. I was hurt deeply when she was angry with me—the love of my life, said Kate. Even when Stephanie rejected me sexually and betrayed me, I still clung to her. I was devastated, drowning, scared. Once I finally took back my life from Stephanie, I vowed that I would never allow that to happen again. I would not let Susan or anybody else break down my defenses. I think that as I became closer to Susan during the first three years of our marriage, unconsciously, I began to fear that closeness would make me emotionally dependent on her, as I had been on Stephanie. I was afraid of what intimacy would do to me. So I withdrew, using the horse business as my vehicle.

I know now that Susan felt the withdrawal intensely. I was only aware of the sexual part of the withdrawal, and I tried, successfully, not to think of that often. Maybe I felt confident that she wouldn't leave me, "as long as we both shall live." I think I still believed in that, because she vowed it on our wedding day, and I trusted her. Without any conscious thought, I believed I could maintain emotional distance from her to protect myself, and she would still love me and stay with me.

In a recent email, Susan told me that once we were married I never gave her a negligee, perfume or jewelry. She wrote, "These kinds of gifts are intimate and are the sort of things that only a husband can give to a wife. I think that you have major problems with any kind of real intimacy, and I think that is the major factor in the destruction of our marriage."

She wrote further that during the last six months of our

marriage, "…you put your hand on my knee once….That was the only time…that you initiated any kind of affection at all towards me."

My withdrawal grew as Susan reacted with understandable resentment.

Chapter Twenty-Three

In 1987 we bought five more horses—three two-year-old racehorses and two brood mares. One of the brood mares was Flying Shopper's mother. We decided to breed our own horses instead of buying them. In 1988 Hopie and East Coast Shopper had foals. We bred them again and also Flying Shopper.

One of the two-year-olds we bought in 1987 was a shiny dark brown colt named Top of the Key. Just before he was ready to race, he injured his shins and had to be rested. A few weeks later Susan called me at the office.

"Top of the Key is very sick," she said. "They don't know what's wrong, but the vet says he has lost strength in his hind legs, and he may have to be put down. Her voice cracked. "I'm going to have Melinda examine him and get a second opinion."

When I got home that night, Susan said, "Melinda knows a vet in Michigan that has had some success in treating Topper's symptoms. I authorized Topper to be shipped to the clinic in

Chino near Melinda. She said she would consult with the vet in Michigan and see what she can do."

"Okay," I said. How much is this going to cost?"

"I don't know," she said, "but we can't just put him down if he can be saved."

Well, it depends at what cost, I thought, but didn't say.

During the next month Susan passed along the reports she got from Melinda. Topper seemed to be improving slowly. At the beginning of the following month I saw the bill from Melinda: $22,000 and change.

Susan was preparing Mark's dinner. "I saw Melinda's bill," I said. "We can't afford that. I want him out of the hospital right now."

"We can't do that, Boyd. He's improving, and Melinda says he has a chance of recovering. But he needs to be in the hospital to continue treatments."

"I don't care. We can't afford it."

"We'll have to afford it," said Susan. "If we're going to be in this business, we have to do what's best for these animals. They're our responsibility. We can't just let them die."

"But we have to run this horse operation like a business," I said. "If we don't we can't stay in it, and we're both having the time of our lives with these horses. How much more will it be?"

"I'll talk to Melinda and see if there is any way to cut costs, and try to get an estimate of how much more it will take."

"Okay," I said. I went to the bar and poured an extra tall Scotch.

Six months later, Topper seemed fine, and we put him back in training. I was doubtful he could race and wanted to sell him for a riding horse, but Susan was bent on giving him a chance. We went to see him race at Bay Meadows. He broke from the starting gate almost sideways. He ran last down the backstretch. It was sad. Around the turn he gained some ground, but when they straightened out in the stretch he lost more ground and finished last.

His jockey jumped off and said, "He has a funny gait. I was worried about him."

The trainer, Allen Severinsen, recommended we not race him again, and we didn't. He became my expensive riding horse. On the way home from the track I added in my head what he had cost us--over $100,000, counting all the vet and training bills and his $14,000 purchase price. I pointed this out to Susan. She didn't say anything.

I understood that we were more likely to lose money in the horse business than to break even. I understand now that my desire to be involved was motivated more by emotion than by a financial investment. But I wanted to try to lose as little money as possible. It seemed to me that Susan did not share this desire; her focus was on what was best for the animals; but we were both motivated by emotion.

Topper's vet and training bills, and the training and breeding bills for the other horses, put us in a deep financial hole. I said to Susan, "The only thing we can do is sell the house. It has appreciated so much in the past five years, we could pay off our debts and still have enough for a down payment on a house that is almost as expensive."

She said, "I really would like a yard for Mark. Living by the beach is nice, but we could have a yard if we lived farther back."

I had been thinking we should move from Manhattan Beach and buy horse property east of Los Angeles. When we went to see our horses at the farms out there we had looked at houses just for fun. We could buy a house with acreage for horses for less than we would get for the Manhattan Beach house. "It would save money to have our horses with us instead of boarding them," I pointed out to Susan.

Susan said, "I could take care of them instead of going back to work." At the time, I thought this was a reasonable proposal. It probably would save us as much money as Susan could earn by working. I didn't feel any resentment.

In June 1988 we sold our house in Manhattan Beach and

moved to a house in Bradbury, a horse community near Santa Anita Racetrack. The large three-bedroom ranch-style house was on almost two acres, and had a swimming pool, a small barn, and three horse paddocks. We were both excited about having our horses living on our property.

I heard Shopper whinnying before I heard the van. Susan told the driver to put the two mares in the front pasture. Shopper ran around and around the paddock like an excited toddler, kicking up her heels and passing gas. We laughed. Hopie did the same. My heart was pounding. It felt as if my children had come home. I soon smelled the manure I loved. East Coast Shopper arrived a few days later with her foal; Linpac Leaf, an injured race horse that we were going to breed, arrived last.

I intensified my study of equine bloodlines and breeding. I have always been an avid reader, but back then my only reading was about racehorses and their breeding, and law. I continued to go to the races a couple of times a week. I told Susan if I could go to the races every day, instead of doing law work, I would be a happy man. I was obsessed, my time and energy directed away from my family. Susan hadn't said anything yet, but I know now she felt abandoned, and I had forgotten about my plan to spend more time with this child.

I tried out numerous systems of betting the races to see if I could make money. After about a year, all of them had failed, and I quit going to the races as often.

The advent of e-mail, fax machines and cell phones made it possible for me to commute to the office three days a week, and work at home two to avoid five long drives a week through rush-hour traffic.

Mark, then four, learned how to swim in our pool that summer. We spent some happy times in the pool and lying out in the sun. He started pre-school at the Church of the Nazarene, which he called the Church of the Tangerine. Lisa was in college at the University of California, Santa Barbara.

Taking care of Mark and six horses on almost two acres was a full-time job for Susan, and a part-time job for me. She spent hours every day cleaning up the manure and mucking out the stalls: shoveling the manure and dirty straw into the red wheelbarrow, dumping it in front of the blue dumpster, and going back for more. A horse, on average, has six bowel movements a day. They are large animals. That's a lot of shit.

Every evening I shoveled the pile Susan had made, so to speak, into the big blue dumpster. Once I counted fifty-four shovels full. We had to be diligent. We lived in a residential area. If we slacked, we and our neighbors would be overwhelmed with odor, flies and who knows what else. The manure began to smell less sweet to me.

Susan stopped cooking. We either went out or I barbecued. By the time we had been in Bradbury six months, Susan complained, "I feel like all I do is shovel shit—literally. This is not what I thought I'd be doing at the age of thirty-seven."

At about the time Susan expressed unhappiness with her work on the property, she also complained that we rarely made love anymore. "I wonder if you really love me," she said once.

"Of course I do," I said. "But you're always too tired."

"I'm not too tired. I snuggle up to you, and you ignore me."

"I think I may be concerned about pregnancy," I said. "I don't like condoms and I sure don't want another baby. Four is enough. I tell you what. I'll get a vasectomy."

"Okay," she said. "I hope that helps."

What I said was sincere, but I wasn't certain that fear of pregnancy was affecting my desire for sex with Susan. I didn't express this uncertainty. I had the vasectomy, but it didn't help.

I'm home in Cambridge until Christmas. I hope that I can gain more insight into my marriage with Susan over the next couple of weeks, before I visit her and Mark at the end of December. I walk down Mass Ave and get cash from the ATM.

I pass India Castle, the Plough and Stars and the liquor store. I keep walking and think more about my sexual rejection of Susan. The cold, gray air numbs my face.

When I'm back at my apartment and sit down to write, what comes out does not ring true. People don't withdraw from their spouses because they gain weight, do they? I don't know. I turn off my computer and go to bed. When I write again the next day, I'm still not clear. A little clarity on this issue comes, months and many writing practices later.

Susan had gained a lot of weight—eighty pounds or more since we started dating, I guessed. I noticed her weight gain early in our marriage. Then she didn't lose much after her pregnancy. I never was attracted to heavy women. Susan talked from time to time about counseling for nutrition and weight loss, but never did anything about it. I suggested it once, and she yelled, "Don't talk to me about my weight." She ran to the bedroom and sobbed.

My lack of desire for her might have been partly the anger that was building over her management of the horse business. But I still wanted sex with Stephanie even after my resentment rose to a much greater degree than I ever resented Susan. I know that emotional overeating is sometimes used as a substitute for love, but Susan had gained a lot of weight before she says that I began withdrawing emotionally. According to her, my emotional withdrawal started in 1986, three years after we were married. She had gained most of the weight by that time.

Even if I wasn't attracted to her sexually, I could have at least given her physical affection. What she may have needed most was the love and closeness that hugging, kissing and cuddling bring. I wasn't doing even that. I realize I will have to return to this issue. There's more to it than I now understand. I must dig deeper.

One day in the spring of 1989, I sat in the family room studying our checkbooks. Once again we were out of money and barely paying our debts on time. We were going deeper in debt every month. Susan came in. I sighed.

She said, "You're looking at our check books. I wrestle with them every day. Maybe I should go back to work, Boyd."

"I've thought about that," I said, "but I don't think it would help. We'd have to pay somebody to take care of the horses and Mark, and it couldn't be the same person. By the time we did that and paid the extra taxes on what you made, we wouldn't come out ahead."

Although I rejected her suggestion that she go back to work, I remember resenting her not contributing financially to the household—another wife who spent without earning. It was an irrational resentment because, in effect, she did contribute by eliminating the need to hire people to care for Mark and the horses. Nevertheless, this resentment persisted, especially when she spent money on the horses that I thought was unnecessary or unwise. Although I was generous with Susan, as I was with Stephanie, I acted as though the money was mine, that I alone had the right to decide how it was spent. I made the money, and I resented it when they spent it differently than I wanted—surprising for a lawyer who understood the concept of community property.

We had another problem: as new foals were born, we were running out of room. We discussed the issue without reaching a solution.

One night, after we had lived in the Bradbury house about nine months, I woke up to the sound of rushing water. In my grogginess, I thought Susan might be taking a bath, until I realized she was next to me, in bed. I ran through the house, splashing through water in the hallway. Water was pouring from under the sink in the kitchen. I ran out the front door and closed the main valve. This was the third time some plumbing connection had broken, resulting in a flood inside the house.

Susan was standing in the water in the kitchen crying when

I walked back in. "We can't go on like this," she said. "I can't live like this. And we don't have the money to fix it."

We charged the cost of fixing the plumbing—a temporary fix, we were told. We rented a big fan and dried out the carpeting ourselves. A half hour after I had re-laid the last of the dry carpeting, the doorbell rang.

"Who could that be?" asked Susan, as she went to the door. I heard her talking to a woman. A few minutes later Susan brought her into the kitchen and introduced us. "This is Jeannie," she said. Jeannie was a pretty, dark-haired young woman. She handed me her card.

"My mother and I are realtors," she said, "and we have a client who is interested in buying your property. You may know values have increased greatly in the year since you bought, especially good horse properties like this. I brought along some comps for you to look at." She handed me a sheaf of papers and pointed to the top sheet. "This one, for example, has a little more land than yours, but the house isn't as nice. It sold last month for $590,000. Anyway, take a look at these, and let me know if you're interested. I think our client will make you a good offer. This property is just what he's looking for."

"Okay, thank you. We'll discuss it and get back to you tomorrow," I said.

I looked at the comps. Our property must be worth around $600,000, I thought. We had a loan of $390,000. After broker's commissions and closing costs, we would net more than $150,000.

"That's an amazing turn of events," Susan said. "We were just talking about running out of room here, and I can't take being flooded out constantly."

"It looks like we could come out really well," I said.

Susan called Jeannie the next morning and told her we were interested in selling. Jeannie said she and her mother would present an offer that evening at eight.

After a few pleasantries and gossip—Jeannie and her mother had lived in Bradbury for thirty years and knew everybody and everything that was going on—"This is a good offer," she said. "No contingencies except a loan, and these are well-qualified buyers."

I stared at the purchase price--$630,000—nearly $200,000 cash net to us. I handed the offer to Susan.

"This is not an offer for negotiating, Boyd," Jeannie's mother said. "We think the property should sell for $630,000, no more, no less. We told the buyers, and they accepted."

We accepted the offer and soon found acreage in Paso Robles two hundred miles to the north, where there were many thoroughbred farms. I was excited about moving to the thirty-eight acres and building a house. I planned to drive into L.A. early Tuesday morning, stay in L.A. and work twelve to fourteen hours a day Tuesday, Wednesday and Thursday, and drive back to the ranch Thursday night.

About two weeks before the sale escrow was to close on our Bradbury property, I came in from work. Susan knelt in the kitchen hugging Mark. She stood up and told him to go play in his room.

"Hi," I said. "How was your day?" She didn't answer. Her face was expressionless.

"Boyd, I want a separation," she said.

"What? Why?" I said. I was in shock.

"I've been unhappy for three years now. We've only made love a few times since we moved here. Every time I try to initiate something, you ignore me. You got a vasectomy, supposedly so you wouldn't be concerned about having a baby. But nothing's changed. You show no affection for me. You pay no attention to me. You don't love me. All I do is shovel shit around here. I've had it."

I was breathless. I felt the tightness of panic. I couldn't think. "Please, please don't leave me Susan. Give me a chance. I'll change. You'll see. I do love you—very much."

"You wouldn't treat me the way you do if you loved me, Boyd. And I can't live with a man who doesn't love me."

"I swear, Susan, I do love you. I don't know what's wrong.

I'm so sorry. I guess I've been distracted by the horses and our financial problems and work. There just doesn't seem to be enough time for us. But I'll change that. I promise. Please give me a chance," I pleaded. "We can start fresh at our ranch." I was in tears.

"I'll be back in a minute," she said, and walked toward the bedroom.

I stood in the kitchen wiping my tears. I was wrung out, dumbfounded. How could this be happening again? I had no idea she was so unhappy, though there had been clues. What would we do with the ranch if we separated? I couldn't move there by myself. I couldn't take care of the horses and work two hundred miles away.

Susan came back, a calm gracing her pinkish face, eyes red from crying. "Okay, I'll give you another chance, but things have to change," she said. "I'm not just your hired hand. I'm your wife, and you have to treat me like a wife."

"Okay, I will. You'll see," I said.

We hugged. "Now let's go to Dominico's for dinner," I said, as my muscles relaxed and the tears dried.

Back on my couch in Cambridge a few days before Christmas, I ask myself what I did to respond to Susan's ultimatum. Nothing. By the time we were settled at our ranch in Paso Robles, I had mostly forgotten about it. Once in a while over the succeeding seven years I'd briefly remember. Then, without committing to any action or resolution, or even discussing it with Susan, I moved on to easier issues. She didn't bring it up either during that time.

Almost this same scenario happened with Stephanie. In neither case did I bother to discuss how we could change to make it better. Nor did I change any of my conduct. Both women made it clear in their own way that the situation was threatening the marriage. Why didn't I do anything?

Maybe writing about it will provide the answer. I write many times about my conduct and try to come up with an answer. What rings most true is somewhat different with each wife. With Stephanie, I felt helplessness, that there was nothing I could do, that I wasn't at fault and it was she who had to change. With Susan, I misjudged her. At the time she threatened a separation and for years after, I thought she loved me so much and that she was so needy, she would never leave me. She also lulled me into believing that it was only a fleeting problem by not mentioning it for the next seven years. That is exactly what I wanted to believe. I remember thinking that she didn't seem to care anymore. I didn't want to face the hard questions, such as why I didn't pay attention to her or give her the respect and affection she needed. Still I think there is more. I'll keep digging and writing.

We moved to our ranch in June 1989. It had a barn with eight stalls, a pasture—we built fencing for three more—a mobile home that we lived in until our house up the hill was finished, a creek that ran in the winter, fruit trees, a well for water, and a gently sloping hill of more than thirty acres edged with oaks.

We brought with us three dogs and a bipolar cat misnamed Felicity. Blaze and Klutzy had run away in Bradbury. We also brought four ducks and soon acquired a rabbit and some chickens. Our eight horses arrived over the first few weeks. Two sick black kittens, apparently left by the previous owners, became ours, generating our first small animal vet bills in Paso Robles.

I was exhausted at the end of moving day, but, sitting on our deck, looking out at the green hills sprinkled with oaks and other trees I couldn't name, I felt at peace in this beautiful place.

We had made the down payment on the ranch, paid off our debts, and spent the remaining $32,000 of the proceeds from the sale of the Bradbury property on Revered Princess, a two-year-old in training, the best-bred and best-looking horse we had ever owned. I don't remember who first suggested we use that money to buy her, but I had no objection. A more rational decision would have been to save it to help pay expenses of the horses we already had. A year later, Revered Princess broke her knee and never raced. We had another brood mare.

Chapter Twenty-Four

The day before Thanksgiving I sat on the front porch of our new house gazing at the brown, almost golden hills dotted by oaks and a few houses. I lowered my gaze to the tree-lined creek bordering the front of our property, then the pastures. The barn and mobile home were darkened in the foreground, shaded by the hill where I sat. Sunlight angled off the ever-green oak leaves, and the house cast long shadows across the hill below. In the evening's chill I shivered a little in my sweat-shirt; the tip of my index finger was numb on my Martini glass. My dog, Red, lay at my feet. I lifted my glass in silent toast to our new home in the country. It felt like a dream come true, but it was one I had never even dared to dream.

My hope was that, within a year or two, the horse business would break even and I could make enough money practic-ing law in Paso Robles, so that my trips to L.A. would be less frequent.

I would be happier as a judge, I thought. I would have

been a better judge than an advocate. I know the right people to get an appointment, but I've chosen to raise racehorses and move here instead. I couldn't support the horses on a judge's salary. I have my family and my home in this beautiful spot. How lucky I am. I'm forty-nine. Growing old here with Susan will be a good life. I'll finally help raise a child to adulthood. He'll go to elementary school, middle school and high school in this idyllic place.

It didn't occur to me that six months before, Susan had threatened to leave me, and I hadn't even tried to change.

I waved at Susan as she fed her ducks and chickens in the pen I had built next to the garage, and she waved back. I got up and walked over to the pen. The fowl were chasing each other away from the grain and greens Susan had thrown them. The rabbit cowered in his cage inside the pen. Jake, the dog, paced up and down, wishing he could get in and have a nice chicken dinner. Susan spoiled all her animals. In addition to the best grain, she bought them fresh produce from the market, which she fed them daily. She talked to them too. It wouldn't have surprised me if she had bought a stereo for them. One of her ducks lived to be twenty-two.

As I did every Tuesday morning, occasionally on Monday, the Tuesday after Thanksgiving, I left home a few minutes before six to drive the three and a half hours to my Marina Del Rey office. At first, while I was working in Marina Del Rey, I stayed in a motel a few miles from my office. A year later, Lisa graduated from college and had a job not far from my office. We rented an apartment in nearby El Segundo. By 1991, two years after Susan and I had moved to the ranch, Lisa, her boyfriend, my son Jeff, who had graduated from high school, and I shared the El Segundo apartment. I stayed two or three nights a week. Jeff worked as a clerk in my firm's office. It was a great bonding experience with my two oldest children.

On Thursday night, or sometimes Friday, I made the long drive back home. It was especially wearing at night. I got home around eleven, and Susan usually waited up for me.

For the first couple of years I didn't mind the drive, and I enjoyed the work on the ranch three or four days a week and the peace it brought me. I moved irrigation pipes to water the pastures so the horses could graze. I made repairs to the barn, landscaped around the house and sometimes fed and bathed the horses. I bought an old mare and rode her down on the riverbed. I grew a vegetable garden for the first time in my life—artichokes, carrots, green beans, cantaloupes, pumpkins and watermelons. It was a happy time for me, and, I thought, for Susan.

I was so obsessed with our horse business I paid little attention to the most amazing international political event since World War Two, the collapse of the Soviet Union. The first Iraq war, the election of Bill Clinton and the war in Bosnia didn't create as much interest as they normally would have either. Once the first Iraq war and the war in Bosnia were over, it was a peaceful time for the country, too. Although we engaged in a couple of military actions in the eighties, until the first Iraq war, we had not been at war in almost fifteen years. The eighties seemed more like the fifties than the sixties or seventies. The youth of the eighties seemed more interested in making money than in peace protests or race riots. It was the "me decade".

One typical Thursday night I walked in through the door from the garage. Susan greeted me in her nightgown with a hug and kiss. I dropped my briefcase and suitcase on the floor. I grabbed her bare ass under the nightgown. "Mmmm," she moaned, and grabbed my ass pushing me into her. I pulled away and walked down the hall to the bedroom. After rifling through the mail—junk and bills—I undressed and climbed into bed. Susan snuggled up against me and kissed me, caressing my back with one hand and putting the other hand down my shorts. I turned away.

"I'm too tired," I said. "I just don't feel like it after that drive and three fourteen-hour days."

"You never feel like it," she said and turned the other way.

An hour later I still wasn't asleep. Susan snored next to me. I knew I wasn't going to sleep, so I decided to get up. I crept out of bed, went to the kitchen, poured myself a tall Scotch and sat down on the living room couch. My nose was stuffed up—the cat hair, I thought. When I had suggested that the cats live outside, Susan said they couldn't because coyotes would kill them at night. We also had two stray dogs that Susan took in, raising that count to five. When I finished the Scotch I felt sleepy, so I went back to bed. The clock said 12:55.

Mark came roaring into our room and jumped on our bed a little after six. "Hi, Dad. The C-14 fire fighting plane flew over yesterday. It was awesome."

"That's nice," I said. "Is there a fire somewhere?"

"Maybe. I don't know," he said.

"I heard there was a fire east of Atascadero," murmured Susan, "but it's out now."

"Good," I said.

Susan got up to make coffee. About ten minutes later she came back carrying two mugs and handed me mine. She picked up *Soap Opera Digest* from her nightstand and started reading. I picked up *Blood Horse*. Saturday mornings were peaceful. We sat in bed together, backs against our pillows, sometimes reading, sometimes talking, feeling no pressure to do or say anything in particular. We had hired a hand to feed the horses Monday through Saturday. I loved these Saturday mornings. Susan said she did too. Mark fluttered in and out. We talked of horses and future plans and our garden and our son. It was our time to communicate, but I avoided bringing up anything unpleasant. So did she.

"We've been invited to the Raines' for a barbeque tomorrow afternoon," said Susan.

"I really don't want to go. I have nothing in common with those people," I said. What I really thought was that Jim Raines was an arrogant ass.

"How can you say you have nothing in common? He's a lawyer."

"I have nothing in common with most lawyers. Go yourself, if you want to."

"It would be too embarrassing explaining why you're not there," she said. "Come on, Boyd, you never want to do anything with other people. It makes me feel so isolated. I'm the one who's here all alone every week."

"I don't need other people, just my family," I said.

As the years passed, this little piece of Saturday morning fabric that bound us together frayed like the fabric on our couch, clawed by the cats. Our Saturday mornings were spiked more often by arguments.

The next Friday night we had our usual dinner at Lola's, the only decent restaurant in Paso Robles then. After a couple of Scotches and a pitcher of Lola's wine Margaritas, we got home and I fell into bed. Susan snuggled against me, her arm around me, stroking my chest. I fell asleep. This was typical on Friday nights.

It's Christmas Eve, and I finish packing for my trip to California. As I think about the first two or three years at the ranch, I am again incredulous at my lack of attention to Susan's obvious needs. She needed to have sex with me. I thought I was satisfied, though not happy, beating off. During our seven years at the ranch, we probably had sex on an average of three or four times a year. Surely, the feel of Susan's body, however heavy, and the emotional closeness of another human being would have been more satisfying than masturbation.

We had sold several of our yearling foals, though for less than the cost of breeding and caring for them. Susan said she hated selling our horses. I told her I understood, but it was too expensive to keep and train them all. I had read that only a quarter of all racehorses bred actually made it to the races; only one in ten made a profit. The reality, I explained to Susan, was that to stay in the business we had to sell as many as we could, race a few, and hope that one would make a lot of money to offset the losses on the rest.

"I understand what you're saying," said Susan, "but that doesn't make it any easier for me to sell them. I feel responsible for them, and if we sell them, I don't know what happens to them, whether they're properly cared for or whether they're sent to the horse butchers for meat overseas."

Although I called her manager of the horse business, I really didn't see it that way. I saw myself as the boss, the final decision maker, not a partner with Susan. I really didn't trust her as a business partner. I realized early on that our goals were different. I wanted the horses to be a business, or thought I did; she wanted the best for each horse. Sometimes these goals could not be reconciled. And Susan's sincere, child-like faith in people, her refusal to question their sincerity in a business transaction was incompatible with my view of doing business. She trusted people she didn't know. I was more skeptical.

The solution was simple. We should have gotten out of the horse business. But because of my belief that the husband had the right to control, I thought I should be able to control it. I thought that if I had control, I could minimize the losses to what was acceptable to me.

We bred Flying Shopper to Skywalker, a winner of the Breeders Cup Classic, the richest horse race in the world at the time. We went to Cardiff Stud Farm just down the road to see her colt an hour after he was born. He was already standing and nursing. A few weeks later, shortly before he and Shopper could be shipped home, we went to see him again. The farm manager said he was a magnificent looking colt. Susan and I brimmed with hope and anticipation for his racing career in a couple of years. Maybe he would be our "big" horse, the one that would make enough money to keep us in the business. In a few weeks, the colt was transported to our ranch, and we put him in a pasture with his mother.

A few months later our helper, José, banged on our back door. "New colt hurt," he said. His eyes narrowed. His lips pursed. I ran down the hill, almost falling. Susan followed. The Skywalker colt was prone in a far corner of the pasture, Shopper standing over him. I ran up to him. His eyes were closed. His head twitched, as if an electric shock was going through him. Then it stopped. His body was still. Susan screamed.

"Oh, my god," I said. "Go call the vet."

As I petted the little guy, his brown eyes opened. I slid my hand above his nose, over his head and down his side—his coat so soft and warm. Susan returned and took up the petting detail. Susan and I stood, tears stinging my eyes and streaming down her face.

The vet's van pulled up in the driveway. Dave, the vet, came in, nodding at Susan, but not speaking. He pulled his stethoscope out of his weathered brown bag and kneeled over the foal. He placed the stethoscope on the colt's belly, then moved it to his chest and neck. After moving his hand over the colt's head, he lifted up his whole body. The colt's head dropped, and his spindly brown legs hung. He opened his eyes and looked at Dave. Dave grunted and laid him back down, shaking his head. He walked over to the corner of the fence, and rubbed his finger on the top rail.

He walked slowly back. "He's paralyzed. His skull and his neck are broken. It looks like he ran into the corner of the fence. Something must have spooked him. We're going to have to put him down."

Susan sobbed, turned around, and walked back toward the house. I held back my tears.

"May I have your consent to put him down? Dave asked.

"Yes," I whispered, and nodded. "Do you mind if I don't watch."

"No," Dave said. "That's not necessary."

I followed Susan up the hill. I could hear her sobs. That's when I started to cry, for the poor baby, for us, for the whole fucking horse business.

During the fall of our third year at the ranch we drove up to Bay Meadows near San Francisco for Horizon Moon's first race. She was Shopper's first baby. I said to Susan, "I don't know if we can afford to keep training her if she doesn't make some money."

"We can't stop now," said Susan.

"We may have to."

A few minutes before the race the tote board displayed her odds: 90 to 1, the longest shot in the race. I bet my usual $20 to win. By this time I had seen many of our horses waiting in the starting gate. While my nerves were on edge, I didn't have the butterflies I used to.

As the horses burst from the starting gate, I saw her number-three saddlecloth near the front. She raced third in the early going. My pessimism turned instantly to hope and then to optimism, as her jockey angled her outside on the turn and she caught the two leaders. My heart pounded. I jumped a little, and stood on my toes to see her make the turn. "Come on Moonie," I yelled. As they straightened out in the stretch, Moonie took the lead. The crowd roared. Down the stretch they came, Moonie in the lead. She crossed the finish line first. Susan and I were thrilled and had our pictures taken with her in the winner's circle.

After watching the replay on the TV monitor, I walked over to the window and handed my ticket to the clerk. He took a big pile of twenties out of his drawer and winked at me. After counting out $2,200 in $20 bills, he handed me the stack.

That and the $4,400 winner's purse will keep her in training another three months or so, even if she doesn't earn anymore, I thought.

I flew back to LA., and Susan drove home. I let myself into the apartment.

Lisa came out of the kitchen. "Hi, Dad. Why the big smile?"

"I'll show you," I said. I put my briefcase on the floor and opened it. I grabbed the hundred and ten twenties, and threw them in the air.

"What are you doing, Dad?" she yelled. "Oh, my god!"

"We're going out for sushi tonight," I shouted. "Horizon Moon won!"

The winnings were a pittance, compared to the money we were spending on the horses—several hundred thousand over the previous five years. And we were behind on our bills. But that night I didn't think about that. I reveled in the glory of the win.

On Christmas morning 2008, I sit in my aisle seat on the way to L.A. I think about my life during those last months of 1991. I was working longer hours in L.A. and at my home office. I had quit working much on the ranch, and we'd hired a helper, Juan, to work full time.

In early 1992 I quit the Hirschtick Firm, opened my own office and an office in downtown Paso Robles to try to make more money. By this time it should have been clear to me that we could not break even with the horses, and no matter how hard I worked I couldn't earn enough to cover the losses. I constantly nagged Susan to cut down on horse expenses. I didn't make the hard decision to get out of the business or even ask Susan what she thought about getting out.

Chapter Twenty-Five

Three weeks after Moonie's win, Allen entered her in a much tougher race. On the turn for home she took the lead. "Moonie, can you do this?" Allen said out loud. Moonie pulled away by three lengths. Down the stretch another horse, Cotton Bloomers, was gaining on her. I held my breath. Cotton Bloomers caught her at the finish line. We walked down to the track and waited for the officials to review the photos of the finish.

Moonie galloped up. "She thought she had the race won and let up," said the jockey. "She never saw that other horse coming." The winner's number flashed on the board: number 7, Cotton Bloomers.

Allen said he would enter Moonie in a stakes race next. Suddenly we were near the top of the horserace mountain. On the day of Moonie's big race, it was raining, and the track was sloppy. Moonie slipped coming out of the starting gate and ran poorly.

A few days later Susan called me at the office. "Allen just called," she said. "Moonie has an ankle chip. She'll need to have it removed, but she should be as good as new." A year after surgery, Moonie won another race and had two seconds and two thirds before we retired her, but she wasn't as good as we had hoped.

For the next two years nothing much changed, except Susan took in more dogs and cats; we sold and raced more horses without financial success; and I worked more hours to support them. I continued to ignore the infrequency of sex in our marriage.

In the early 1990's a nationwide recession hit California especially hard, fueled by a major earthquake in L.A., devastating fires that destroyed hundreds of homes and the second L.A. Riots. For the first time in my life California real estate prices declined significantly. The ranch became worth less than what we had put into it. There was no hope we could sell our yearlings for what they had cost to breed. Nationally, the recession destroyed any remaining hope of reducing poverty in the United States. Bill Clinton, always a centrist, moved further to the right to be re-elected. While the rich got richer, Clinton and the Republican Congress ignored the accelerating poverty in the richest country in the world. But these events didn't have as big an impact on my consciousness as they would have twenty years before. I was too obsessed with horseracing and stressed by the debt we were in.

At home one weekend I sat on the couch, the cat urine odor pushing me toward nausea. The upholstery on the couch and the recliner had holes from the cats clawing them. I didn't know what I could do to get the cats out of the house.

Every surface in the house was piled with junk and gathering dust that mingled with the cat hair. It made me feel dirty. Susan kept stuff in moving boxes that were still scattered around our bedroom five years after we had moved to the ranch. I told her I would put it away or throw it out. "No," she said. "I need to take care of it one of these days." She never did. It accumulated a layer of dust that could grow vegetables.

Six years after Susan's ultimatum, sitting out on the back patio, I gazed at the golden hills turning darker. The sun had just sunk below the top of the hill, turning the cloudless sky a deeper blue. The red, white, and yellow wildflowers gradually disappeared from view. The oak trees on the east side of the hill were their darkest green. It hadn't rained in months. I imagined their roots burrowing deep into the water table. On the farm to the west, Mr. Steven's barley turned from gold to brown in the waning light.

I sipped a Martini before firing up the barbeque to cook the steaks. I had put the baked potatoes in the oven. I gazed at the view, as I often did, and thought about how peaceful this place was. It flashed through my mind, as it did every few months, that Susan and I hadn't had sex in a while. *How long has it been? A couple months,* I thought. *I'm so tired when I get home from L.A., but I know that's not the reason. She just doesn't turn me on. She must weigh close to two hundred pounds. I can't tell her I don't want to have sex with her because she's fat.* More than a year ago, I suggested she could lose weight by joining the new gym in town. She yelled at me not to mention her weight. "It's too sensitive a subject," she said. "I don't need you to tell me I need to lose weight. You think I don't know that?" She walked down the hall to the bedroom and slammed the door. *So what can I do? She's made it clear again I can't talk to her about it. She hasn't mentioned sex lately, so maybe she doesn't care.* These were my thoughts.

As I write this, I realize that my failure to satisfy Susan's sexual needs was no different from my failure to prioritize any of her needs. Her weight did make her less attractive to me, but denying her sex was part of a general pattern of lack of attention to her. It couldn't have been her weight that made me withdraw physically. That now seems ridiculous. It wouldn't have been any sacrifice to make love to her. It would have been better than no sex at all. Guys are notoriously not picky when it comes to sex.

Writing practice has finally exposed the absurdity of that conclusion. Susan often failed to tell me her needs, but she had made clear when she threatened to leave me that she needed sex. I didn't listen. Listening is an act of love. I also didn't consider that you don't have to be aroused to show affection. My experience with Stephanie's rejection should have helped me empathize with Susan.

It wasn't just about sex. It was part of the larger picture of my ignoring Susan's needs, having a vague awareness of what I was doing and not facing the issue—the same pattern I had established with Christie and Stephanie. And I took for granted that Susan would stick with me "for better or for worse," despite what she had told me.

Susan also needed a social life, as one of a couple, not by herself. I thought I didn't have that need then, and I ignored her need.

The evening wind came up. The dreams we had originally had become nightmares. We had lost hundreds of thousands of dollars on the horses. We were in debt over $200,000 from the horses and vet bills for chickens, ducks and rabbits, as well as dogs and cats. Unlike Stephanie, Susan was not extravagant in any other way. But she spared none of the money I earned on the animals, I thought.

I got up and walked into the family room, through the living room, past the dining room and down the hall to the master bathroom. Fourteen cats and seven dogs had destroyed the inside of the house. If you walked through the house bare foot, you could feel the cat urine soaked into the carpet. The cats had shredded all the upholstered furniture. Every surface in the house was covered with animal hair. I shook my head in disgust. I felt helpless again.

I went back to the kitchen, washed the artichokes and cut off the stems. I set the artichokes in the pot, and ran a little water. After adding a few drops of lemon juice and a little oil, I lit the burner and put the pot on it. That was about as much as we could cook in the kitchen. We couldn't cook a meal. The counters were covered with cat hair, and, around dinner time, with cats and their food. Susan said the dogs would eat the cats' food if she didn't put it on the counter. I went back out and stared at the darkened hills.

I took the steaks off the barbeque. The juice from the medium-rare meat pooled on the sides of the plates. I carried them toward the slider. Susan opened the screen. In the kitchen I got out another plate, cut a little out of each of our steaks into bite sized pieces, and put them on a plate for Mark. I took the tongs from the drawer and pulled the artichokes out of the pot, dropping them into bowls that Susan had taken out of the cupboard. I grabbed the baked potatoes, quickly put them on the counter and shook my burning hands.

"Oh, for god sakes, use the mitt, Boyd," said Susan, scowling and belatedly handing it to me. I took the bowls and plates out in two trips. Susan brought the large bowl for the artichoke leaves. I went back in the kitchen and poured Mark's milk and two glasses of Cabernet Sauvignon. It was cold out that night. We had all put on sweatshirts, but we ate outside because the dining room table was covered with junk. In winter, when eating outside was unbearably cold, Susan shoved all the junk to one end of the table, some of it falling on the floor, where it remained.

Susan and Mark chatted, as we ate our steaks. She never cooks anymore, I thought. On the three or four nights a week I'm home, either I barbeque—even in the winter—or we go out. I didn't know what she and Mark ate when I was in L.A. She hadn't cooked much since we lived in Manhattan Beach, seven years ago. I was pissed, as I thought about it, but I didn't say anything. After we ate, Susan washed the dishes, and Mark and I watched the last couple of innings of the

Dodgers game. Susan came in, sat down in her recliner, and picked up *Prevention* magazine.

I said, "Mark, it's ten-thirty. You should be in bed."

"Oh, it's Friday night," said Susan. "He can stay up."

I opened a *California Thoroughbred*. About eleven-thirty I got up and said, "I'm going to bed."

Susan yawned. "Yeah, me too. Get your pajamas on, Mark."

I sat up in bed reading, waiting for Susan to come to bed. When she climbed in, grunting, I thought again about how fat she had gotten. She picked up her magazine.

A minute later I put mine down, yawning. "You know, we never have a chance to just talk anymore like we used to. All we talk about is our financial problems and the problems with the horses, and we usually end up arguing about that."

"I know," she said. "You call me from the office or the road and fight with me about the horses. We're here now though. Talk."

"It's almost midnight. I'm too tired now. If you would just make Mark go to bed when most kids his age go to bed, say nine o'clock, we would have some time to ourselves."

Susan didn't respond. I had learned long before that when she didn't respond, it meant she disagreed with what I wanted and wouldn't do it. I sighed, turned off my lamp and lay down, turning away from her.

As I write this I realize that complaining about Mark going to bed late was just picking at Susan. I did that a lot. We had major issues in our marriage. That was what I should have been talking to her about—sex and my lack of attention, getting out of the horse business, the cats and dogs, our lack of a social life, the resentment we had both built up. I was aware of all of this, but I ignored it. So did she. It had infected our marriage like a bleeding ulcer, but we sought no cure.

Susan worked with me in the Paso Robles office most Mondays and Fridays dunning clients to pay, preparing and sending out bills and paying bills. I heard her talking to my biggest client on the phone. He was behind on his bills by nearly $100,000. We were really hurting because of it, and couldn't pay our horse expenses. I heard her chatting about his family and about Mark. Finally, she broached the subject of his bill. My phone rang, so I didn't hear the rest of her conversation. When I hung up, she came in and said he had promised to apply for a loan on property he owned, and should be able to pay his balance in full the end of next month.

"Not a moment too soon," I said.

"Yeah," she said and turned around. She turned back toward me. "You know, it would be nice if you complimented me once in a while on the work I do for you. It's really hard not knowing if you even notice."

"I've told you several times what a great job you do collecting money from my clients, and the billing," I said. "What am I supposed to do, compliment you every day?"

"No, but a little more often would be nice," she said, as she walked out the door and fell into her chair.

God. Nag, nag, nag, I thought. I never do anything right. Nobody tells me what a great job I'm doing—well, rarely. I have to be self-motivated. I'm surely not motivated by my clients. What I didn't see is that if I gave her more attention at home, maybe she wouldn't need it at work as much.

My practice in L.A. had expanded, but not enough to keep up with the horse expenses. When I came home for the long weekends I spent more time at the Paso Robles office I had opened. More often I went to L.A. on Monday instead of Tuesday, or stayed until Friday night.

My shoulders began to hurt chronically. When I couldn't raise my arms above my shoulders, I went to an orthopedist in Paso Robles. He said I probably had a strained rotator cuff. I thought it was from throwing out hay to the horses on Sunday, Juan's day off. But I now believe it was tension from driving during the long weekly commute.

Susan and I had been together twelve years. Lisa had spent every Christmas with us. She called and told me that she and her husband wouldn't be coming for Christmas. She said, "To be honest, there's so much cat hair, no matter what I take, my allergies make me miserable. Last time even the medication my doctor prescribed didn't help much. And Jim can't stand the odor. He says it makes him nauseous the whole time he's there."

"Okay. I'm sorry, Lisa, I'll miss you." I plopped down on the urine soaked couch. I looked over at the hole in the drywall chewed by one of the dogs, the psychotic golden retriever Susan took in. I hate being here, I thought.

Jennifer came to visit during the summer, but she took so much Dimetapp to keep from being asphyxiated by the cat hair and dust, she slept most of the time. My nose was congested when I was home.

One night when I came home from L.A. I walked in and was overwhelmed by the pungent smell of chicken shit. I walked toward the kitchen. There was a cage on the kitchen floor with a Rhode Island Red in it. Shit seeped over the bottom edge onto the floor, like an overflowing toilet. I dropped my briefcase and headed for the bedroom. Susan was sitting up in bed, reading.

"What is that in the kitchen?" I asked.

"Flora," she said. "I took her to the vet this afternoon. I'm afraid we're going to lose her."

"You took a chicken to the vet?"

"She hasn't eaten all week. Steve thinks her kidneys are failing."

"I can't believe you took a chicken to the vet. No wonder we have a $2,000 past-due bill with Steve," I said.

"Flora wasn't eating. What else was I supposed to do?"

"Let the fucking chicken die in peace," I said.

"I can't do that. Boyd. You don't understand. I feel responsible for these animals. When I own them, I am responsible to take care of them for the rest of their lives. That's just the way I feel, whether it's a chicken, a dog, or a horse."

"You just care about the animals. You don't care about my feelings. I'm miserable living this way, and I'm the one who has to work to pay for all the animals," I yelled. I was standing over her at the side of the bed.

"Get away. Stop shouting," she said. "Maybe if you showed more affection for me I wouldn't have to seek affection from animals," she said.

I wanted to say, maybe if you weren't so fat I would show you more affection, but I couldn't do that. It would hurt her too much, and that would be the end of our marriage.

I got home from L.A. one night and went to bed. Susan was in bed reading. I heard soft, small meows coming from the closet. I raised myself up on my elbow.

"I brought home three kittens from Rio Vista. God knows what they would have done with them," said Susan.

"Susan, please take the cats back. Cats are ruining the house. The whole house reeks of cat urine. There's sand everywhere from their litter boxes. The dogs jump all over me as soon as I get out of the car. They've even scratched my car."

"I can't take them back, Boyd. I would be sentencing them to death."

"Why do they all have to be in the house?" I asked. "We can't even prepare food in the kitchen, since you insist on feeding the cats on the kitchen counter. Let's keep the cats in the garage."

"We can't do that," she said. "They would have no way to get away from the dogs, or each other, no place to sleep comfortably. I've told you that before. And I would have no contact with them."

"What about my comfort? You don't care about that." I got up and stomped into the living room, where I sat seething for a while. When I went back to the bedroom, Susan was asleep.

We pulled up the carpet in the dining room, the hall, and the second bathroom and had tile laid so the cat urine could be cleaned up. We put new carpeting in the living room. We got a new sectional couch and a new recliner. Susan promised to spray the furniture to keep the cats off it. Within a year they had clawed holes in it, and it reeked of urine. When I got up in the morning to pee and wash my hands, the usual cat poop from Felicity stared at me from the sink.

Sam, the client who owed us so much, paid us $100,000. We used $70,000 of it to pay down the horse debt. Another client who had been behind paid $25,000 that same week. Instead of holding money in reserve, in August 1995 we took $40,000 to the yearling sale at Del Mar and bought the two best-looking yearlings we ever had.

I decided to buy these yearlings. I couldn't blame it on Susan. I had the impression—perhaps it was her lack of enthusiasm—that Susan disagreed, but she didn't express it. As I drove home from Del Mar, excitement ran through me. These horses are our best chance, I thought. If they don't make money next year, we'll be finished in the horse business.

The horse business was the first endeavor that I had been passionate about since working for legal aid. I was obsessed and didn't recognize the damage it was causing me—or my marriage. I had never objected to losing some money on the horses, but originally I was just willing to use the equity in our property. I had let it get way out of hand, and like any compulsive gambler, I was trying to recoup my losses by playing at higher stakes.

One day in early fall 1995 I gathered information for our accountant so he could prepare our 1994 tax returns. I began adding up the losses from the horse business for Schedule C. When I got to the last item, the calculator read over $190,000. I shook my head. I went into the living room and showed it to Susan.

"That is the loss from the horses," I said. "We have to do something. We can't continue this way."

"We have some good horses coming to the races," she said. "We can't stop now. I'm sure we'll do better next year."

"Yeah, but where will the money come from to continue training them? Rio Vista has cut us off. Cardiff has cut us off. We're behind on our payments to San Miguel."

"Sam'll pay us again next week. We'll be all right," she said.

"If he does, you're a miracle worker. I don't think he'll pay. I don't think he can anymore."

"I want to nominate our foals to the Breeder's Cup," Susan said.

"We don't have the money to do that," I said. "That's $2,500. We need that to train the horses at the track. The chances of those foals ever running in a Breeder's Cup race are so remote it's foolish to spend the money."

"It hurts me not to nominate them. It's saying we don't have any faith in them. We might be sorry two years from now."

"I don't think so," I said.

The next month I sat at our patio table waiting for the barbeque to reach the right temperature so I could put on the drumsticks. I had brought out the mail. I opened one of our Visa Statements. In the long list of debits was one for $2,500 to the Jockey Club, Louisville, Kentucky. It was the charge for Breeder's Cup nominations. Holding the statement, I slid open the patio door. I roared into the living room where the TV blared, grabbed the remote control and hit "mute." I threw the statement in Susan's lap.

"I can't believe you nominated the foals," I said, surprising myself for speaking so softly. "You lied to me. You have never done that before. You have always been honest with me. This is an act of complete dishonesty. I don't know if I can ever trust you again."

"I never agreed not to nominate them," she said. "I know you said not to. I'm sorry. I couldn't help it. I couldn't not nominate them. It would be admitting they're no good."

"That's absurd, Susan. Only one horse in a thousand runs

in a Breeder's Cup Race. That doesn't mean the others are no good. Anyway, the point is you were dishonest."

"No, I never told you I wouldn't nominate them. But I'm sorry. I shouldn't have done it. What else can I say?"

"I don't know," I said. "We have to get out of this business."

I grabbed my car keys and drove to A.J. Spurs, and went to the bar. I drank a Martini, trying not to think about anything. But I kept turning over in my mind: how do we get out of this business and lead a normal life? It wouldn't have been difficult—just sell all the horses we could. I didn't have the courage to do that. I continued to blame Susan and dream of success that deep down I knew was folly; we were careening down a trail to destruction.

Chapter Twenty-Six

Caro's Gem, one of our potential racehorses, was training at Del Mar with David Bernstein. She was due for her last workout before a race when Susan called me at my office.

"Bernstein says something's wrong with Gemie," she said. She's running a fever and won't eat. The vet drew blood, and we're waiting for the results."

"Shit, I said. "Why does this always happen just before they're ready to race and we've spent $20,000 to get them ready?"

"I don't know. Maybe, it's the stress from training. Maybe these animals were not meant to do what we're asking them to do," she said.

When I get home I'm going to have a serious talk with Susan about selling all the horses at the races and all the foals and yearlings and getting out of this business, I thought. But I didn't.

After a delightful Christmas dinner at Lisa's and a night in her guest room, I drive toward Susan's for the four-day visit. During the three-hour drive I think about our situation around Christmas back in 1995. I was like a kitten chasing its tail, devoting energy to multiple problems but not long enough to solve them: juggle debt to keep our horses in training, try to earn money to pay obligations; collect from clients who weren't paying; try to get the law work done to pay for it all; and spend some time with Mark. My shoulders hurt all the time. I developed diverticulitis, a painful inflammation of the large intestine. These pressures distracted me from the central issue—what was happening to our marriage. Our life together had disintegrated. This was my third marriage. Why didn't I make salvaging it my first priority? The answer will require more writing practice.

After three days of high fever and not eating, Gemie wouldn't get up, Susan told me when I got home. If a horse cannot stand, it cannot live. The bottoms of its feet become infected, and a disease called laminitis develops. The bones of the feet protrude, and if the horse is not euthanized it dies a painful death.

The next morning Susan called me at the Paso office. "Bernstein called and said the vet recommended that Gemie be euthanized." Between sobs, she said, "I told him to get a second opinion. He said he would. I'm going to call Melinda and see if she will go down and see Gemie."

"We can't afford big vet bills right now," I said. "We have too many horses in training."

"I can't just put her down without knowing if something can be done," said Susan.

Susan found a vet to treat Gemie. The scenario was similar to Topper seven years before. I complained and whined, but I didn't do anything but make the money to pay the vet bills. I could have called the vet and instructed her to send Gemie home or euthanize her. I wanted to, but I didn't.

More than $100,000 in vet bills later, Gemie came home alive, but unable to do anything except hang out as an expensive pet. As I drove home from L.A. one night, I added up our horse losses for the past year in my head--more than $200,000, for the ten years we had been in the business more than a million dollars. I felt sick to my stomach. I wasn't sure who I was angrier with, Susan or myself. I was fifty-five years old, a successful lawyer, with a negative net worth. My insecurities as a man, the ones that made me need Christie and Stephanie and devastated me when Stephanie rejected me sexually, plagued me again, this time in the form of financial failure. Based on what my father had taught me, a man who is a successful lawyer should have money and substantial material worth. I had sold my soul for that and failed to achieve it.

I didn't talk to Susan when I got home. What more was there to say? I worked late at the Paso Robles office on Friday. We went to A.J. Spurs for dinner Friday night, as usual, but barely spoke. When I turned over to go to sleep, I realized that Susan hadn't spoken to me about anything for months, except to convey information about the horses or about my law business. I awoke with a slight hangover. A few minutes later I felt anxious. Then gloom set in. It seemed like the last years with Stephanie again. I had lost control of my life. I couldn't stop the animals from destroying the house. I couldn't stop Susan from spending more than I could make. To pay for it all I had to keep making that exhausting, painful drive back and forth to L.A. Sam wasn't paying anymore, but his case was so close to trial the court wouldn't let me withdraw. I felt I had no control over any of it.

I arrive in Paso Robles the day after Christmas 2008 and drive down Linne Road past the ranch a quarter of a mile to Cass Winery, where Mark works. Susan still owns the ranch. She has planted twenty acres of Syrah and Cabernet Sauvignon wine grapes and is a realtor. She has five of our horses left. The others were sold or have died. I feel melancholy, as I have every time I visit the ranch. Sometimes on my infrequent visits, when I see the ranch, I don't remember the stress of the horse operation or my disintegrating marriage. I think about the beauty of the countryside and the peace it brought me for a while.

I sit at a table at Cass with a glass of wine, waiting for Mark to get off work. I think about the helplessness I felt twelve years earlier and almost shake my head. Once again, though I thought I was helpless, I wasn't. I could have taken control of the money and sold all the horses. I could have told Susan we needed counseling to try to repair our marriage; told her how much I hated making that drive after seven years, and suggest we move back to L.A. But I didn't discuss any of this with her. And she remained mute.

When I came back from my L.A. office to the ranch a few days before Christmas of 1995, I decided to try to communicate better with Susan. Her cold shoulder was depressing me. First, I'll get her a nice Christmas present, I thought. She doesn't have a decent winter coat, and every winter she gets soaked from rain.

I drove an hour to the London Fog outlet in Pismo Beach. I picked out a nice, warm, waterproof coat, a pair of rain boots, an umbrella, and a blue wool scarf, and had them gift wrapped in four separate boxes. When I got home and carried the packages into the house, she said, "What's that?"

"Your Christmas presents," I said.

"I see," she said and turned away. I put them under the tree.

At our annual unwrapping ceremony on Christmas morning--Susan, her parents, Mark, and me—I was excited to see her reaction. She opened the boots first. She said nothing. She opened the coat, and said nothing. The same when she opened the umbrella and the scarf. Afterwards I followed her into the hallway. "You didn't like your presents, Susan?"

"I'm going to take them back, Boyd. I don't need those things. I told you what I wanted, a sweater. You always do that. I tell you want I want, and you don't listen. You get me something else. Why can't you just get me what I ask for?"

"Well, fine. Take them back," I said.

"You did the same thing when you bought my engagement ring," she said. "I wanted to help pick it out, but you just went and bought it. I have never liked it."

"I see," I said. I held back my anger.

"I'm sorry to hurt your feelings," she said, "but I don't understand why you just can't get me what I ask for."

"I was just trying to surprise you," I said. "And I thought you needed a nice coat." Susan's dad walked up, and the conversation ended. My feelings were hurt. I had tried to do something nice for her as a prelude to more communication. I never tried to communicate after that.

I was angry about the engagement ring comments. She never told me she wanted to help pick it out. How was I supposed to know? Just as she had never told me she wanted to go to Paris on our honeymoon. She should have suggested it, if that was where she wanted to go, or even insisted on it. I would have accommodated her on both counts. She collaborated in the buildup of resentment. On these occasions and others, Susan seemed to expect me to read her mind and resented me when I didn't.

Over the Christmas holidays we had guests: Susan's parents, Jeff and his girlfriend, Jennifer for a few hours with her boyfriend.

Jeff and I were talking in the kitchen when Susan came in. "Jeff," she said, "how old is Anne?"

"She's seventeen. Why?"

"I just want you to know that I will not allow you to sleep with her in my house." I looked away. Oh, god, I thought. What difference does it make? "Especially since she's under age. It's a felony, you know, and I am not going to accept it in my house," she said.

"Not a problem," said Jeff. "It's your house." It's also mine, I thought, but I didn't say anything.

Jennifer had gone to study at the University of Wales for her junior year. She told me she wanted to come home for the holidays, and I sent her money for a plane ticket. When she came by with her boyfriend, she told me she was having the time of her life in Wales. She had made Welsh and English friends, and the university program of directed study was fantastic. She had never read so much in her life. "One more year back at Cal Poly, and I'll have a degree in English," she said, "if I don't decide to stay in the U.K."

"You like it that much, huh."

"Yeah, I do, except for the food. The food is terrible. I'm living on potatoes and Guinness. But I really did need this time back here. Thanks for the plane ticket, Dad. I really appreciate it." She gave me a big hug. "You should come and visit."

"Maybe I will."

"You could come over spring break. We get two weeks. We could travel around Wales and England."

"I'll let you know," I said. It sure would be a nice break from Susan and the horses, I thought.

After Jennifer left, in bed that night, Susan said, "I'm really mad at Jennifer. We pay for her to come home for the holidays, and she arrives with her boyfriend and spends all of four hours with us before she leaves with him for vacation."

"Well, she's twenty-one. That's the way twenty-one year olds are," I said. "Would you want her to be here when she doesn't want to?"

"No, I just expected a little gratitude. That's all," she said. She turned away and was soon snoring.

Jeff and Anne were saying their goodbyes the next day when Susan walked up carrying a can of Coke. "Jeff," she said, "I bought a six-pack yesterday. This is all that's left. Mark said he drank one. You're the only other one who drinks Coke. That means you drank four of my Cokes in less than twenty-four hours. I would appreciate your being more considerate."

"Sorry," said Jeff, "but I only had one."

"That's impossible," said Susan.

"Come on," I said. "It's only Coke."

Jeff opened the door, with Anne in tow, and headed for his car. I gave Susan a frown and caught up to them. "Sorry, Jeff," I said.

"That's okay, Dad. It's not your fault. But I have to tell you, I won't come back here anymore. I'm obviously not welcome, and I won't put up with being treated like a little kid. I'm twenty-three years old, and what does it matter if I did drink four Cokes, which I swear to you I didn't. It was her precious son who drank them."

"I'm really sorry, Jeff," I said, and hugged him.

"We'll get together elsewhere, Dad," he said.

Susan continued to be uncommunicative, and so did I. I buried myself in work and trying to keep the horse business afloat.

After Mark gets off work, we drive into town for dinner at a lovely restaurant in downtown Paso Robles—since the area has become a prime wine-making region, gourmet restaurants have opened to serve the more sophisticated residents and tourists. We drive back to the ranch, and Mark goes to his mother's bedroom to use the computer. Susan is in bed, so I say goodnight and go to the guest room. I try to read, but I think of those last months with Susan. I get up, grab my notebook and write about them.

In March I decided to visit Jennifer in Wales the first two weeks of April. When I told Susan, she frowned and said nothing. There had to be a part of me that knew my marriage was over. Jennifer and I had a grand time, a week in Wales and a week in Ireland. It was a great father-daughter bonding trip that launched a close, wonderful relationship.

When I got home from that trip, Susan ignored me. She didn't even give me a hug. Then, when Mark was not around, she said, "I'm really upset with you. You go away to Europe and leave me to deal with all the financial problems, all the creditors screaming to get paid, the horse problems. What could I tell them? 'Oh, Boyd took a trip to Europe.' I can't believe you did that. It shows no consideration for me."

"It's something I had to do," I said.

"Yeah, well, fine," she said.

In late April and May we had minor successes with the horses. On Memorial Day weekend we stood in the winner's circle at Golden Gate Fields. They took the win picture. It was the fifth win picture in six weeks, one more win than we had in the previous ten years. I was thrilled, but only for a few minutes.

As we drove home, I told Susan, "You know these wins have been great, but the purses have barely scratched the surface of our financial problems. We need a horse to win big races, not these low-level ones."

"I know," she said.

We sold one of the winning horses for $12,000. I couldn't convince Susan to sell him, but we owed our trainer so much that he said we had to sell or he would quit training our other two horses. The farm in San Miguel had stopped training our two-year-old, Limitless Flight, because we were behind on the bills. We used some of the purse money to pay part of that bill so they would resume.

By July Limitless Flight was ready to send to the track, but the farm wouldn't let him go because we still owed them money. In the Paso office Susan was sitting at the computer. I walked up to her and said, "I need to talk to you before I go down to L.A. We have to sell all our babies and racehorses. But I think we should keep Limitless Flight, and send him to Santa Anita. His trainer thinks he can compete down there. Maybe he can make some money to pay off some of this debt.

We owe over $200,000, you know."

"I know," she said. "I'm the one that deals with these bills day to day, every day. You don't."

"Do you agree we should keep Limitless Flight and sell the rest?" I asked.

"What do you mean—we?" She asked.

"Well, we," I said. "They belong to both of us. What are you talking about?"

"Boyd, you do what you want. I don't want to be married to you any more." She started to cry.

"What?" I said. "You can't mean that."

She stopped crying. "Oh, you bet I mean it."

I stepped back. My breath left me.

When I could, I said, "Susan I know things have been tough lately, but if we sell the horses and get out of debt and this crazy horse business, we can get back to normal. Let's move back to Manhattan Beach, so I don't have to make this horrendous drive."

"It's too late, Boyd. I can't take it anymore. These past few months I deliberately stopped talking to you and ignored you to see what would happen. I thought that might jolt you into reality. But you didn't even notice. Instead you just went off to Ireland. You don't love me. I don't believe you ever did, and I can't live with that. I've been miserable for years. I told you I wanted to leave you before we ever moved up here. You promised to change, but nothing has changed. You still show me no affection. We've only made love twice in the last year. I used to try to initiate it, but I gave up. It was too humiliating."

I realized she was right. I felt guilty and confused. "I'm sorry," I said. "Let's go to counseling and try to make it work."

"I think it's too late, Boyd. I'll think about it and let you know." I knew that meant no.

"I have to get down to L.A.," I said. "Please consider counseling. Let me know." I said it because it seemed the reasonable thing to do. I had always wanted to be reasonable.

I picked up my briefcase and walked out the door.

Chapter Twenty-Seven

As I drove away from Susan, my mental haze became shock. Then the shock seeped out, leaving a strange combination of fear, sadness and relief—fear of loneliness; sadness from another failure as a husband; and relief at the thought of regaining control of my life. Suddenly, I felt empowered. I could sell all the horses that could be sold, and Susan couldn't stop me. She couldn't support them. I could move to L.A. and work hard to earn the money to pay off the debt, just as I had done when I left Stephanie. There would be no more arguing with Susan. I would have my own space, without the clutter and animal filth. If she wanted to go into couple's therapy, I wouldn't refuse; but I knew she wouldn't. Susan, like the others, was not willing to stick it out for better or for worse. My offer of counseling was half-hearted. Maybe Susan had picked up on that.

Then an aching, quiet melancholy enveloped me. I would not grow old with a partner on that bucolic ranch. I would not live with my son beyond the age of twelve. I thought about our pitch-and-hit games, one of my few pleasures during the previous two years, besides watching the horses. Except for the fenced pastures, we had what seemed like an endless back yard—more than thirty acres. Far behind the house, I would overhand pitch a hard ball to him, which he hit—or not. I'd catch them—or not, and had to apologize for hitting him—more than once. When he hit the ball over my head, and I chased it, he laughed without restraint. In ten minutes I'd be out of breath and have to rest. I didn't mind; it was good exercise. It reminded me of the good times with my own father, when I pitched, and he caught and called balls and strikes.

Loneliness interrupted. Once again, I would have nobody to come home to. I cried softly, the tears obscuring my view out the windshield, like rain without wipers. But I wouldn't have to make that terrible drive every week. I could be out of debt in less than two years, I figured. Then I could cut back on work and enjoy life.

Lisa and her first husband had moved to a new home forty miles away, and when I was in L.A. I had been staying with Eric, a former associate, and his wife, Darby, for about a year. Now it would be full time. It was pleasant living with them, and they only charged me $400 a month for my room. I breathed easier, sinking down in the driver's seat.

A few minutes later, anger rolled in like the surf outside my window. Susan claims she was miserable the whole seven years we had lived in Paso Robles—and she didn't tell me. *Now she won't even go to therapy—after thirteen years she won't do anything to save our marriage. She deliberately stopped communicating with me to see what I would do--what is this, a game?*

Over the next few days, I decided that once again I had married a needy woman—not as crazy as Christie and Stephanie, but crazy in her own way—the cat lady, my children called her. All three wives had been too needy, I thought. I simply had used poor judgment in choosing wives.

Both Susan and Mark are at work, so I have most of the

day to sit in the house and think and write about our marriage. I still haven't told Susan I will not move back. I walk out to the pasture behind the house and watch the five remaining horses graze on their alfalfa. I hear that sound once again—the crunch, crunch of them chewing, and I am nostalgic for the good times living on this ranch. I love it here, I think. Too bad I had to leave. Should I come back?

The patio chairs and table I used to sit at are gone now. Susan never did like the outdoors, I think. I walk back in the house and sit on the couch. It smells of cat urine and some kind of cleaner Susan uses to mask the odor. I go into the guest room, turn on my computer and write a conclusion to my memoir. It's redundant and vague. I'll have to keep working on it. When I'm writing about something that makes me sad or angry or brings my insecurities to the surface, I tend to skip over the surface and not dive deep. I need to go deeper.

My conduct during my marriage to Susan was a now familiar pattern cut from my insecurities. I married a woman I felt superior to, one I thought I could control. After the newness wore off, I ignored my wife and focused my attention on work, and, in Susan's case, horse racing and breeding. I didn't consider my wife's needs. I had never sufficiently relinquished the model of my parents' marriage. At the basic level I still believed that if I was a good provider and didn't abuse my wife, she would stay with me, for better or for worse, and I could focus on other things. I didn't see marriage as a partnership, although if you had asked me I would have said it was. I knew it should be, but that it had to be was down there some place deep within me.

I think of David and Lisa again. David is ambitious, but his family seems to be the most important element of his life. Achievement at work is a means to an end for him, not an end in itself. For me achievement as a lawyer and then a horse breeder was a means to placate my insecurities as a man, rather than a means to a satisfying family life.

My sexual insecurities were a huge factor. They must have

come, in part, from my experiences as a child. But I wonder, though I cannot know, if my father had severe sexual insecurity and somehow passed that on to me. He didn't marry until he was forty-six. Since few middle-class women in his generation would have sex outside of marriage, I would guess he had very little sex. Given my mother's view of sex, he may not have had much during marriage. This—and who knows what else—could have caused him to be sexually insecure. Perhaps evidence of this is that he seemed to have extreme fear that his son would be Gay. He told me when I was in high school that if he ever saw me with a tennis racket, he would disown me—this because years before, a male tennis star had been exposed as Gay. He forbade me to play with a boy who lived down the street, because the boy was effeminate and may have been Gay.

My fear of becoming too close to Susan, and being hurt again as I had been with Stephanie, drove me to withdraw further. When the warning signs shouted at me, I stubbornly covered my ears, and when the relationship became almost unbearable, I felt just as helpless as I did with Stephanie.

Susan and I had our unexpressed contract too. I expected from Susan unrelenting peace and serenity. I couldn't bear the thought of going through the tumult that I had endured with Stephanie. I wanted no crises, no conflicts, and no arguments—just serenity. I naively thought Susan could and would provide that. Nobody could have. And I wanted the control that I had lost with Stephanie. I didn't ever want to give that up again. I still needed and expected to be wanted sexually, perhaps even more with Susan, since Stephanie had betrayed me.

Susan expected attention and notice, as Stephanie had. Susan may have needed my affection more. But I think she also expected a partnership, not a relationship that I controlled. I defaulted on everything Susan wanted. I wasn't a partner; I insisted on control. I withdrew my attention and affection. I broke the contract first. When Susan didn't get what she expected, she fought my control, showed, though rarely expressed, her resentment of my lack of attention, and broke the serenity. My male ego remained intact because she made it clear that she wanted to have sex with me. I was the one who withheld it this time.

Susan, Mark and I go out to dinner the next evening, and the conversation is pleasant. Susan and I talk at the ranch after dinner, while Mark retires to the computer.

Her conversation is pleasant, but small talk, much of it about other people that she knows and I don't know or care about. She talks nonstop about nothing that interests me, and I don't stop her. Susan usually talks a lot, as if silence is something to avoid. I'm bored. Maybe I was bored during our marriage.

I drive to Monterey December 30 to visit Dora and don't think about Susan until the day after New Year's as I'm driving back to Lisa's. I wonder what it would be like to live with Susan again. We have nothing in common now. She doesn't have the passion for art, music and literature that I have. She doesn't appreciate good food like I do—she still won't eat anything warm and green, as she puts it, or anything that swims. She doesn't share my interest in travel, the outdoors, history and other cultures—or even baseball anymore. She loves auto racing. She's a nice, good-hearted woman, but I still have no passion for her. As I drive on the 101 past Paso Robles, I feel melancholy. I realize I will never go back to Susan, and I know I've made a good decision. The melancholy disappears.

It occurs to me that I didn't have much to drink while I was at Susan's and Dora's, except tasting wine at the winery where Mark works and only one drink while I was at Dora's. I didn't have any alcohol the week before in Boston. Something has fallen into place. I know now I can and must drink only to enhance living, not to avoid it. I have finally conquered that demon.

Back at Lisa's, I send Susan an e-mail telling her that I will stay in Boston. I lie down on the guest room bed to take a nap, but I can't sleep. Although I have discerned much about my role in the destruction of my marriages, I still don't understand why I didn't internalize that I could not duplicate my parents' marriage. Why didn't I pay attention to the evidence, visible all around me, that in my generation marriage would not work as a male dictatorship, however benevolent, but had to be a partnership that required constant attention; otherwise, unlike my mother, women would resist and eventually leave. A woman born forty or fifty years after my mother had needs different from hers. And my mother's needs didn't change drastically. She was married from 1930 until 1963, when my father died. There had not been anything like the dynamic social changes that took place as my generation began marrying.

I must also consider that my parents' marriage may not have been what it appeared to me. Everyone expects from his or her partner attention, notice. My father may have given her that. Perhaps I was trying to duplicate something that was not only outdated and inauthentic, but never existed—like building a sculpture of an airplane, and then expecting it to fly.

When I get back to Boston, I decide to look for a writing group. I Google "writing groups boston." Up comes Collaborative Therapy. It's not really a writing group. It's a husband-and-wife team of psychotherapists who specialize in counseling writers and other artists.

A week later I sit in Anne Wynn's office telling her about my marriages. At a subsequent session I raise the "why" questions that plague me. Anne points out the obvious. The destruction of my marriages was not just my doing. My wives collaborated. Their conduct too was influenced by belief systems and neuroses passed on by their parents. None of my wives constructively expressed their needs. They responded destructively—Christie usually with silence; Stephanie with counter-attacks, drugs, alcohol, and sexual rejection and betrayal; Susan with defiance and silence. My wives share with me the responsibility for their suffering and mine.

At the end of the session Anne says we'll discuss this issue further next time. My wives' collaboration doesn't relieve me of my guilt. My mood walking to the T to ride back home is as dark as the winter sky. Have I lived my whole life as a puppet of my dead parents?

The next week, as I trudge through the cold, icy rain toward Anne's office, I plunge into guilt. I didn't destroy abstract marriages. I profoundly damaged the lives of three women I once loved and four children I still love. It is this guilt that has agonized me the most lately, as I've thought, talked and written about my marriages. It has robbed me of sleep, disgorged waterfalls of tears down my face, and plunged me into deep sadness.

"How do I deal with the guilt?" I ask Anne.

"You're not guilty," she says. "You did the best you could." She explains that the impact of our parents on us is enormously powerful, especially on our fundamental beliefs, the way we see our world. At a young age we learn from our parents to see the world and operate within it. Each generation is damaged by the previous one. The more attention the parent pays to the child, the stronger the impact. With me, an only child whose parents doted on him, the impact was stronger than on many others. They protected me from outside influences for as long as they could. Anne suggests I read books by Alice Miller, who, she says, spent a lifetime studying the impact of parents on their children.

As soon as I get home, I order three of her books. With scientific support, Alice Miller persuasively argues that our fundamental belief systems, such as our beliefs about how family members relate to each other, are whatever our parents taught us. A striking example she cites is that most people who were beaten or abused sexually as children will beat or sexually abuse their own children. Many children of alcoholics grow up to be alcoholics, despite their experience with the destruction and pain it causes. Few people can exorcize those fundamental views of how to operate in the world, even after years of psychotherapy.

In April spring has still not come to Boston. I'm wearing my winter coat on my way to Anne's office. I discuss the Miller books with her. She says I should be proud that I have gained the insights I now have about my marriages. Many people never gain such insight. I smile and nod my head up and down. I am proud. I decide to walk the two miles home. It's cold, but I hardly notice. The guilt I have been feeling recedes somewhat.

Something else nags at my conscience. What about the children? They were innocent. I damaged them, as my parents damaged me. Yet although they have their own issues and flaws, as we all do, they are all productive and reasonably well adjusted. They have been able to work through whatever destructive influences I had on them. They fill me with pride. Their mothers and I did something right—we loved them—to the full extent we could, while we passed along good traits and bad. We did our best. I treasure the close relationships I have with them. The guilt that is left—I'll just feel it. There are worse things. Maybe, guilt, like loneliness, is part of the human condition.

It is late spring, when New England finally shakes off the doldrums of a cold, dark winter. I feel like I haven't yet penetrated the core. There is something else that kept me ignorant during my marriages.

In June I leave for Taos, New Mexico for another Natalie Goldberg weeklong writing retreat. We keep silence, not talking to anyone, except in class. We do sitting and slow walking meditation, as well as writing exercises that we read aloud to the group if we choose. The silence and meditation soak me. I feel my writing going deeper.

On the third day I feel sick, something like a hangover, though I hadn't had a drink in days. I struggle through the day, and as soon as the evening session concludes, I go to my room and lie down on my bed. I feel exhausted, but I can't sleep, and I can't get up. My head is heavy. My body feels like it's sinking into the bed. I panic. I'm afraid I'm having a heart attack or stroke, or something. I think about my father's heart attacks. In four months I will be the age he was when he died.

Then a vision of my mother appears in my mind's eye. I'm picturing her as she looked when I was a boy. I remember her sitting across from me in the breakfast nook, telling me how she had tried to get pregnant for seven years, how ecstatic she was when the doctor told her she was pregnant with me, how she panicked when he told her at six months she had an ovarian tumor that had to be removed, and she might lose me; telling me how, from the time I was born, she loved me more than life itself, more than she loved my father; that she had no reason to live, except for me. She told me this more than once. I remember how she used to keep things I did secret from my father so he wouldn't spank me. I realize for the first time that my mother used me to fulfill her own life.

I needed and expected my wives to love and accept me unconditionally, as my mother did, "...for as long as we both shall live." I didn't have to pay attention to their needs. They would love me and stay with me no matter what. My beliefs were so deep and strong that even after two failed marriages, I still clung to them—unconscious of their effects on my marriages.

I fly out of bed and write these thoughts in my notebook. Back in bed, I fall asleep immediately. The next morning I feel better. In our morning retreat session I read aloud what I have written about my mother. When I finish, I feel ecstatic. "Now you're getting somewhere," says Natalie. "Put that in your memoir."

The final day I write about my father's role of dominance and control of the family. He ran the show. He showed virtually no affection for my mother in front of me. Likewise, he showed little affection for me. Not once did he discuss sex with me, except to warn me about Gays. When I got my driver's license, he warned me not to pick up female hitchhikers. A friend of his did, he said. She screamed, "rape," and although he never did anything, he was arrested and went to prison. Yes, women are scary creatures. He showed me by his own lack of self-expression that emotions had no legitimate place in life, were a weakness possessed mostly by women and some foreign men. My father's guidance was confined primarily to working hard to get ahead in the world. That I did.

After I return from the workshop, I read to Anne what I have written about my mother. She sits and nods, her expression pained. She suggests, "You weren't bored or lonely as a child, as you've told me you were. You were depressed because of the burden your mother placed on you. She made you, a little boy, responsible for her happiness, her life. You were petrified that you couldn't carry that burden and your mother would die." I tear up.

No wonder I was so devastated by Stephanie's rejection and betrayal. Mommy had betrayed me. I still loved Stephanie and couldn't leave her, because my love for Mommy was unconditional. I couldn't get out of the horse business until after Susan asked for a divorce. To do so would have been defying Mommy. Even today I find it difficult to say no to a woman—something I will work on. We just keep plugging away, don't we?

Anne asks me if my mother was thin. "Yes," I answer. "So were Christie and Stephanie." Anne smiles. Bingo, if I was looking for my mother in my wives, Susan's weight gain would cause my loss of desire for her. But, Anne quickly adds, it doesn't explain or justify my withdrawing all affection or failing to address the issue of my sexual rejection of Susan.

Months later, during another Boston winter, I rewrite this chapter for what seems like the millionth time. I wrote the first draft of the memoir in six months—the real first draft, not the one I threw away. I have been digging and revising, gaining new insight and rewriting for nearly a year, like a runner in training achieving new "personal bests." I hope some are personal bests, though, like most writers, I am plagued by self-doubt.

During my third Boston winter I drive up to my favorite bed and breakfast near Windsor, Vermont, the Juniper Hill Inn. The unseasonably warm weather allows me to walk up the snowy path to the old mansion in my shirtsleeves. I check in, and Robert, one of the owners, comes out to greet me, as usual. I tell him I've come up to finish my book. After slowly walking around the spacious living room, looking at the familiar paintings and artifacts from Robert's travels, I sit down on the winged back chair that faces the front door and put what turn out to be the finishing touches on my conclusion.

I wanted from marriage somebody to allay my sexual insecurities, to adore me, to hug and kiss me when I got home from work and tell me I was okay and my world was thriving, to produce children for me and care for them, and to encourage me when I was feeling low and inadequate. I wanted a housekeeper and a cook and someone to do my errands and laundry and keep fresh sheets on my bed. But I didn't want someone I had to pay attention to, notice, comfort in times of need, listen to. I didn't want to try to provide for her needs or even allow her to try. And I surely did not want a partner to deal with. I didn't pay attention to my wives because I didn't want to.

Deep down I knew this vaguely, but on the rare occasions when a hint of realization clawed its way through the brush and thistles, the fog and murk, up to my consciousness, I beat it back with devastating psychic force, and with alcohol.

Before now, I had little understanding about the failure of my marriages. I had stopped at the conclusion that I had married overly needy women. What bullshit that was. What does "needy" mean in the context of a marriage or any partnership? Every individual has needs. Everybody also has wants—a nice dinner out, good-looking clothes, a vacation in the Bahamas, a game of golf, a massage, a fast car. None of these are needs, but maybe having such a want fulfilled once in a while is a need.

Simply labeling my wives as needy is meaningless. The relevant questions are: what does she need from me, and am I willing to fulfill those needs? If she can't handle my having female friends, am I willing to give them up? If she won't allow me as much time alone as I want, am I willing to live with less? If she needs frequent physical affection, am I willing to provide it? I didn't ask those questions. If I had asked them and answered them honestly, the answers for all three wives were, no, I was not willing to fulfill those needs.

I shut down the real me who didn't want the demands of a wife and family and listened only to the part of me that wanted the goodies—sex to allay my insecurities, a family for its status—the part my parents and my society taught me. Then, after twenty-seven years of three failed marriages, I buried the whole thing for another twelve years.

I also shut down the authentic me, the me that didn't want to work the better part of a lifetime helping the rich get richer, that wanted to teach, help those who needed it, create and learn. I allowed someone else, the inauthentic me, to carry on my life. The real me surfaced occasionally, but it brought stress and fear. Before long I buried it again.

Perhaps I unconsciously did not want to meet the demands of marriage because I was an only child with no relatives my age and few neighborhood children to play with. I simply had no experience in the types of relationships that would have taught me how to interact in a marital partnership. When I reached adulthood the concepts of partnership, which required giving up control and complex human interaction, were unfamiliar and scary. I had always been a loner. So I avoided the responsibilities of partnership, unaware that my avoidance would doom almost any marriage.

Writing about my marriages has, little by little, unearthed

this lifelong, mostly unconscious struggle between the authentic and the inauthentic me, finally bringing the authentic me to the surface. This realization brings me a profound paradox of sadness and peace—sadness that I spent nearly a lifetime losing this struggle; peace that I have finally won it and can live authentically with the life I have left.

While writing this memoir, I dated a nice woman for nearly a year. She told me that she wanted to move our relationship to the next level—beyond just dating. She made it clear that she was looking to get married, and I might be her future husband. I realized then that I did not want to be married to her or anyone. I told her, and we broke up.

I never should have married. But I did. I couldn't effectively deal with what has become in the past sixty years or so a tricky, difficult relationship. I am not alone in that failure. Do I regret ever getting married? All experiences shape who we are. If I hadn't married these women, I would be a different person. And who can say I would be happier or more fulfilled? My wives helped shape who I am. I don't regret who I am, so I don't regret the marriages. And I can't imagine not ever having known my four children.

My journey to Boston to live with Kate stimulated me to write. Boston is a good writing city, especially in the winter when so often it is cold and wet and dark. There are a lot of writers here, and though I don't know many of them, I have a sense that I'm doing what should be done here. Writing, for me, is a kind of psychotherapy—better. It digs up things that talking doesn't. It has exposed me to myself. Writing practice is a way of slowing down and digesting our memories. It provides a chance to figure out how we got where we are.

Though we never fully understand, through writing I see closer than ever before some of the things I buried, something like the authentic me. I want to help those I love, to make a difference in their lives. I want to create something the world wouldn't have if I hadn't lived. I don't need material things beyond the basic necessities, and I won't make sacrifices to get them anymore. I yearn to experience how others in different cultures live their lives. I receive life, instead of chasing it.

I want my children and grandchildren to know the me I have discovered and the process I went through. My parents told me little about their lives or the lives of my grandparents and great-grandparents. There was so much I never asked them. I really didn't know my parents—a terrible loss. If my journey to understand myself and my marriages interests others, I would be grateful to share it. But I wrote this memoir for me--to get as close to me as I could, to find the authentic me. Writing got me closer. But I'm not finished. I hunger to understand as much as I can before I die. I will continue to write what I buried, to dig deep.

Acknowledgements

I first want to thank Adena Atkins, without whose help, ideas, hours of reading and critiques, and especially her constant encouragement, this book would not have been written.

Several people who read it and commented also provided immeasurable help and encouragement, among them, Jervey Tervelon, Daniel Evans, Kia Penso and Marsha Bielawski.

Natalie Goldberg taught me more about writing memoir and living life than I could ever acknowledge. Not just Natalie, but my fellow students in her workshops, especially the 2009 Intensive, contributed significantly to my ability to tell my story.

CPSIA information can be obtained at www.ICGtesting.com

260838BV00003B/1/P